German Cooking

Marianna Olszewska Heberle

D1502258

HPBooks

Acknowledgments

Special thanks to Tom and Lois Holtz Heberle, whose traditional and creative renditions of their German parents' recipes helped show how healthy and versatile German cooking can be.

HPBooks
Published by The Berkley Publishing Group
A division of Penguin Putnam Inc.
375 Hudson Street
New York, New York 10014

Copyright © 1996 by Marianna Olszewska Heberle

Book design by Richard Oriolo
Cover design by James R. Harris
Cover photograph by Zeva Oelbaum
Interior illustrations by Michelle Burchard

First edition: September 1996

Published simultaneously in Canada.

Visit our website at
www.penguinputnam.com

Library of Congress Cataloging-in-Publication Data

Heberle, Marianna Olszewska.
    German cooking / Marianna Olszewska Heberle.
        p.   cm.
    ISBN 1-55788-251-7
    1. Cookery, German.   2. Food habits—Germany.   I. Title.
    TX721.H43   1996
641.5943—dc20   96-966
                                                                                CIP

Printed in the United States of America

19   18   17   16   15

Contents

Preface

*G*uten tag! Welcome to the wonderful world of German cuisine! If you've been here before, you know what an interesting, delicious experience it is. If you've never knowingly ventured within its boundaries, you're in for an enriching series of pleasant surprises.

What comes to mind when you think of German cooking? Sauerkraut and pork? Sausages? Dumplings? Rye bread, simmered cabbage, dill pickles and Black Forest cherry cake? Soft pretzels and German beer? Although all of these are fair game, individuals who have been exposed only to overcooked or otherwise poorly prepared German recipes may mistakenly infer that German cooking is rather monotonous, relying too heavily on a few bland sauerkraut and sausage dishes, for instance. Such a generalization is both misleading and unfair. Indeed, you'll see that German cookery—like Germany and the Germans themselves—cannot be described and classified in simple terms. All three display far more variety than may at first be apparent.

You're going to discover that German cooking, while steeped in centuries of tradition, has also been strongly influenced by outside forces, including a recent influx of foreign immigrants, and continues to evolve against a backdrop of modern life-styles, with attention focused on nutritional sciences. For sure, German cookery—once you get beyond the most traditional dishes—is not as distinctive as Chinese, French, Italian, or even Polish. And the days of Germans eating foods simply because their ancestors did are long gone. Now it's a combination of old and modern—what survives from both worlds. Germans simply like good food tastefully prepared. That's what the recipes in this book are all about. That's what the Germans of today are eating, whether dining at home or in restaurants. Together, the dishes represent the fare found from west to east and north to south. Yet all told, German food is savory and substantial, with plenty of meat, sauces, and meat-based flavorings. In households and restaurants the helpings are generous, the service efficient and the presentations simple and direct.

Why a new German cookbook? Certainly a lot has happened in Germany during the past ten years: The crumbling of the Berlin Wall. The joining of East and West. Internal strife. Political struggle. Steps, then bounds toward democracy. A changed present and a taxing yet promising future. All of this has stirred ethnic fervor in the hearts of anyone with even a slight German background and has instilled those same individuals with the desire to learn more about their cultural heritage. An interest in history and cultural materials has been ignited and Germany's long tumultuous past, good and bad, has been thrust into the limelight. Consider the publicity generated by the book and movie *Schindler's List,* for example, or the recent anniversaries of D day and the end of World War II.

Due to the positive national climate and the opening of the new eastern horizon, travel to Germany is reaching levels never experienced before. Airlines have scheduled additional flights and travel agencies have revised their information to include packages and literature that reflect the travelers' interest in lands once hidden behind steel curtains. Accessible now are historic Berlin, heading toward its former status as the capital of Germany; Dresden, with its celebrated architectural and artistic treasures; and Leipzig, that music lover's mecca, where Richard Wagner was born, where Mendelssohn and the Schumanns lived, and where Johann Sebastian Bach is buried. With all this attention on Germany and things German, it's only natural that German cuisine is likewise receiving renewed interest.

I hope you'll find *German Cooking* to be a book enjoyed by anyone fond of hearty, delicious recipes.

Now, *Guten Appetit!*

Introduction

❧

*T*o help understand how and why such incredible regional and culinary diversities are found within Germany—a country consisting of only about 136,000 square miles, near the size of Montana—some explanation is in order.

German Geography

Important to any cuisine are geography and climate. They can't help but influence the availability of ingredients and the overall development of national and regional cooking customs. Despite being a relatively small land mass, Germany can be divided into three naturally occurring geographical zones or belts which make up most central European terrain. These zones exist independently of present or past political borders, which have been frequently

changed during periods of conquest, partition and other means of empire building and losing. Instead of the German East-West division most people immediately think of, more
meaningful divisions are found from north to south. Precisely named for our purposes, they
are the Northern Zone, the Central Zone and the Southern Zone. Again, these zones pass
through and include corresponding sections of Germany and encompass parts of neighboring countries as well.

The Northern Zone

The Northern Zone consists of a lowland plain that stretches from the Netherlands to Russia,
where nearness to the Baltic and North seas, Scandinavia to the west and Poland and Russia
to the east have had marked influences upon Northern German cuisine. The federal states
falling within the Northern Zone are Schleswig-Holstein, Hanover, Saxony, Hamburg, Bremen,
and from former East Germany, Mecklenburg and Brandenburg-Vopommern, with Berlin in
its center. Thus most North German cooking reflects a cold and damp climate, offering hearty
soups, plenty of herring in all forms, plus fresh fish and seafood—flounder, salmon, eel, lobster, crab and shrimp, among others. There are lots of pork and poultry entrees, often roasted
with prunes or apples or red cabbage. Potatoes and beets as well as grains such as barley, rye
and oats are important northern ingredients. Cabbage is ever-present, as are pickled meats
and roast duck and goose. Sauces are as likely to contain sweet and sour creams, or generous
amounts of vinegar and lemon juice, as do many Russian, Polish and Slavic dishes.

The Central Zone

The Central Zone is a departure to the south from the level northern plains to rolling hills
that eventually lead to the dramatic mountainous southern lands. The central states include
North-Rhine Westphalia and Hesse, plus the former East Germany's Thuringia and Saxony.
Germany's Central Zone, a land punctuated by large stretches of forests in fertile valleys, is
home to vineyards; orchards; tilled fields of rye, cabbage, turnips, sugar beets and potatoes;
and pasture lands that support small and large herds of cattle and sheep. Despite the cattle
and despite the sheep, pork reigns supreme in central Germany. Westphalian ham, the
most famous of all German meats, is traditionally prepared from pigs who feed on the wild
acorns of Westphalia's numerous oak forests. Frankfurt, the number-one city of Hesse, has
given America the "hot dog" and other Central German specialties, including Thuringian
Bratwurst, potato dumplings, sauerkraut, beefsteak tartar and sundry baked specialties
such as stollen and delicious spicy cookies of all kinds. Saxony features sweet-and-sour
recipes in which raisins, pears, dried fruit and wine play supporting roles.

The Southern Zone

The Southern Zone consists of rugged hills and steep terraces that lead to the Alp Moun-
tains. In the Southern Zone you'll find Baden-Wurttemberg, the Rhineland-Palatinate, the

Saarland and Bavaria. You'll see more dairy and some beef cattle farms, plus huge fields of grain growing on the plateaus—barley to supply the breweries and wheat for feeding the German passion for breads, rolls, pretzels and other baked goods. Acres and acres of white-wine grapes follow the banks of the Mosel and Rhine rivers. Potatoes are a mainstay product, and the famous "Heaven and Earth," made of potatoes and apples, hails from the Rhineland. Game birds, roast pork and wild pig and, of course, sausages are found everywhere. Baden, with its close proximity to France, features many of the finer points of not only German but of French and other styles of European cooking as well.

In addition to Germany's three major land zones, its central position within Europe also has had a considerable effect on its cuisine. Throughout the centuries, many influential Germans have chosen mates from neighboring countries who brought their own servants, including handmaids, craftsmen, gardeners, and chefs. Able to bring only so many ingredients from their home regions, the new chefs eventually had to adapt their own cooking styles to prepare ingredients found locally in their new surroundings. Little by little, an exchange of cooking skills took place.

German History

But geography and locale are not the only things that influenced German cooking. So did German history. Indeed, for most of its existence, Germany had been a patchwork of tiny independent kingdoms and states. And even when those individual principalities were forcibly united under one foreign occupation or another, no unified culinary style emerged.

Formal banquets staged in Germany during the Middle Ages easily rivaled those of England for their grandiose accompaniments, with numerous courses of meticulously prepared dishes, some gilded with gold or silver foil, others less ornately decorated with fur, fin and feather. Entertainment between courses helped the diners alternately renew their hunger and extend the length of a feast up to eight hours. Food for commoners in those times did not vary much. It still consisted of gruels and breads and fruits and vegetables gathered or grown. Fish was more readily available to the commoners, with carp, pike, and native panfish plentiful. Ingredients for the commoners depended on what could be found (and was permitted by the ruling classes) in the forests, fields, rivers, lakes, and seas. For the gentry, huge legs or rib cuts of oxen or beef were roasted on spits over open fires, as were smaller roasts from wild pigs. Kings and nobles were allowed to hunt practically anywhere they pleased, but harvesting game from the land—even though it may have been living in their own backyards—was out of the question for peasants. To stay in touch with their servants, some German rulers made a habit of staging periodic feasts for everyone—with roast oxen, hares, lambs and fish supplied for the entire population.

Into the Renaissance, the cities of Germany gained more power and autonomy. There arose numerous craft guilds, associations that strictly regulated their members' behavior. There were guilds for each trade or profession, and the guilds wielded almost supreme power over what their members could do. For example, cooks who ran restaurants were not permitted to slaughter the animals they cleaned and prepared. Bakers were not allowed to grind their own flour; flour-grinding was instead accomplished by trained members of yet another guild. Some kitchens, in fact, could be used only for roasting meats. Others were permitted just to boil their ingredients. As members of the newly developing bourgeoisie or rising middle class took their place within Germany, they dared to prepare many of the more extravagantly cooked dishes previously reserved for the noble classes.

In the mid- to late-1700s, Germany fell under considerable influence from the French. Handwritten cookbooks became popular. Food took on a more sophisticated look, with smaller portions. Glasses replaced large metal, wooden, or bone drinking goblets. All aspects of dining tended to become more refined. Yeast pastries were in vogue. A baroque style replaced coarser ways of doing things. The use of silver and gold forks and spoons became popular substitutes for eating with fingers. Class differences were becoming more obvious. Aristocrats, bourgeoisie, workers and peasants all ate differently and lived far differently, with strictly prescribed life-styles.

While this French influence was under way, the powerful kingdom of Prussia soon enveloped German lands, with relentless military expansion under Frederick the Great, who preferred to speak French instead of his native German. Within this scenario, the arts were still heavily supported, showcasing Joseph Haydn, Ludwig von Beethoven and Wolfgang Amadeus Mozart. Goethe and the romantics, Schiller, Schumann, Richard Wagner and Johannes Brahms created intensely German music and literature.

In 1806, Napoleon invaded Prussia, and for seven years Germany was part of the French Empire. Napoleon himself was a rather fussy eater who imported chefs from his home country to provide rich and nourishing dishes for French officers and others under his command. By the time Napoleon was defeated, first at Leipzig and several years later at Waterloo, the French chefs had exerted a major influence on German cooks who were kept on by Napoleon as kitchen helpers for the flamboyant master French chefs.

Finally, in 1871, William I was declared the first Kaiser of the United German Empire and Germany was unified. Before 1871, there had *never* been a unified German nation. Instead, the German territory had alternately consisted of a loose collection of tribes, fiefdoms, dukedoms, principalities, and tiny kingdoms, each with its own way of governing and living. In general, the industrialization of many of its areas improved living conditions for the middle classes. The middle classes once again began imitating the social and cooking habits of the aristocracy. Unfortunately, another outgrowth of industrialization was the effort to increase Germany's military might. Inevitably, World War I was triggered by the assassination of the Archduke of Austria and the German invasion of France.

Four years later, in 1918, at the end of the war Germany was completely humiliated and demoralized by the Versailles Treaty, which forced Germany to give up its overseas colonies and much of its European lands, including returning Alsace-Lorraine to France.

By 1923, Germany was mired in financial ruin. Inflation was out of control. German citizens had struck what surely must have been bottom, the worst conditions in Germany since the end of the Thirty Years' War. Enter Adolph Hitler to lead Germany out from under the oppressive and unfair demands of the Allies. In 1934, German President von Hindenburg died and Hitler declared himself Führer (Leader) of the Third Reich (Empire). Nazi philosophy and behavior permeated the country with their racist and anticommunist policies (although not all Germans were swayed by Nazi beliefs). Germany then turned its industrial might to weaponry and preparations for war.

Enter the horrors of World War II. By the end of the war, Germany was in complete shambles. Most of the major cities were in ruins. There were almost no working transportation or delivery systems. No utilities. Nowhere to buy food, clothing, or other commodities. People were starving, with food allotments of fewer than 800 calories per person, per day, mostly from potatoes, cabbage, and bread. Meat was nearly impossible to come by. Known to Germans as the famous "Zero Hour," an entire new start had to be made, overshadowed by the haunting difficulty of facing the Nazi war crimes.

As result of World War II and the later land divisions, about 12 million Germans either moved to other parts of Germany or Europe, or were forcibly expelled, most toward the West. These mass migrations—the result of German expansion into adjacent lands and then her defeat and withdrawal—resulted in the return of Germans to their mother country with various cooking habits and tastes they had adopted from their temporary occupation of neighboring countries.

In 1945, at the Yalta Conference, France, Britain, the United States and the Soviet Union temporarily divided Germany into four military zones. The Russians got the eastern and central parts of Germany, which they occupied and which later became East Germany. The Americans got the southern regions. Great Britain got the northwestern sections and the French received lands adjacent to their own country. Berlin, likewise, was quartered among the Allies.

To prevent the disastrous situation that developed after World War I, when the Treaty of Versailles penalized the German population so heavily, the Allies orchestrated the Potsdam Agreement, which was meant to help rebuild Germany as a democracy. Unfortunately, the Soviet Union decided to pull out of the Potsdam Agreement. On June 24, 1948, the Russians began to blockade Berlin by sealing off all land traffic leading through their part of the country to the West. In response, the United States and England carried out a huge airlift, flying millions of tons of supplies into the city to support West Berlin against the plans of Stalin. Stalin gave up the blockade in April 1949.

France, Great Britain and the United States combined their zones into the Federal Republic of Germany, or West Germany. Eleven federal states made up West Germany and elections for local parliaments were held. However, the Soviet-held territory became the Communist German Democratic Republic and remained under Communist control.

In the early 1950s in West Germany, there was considerable prosperity and growth, aided by support from the Marshall Plan, which helped rebuild devastated cities and the economy. It did wonders for the West German people, who called it the *Wirtschaftscwunder,* or "the economic miracle." Families acquired television sets, modern homes and kitchen appliances, and all the trappings of modern life. The disciplined, thorough, methodical manufacturing capabilities of the Germans were in evidence everywhere. Thousands of Volkswagen "Beetles" were driven within Germany and many other countries.

In 1961, to stem the rising tide of refugees who were leaving the largely rural and repressive East Germany for the West, the Berlin Wall was constructed. For years the Berlin Wall stood as a symbol of Communist repression. By 1989, East German discontent culminated in mass demonstrations and huge numbers of refugees began leaving the East for the West. Finally, Communist power started collapsing in one country after another across Eastern Europe, and the Berlin Wall fell.

In 1990 there was considerable political instability within both Germanys. Free elections were held in East Germany. The economic union took place first and a few months later, the political union, with five new states created out of the former East Germany. In 1991, a decision was made to move the capital from Bonn, which had ruled West Germany since 1949, to Berlin, the popular capital of Germany before the end of World War II.

After forty-five years of living in contrasting East-West political and economic systems, different attitudes toward living standards, work ethics and even how to spend free time have developed. East Germany has a lot of catching up to do with its railway, roads and telecommunications, and the needed modifications have put a strain on the reunified country's economy. Adding to the financial burden are outsiders or individuals from the Mideast, Africa, and Asia who are seeking political freedom and employment within German borders, attempting to take advantage of the strong sense of social welfare displayed by modern-day Germans—a sense which recently has been strained to the breaking point.

Thus the traumatic and unsettling history of Germany, when combined with its markedly different geographical zones, has resulted in a country having so many culinary specialties, styles and traditions. Thanks to German unity and modern methods of transportation and communication—including the publication of cookbooks—numerous facets of German cooking are being shared not only within Germany, but throughout the world.

Ingredients

The foods of modern Germany directly reflect the German devotion to fresh and unadulterated ingredients. Germans demand that their foods be as fresh as possible, without chemical additives, sprays, or preservatives. They would rather shop more often than settle for ingredients having long shelf lives at a sacrifice of freshness, nutritional value, and taste.

Again with thanks to modern methods of transportation, German specialty foods such as pickles, mustards, sauerkraut, cheese, sausages and soups as well as beers and wines are available in large food markets throughout the world. Gourmet food mail-order catalogs supply the same kinds of ingredients to individuals who do not live near the larger food stores. Beyond authentic German ingredients, the good-quality fresh meats, dairy products and produce that make up most of the recipes in this book can be found practically anywhere.

Festivals & Holidays

When German festivals are discussed, the conversation inevitably turns to beer, wine and food—all of which play important roles in endless numbers of festivals and celebrations held for religious and secular reasons. Some festivals are historical celebrations. Others are planned for modern reasons—the dedication of a new school or factory, for instance. There are local annual celebrations all over the country and there are international festivals too. Travel agencies publish enormous lists of festivals and similar going-ons in their "things-to-see-and-experience" brochures.

Fasching season takes place in January, with carnivals, street fairs, parades and masked balls throughout the cities and towns of southern Germany, especially in Munich, Cologne, Mainz, and Dusseldorf. This early-year partying finishes up in early February. It was originally a religious observance, held to usher in the beginning of Lent by providing fun-loving Germans with a "last" chance for drinking, eating and engaging in the more hedonistic pleasures. Sporting events are also accompanied by eating and drinking festivities for ski marathons, tennis tournaments, horse racing, bicycling, and other competitions.

Beer and wine festivals, generally held during spring and/or fall, celebrate everything from religious events to grape harvests. Munich's sixteen-day-long Octoberfest is, of course, the beer blast to end all beer blasts. It began over 185 years ago, on October 12, 1810, to be exact, as an outdoor wedding reception for the Crown Prince Ludwig, later King Ludwig I. It was prompted by a horse race in which the "promoter," a friend of Ludwig's, won before a rousing crowd. Because everyone was having such a good time, the partying lasted through the night and into the next day. Even after the bride and groom had long since departed, the celebration continued. It was so much fun that the people of Munich decided to do it again and again and again. So it was and so it continues to be held in the same meadow, having been canceled over the years only during times of plagues and war. A half-dozen major breweries each sponsor huge festival tents, as do a select number of private businesspeople and other entrepreneurs. At any given time during Octoberfest, the interiors of the tents are packed with Germans and visitors who sway and sing and stomp their feet to the "oom-pa-pa" beat of colorful Bavarian brass bands while eating and drinking all the while. Between 8 and 10 million participants pack themselves into Munich over the partying period, and although there are about 75,000 seats in and near the tents, sometimes it's practically impossible to find an empty spot. The partygoers drink upward of 5 million liters of beer, eat thousands of roast chickens, grill sausages by the ton, consume tens of thousands of pork knuckles and whole herds of oxen roasted whole on spits. It's truly memorable culinary chaos.

There are music festivals linked to many of the great German composers and Munich's Opera Festival in July. There are plum harvests, onion fairs, asparagus festivals and apple days. There are celebrations for practically anything.

Although most German festivals come with or encourage behavior similar to that encountered in the New Orleans Mardi Gras, German celebrations of Easter and Christmas are more reserved. At Easter, the Easter Bunny hides colored eggs throughout the house and yard for children to find. On Easter Sunday German families sit down to carefully prepared meals of whatever entrees they favor.

On December 6, Saint Nicholas Day throughout Germany, children check stockings or boots hung on their windows or doors. If the children have been good, they'll find candies, cookies, nuts and fruit. If they've not been so good, they're likely to discover a half-pretending parent standing there with a switch in his or her hand. Santa Claus—the German Saint Nicholas—may also appear on the eve of December 6 to ask the children if they have been good or to hear their prayers.

During Advent, the four weeks before Christmas, an Advent wreath may be hung in the dining room or placed on top of the table. The wreath contains four candles representing the four Sundays before Christmas. As each Sunday arrives, its respective candle is lit. On Christmas day, all four are blazing at once.

Christmas day is a time for going to church, for relaxing, for enjoying one's family and for eating. Apples, nuts and almonds weigh largely in German Christmas cooking. Traditional Christmas foods include baked carp, roast hare or roast goose stuffed with chestnut or other fillings, turkey, venison, wild pig, chicken, roast beef, roast pork and roast veal, which are all enjoyed by Protestant and Catholic families alike, who, although they may worship differently, celebrate the coming of the Christ Child. The day after Christmas is the time to exchange visits with friends and enjoy Christmas cookies and a glass of wine.

German Jewish Traditions

Entwined with and happily embracing German (and Eastern European) cuisine is the many-faceted discipline of traditional Jewish cooking. It's easy to see how compatible these cooking styles are; in fact, many specific foods are equally shared, including dill pickles and horseradish, herring with its numerous variations, old-fashioned rye breads, nourishing vegetarian bean, lentil, cabbage, and beet soups, crispy potato pancakes, plus noodles and dumplings. Of course, one major difference is the absence of pork from Jewish dinner tables, but sundry beef, veal, lamb, and poultry dishes take up the slack. Stuffed cabbage leaves, roast brisket, beef stews, corned beef, veal rib roasts, and roast legs of lamb are partaken with a wide variety of garden vegetables. Chicken soup is a favorite in every Jewish household, and many "German" cakes and strudels and puddings grace Jewish dessert tables.

Although German Jewish holidays follow the central Jewish calendar, they are somewhat influenced by available traditional German and Eastern European ingredients.

September's Rosh Hashanah features a multi-course festive meal, often with chicken soup, baked beef brisket, potatoes, carrots, green beans, cabbage, fresh fruits and sweet honey-laden or coated cakes.

Yom Kippur comes ten days later, a day of atonement and fasting, before which a traditional pre-fast dinner is served. Sukkot is a seven-day holiday that begins five days after

Yom Kippur and commemorates the forty-year journey of the Israelites from slavery to the Promised Land. Its menus include stuffed cabbage, stuffed vegetables, and lots of fresh fruit—signifying fulfillment and bountiful harvest.

Chanukah arrives in late December, and celebrates the rebellion of the Palestine Jews against the tyrannical ancient Syrian-Greeks more than two thousand years ago. Traditional Chanukah foods include potato pancakes, roast goose, roast duckling, and fried doughnuts.

Passover, the most widely celebrated Jewish holiday, recalls several historical festivals—of the paschal lamb and of unleavened bread, both related to the Exodus when God "passed over" Jewish houses, sparing firstborns. Matzo, or unleavened bread, is always eaten at Passover, and so is horseradish, bitter vegetables, such as radishes or watercress, and lamb as ceremonial dishes, followed by a rather elaborately prepared multi-course meal beginning with hard-cooked eggs and other appetizers, then proceeding with soup, baked fish, roast chicken, vegetables, fruit, and dessert cakes.

Appetizers

Vorspeisen

Due to the German tendency to eat many times throughout the day and evening, appetizers or, at the very least, appetizer-size portions, have always played a supporting role in day-to-day eating habits. Recently, many foreign businesses have been set up in German towns and cities. Naturally, along with these businesses have come people to run them. Consequently, restaurant operators have also moved in. Italian, Greek, Slavic, Chinese, and American cuisines have all made inroads, not only with their own nationals but with the German population as well. It's certainly common to find Germans, in addition to carrying the traditional pretzel and sausage or lunch meat and cheese sandwich that's eaten in outdoor markets, to be walking between business appointments while munching on bags of French fries (*pommes frites*), gyros, or sundry Middle Eastern snacks. Hamburgers, popcorn (with sugar on it instead of salt), and pizza are readily available, too.

There are snack stands or stand-up snack bars located on busy shopping streets, in parking lots, train stations, and markets where sausages of all kinds are dispensed—grilled, roasted or boiled, in all shapes and sizes. There are rolls filled with cheese, cold cuts, special fillings, or even fish.

Fast foods have become and are becoming more popular all the time. They hail from Wienerwald, McDonald's, Pizza Hut, Burger King, and Nordsee fish bars among the many. More traditional restaurants are everywhere, too, in department stores, butcher shops, and outside pubs and taverns. All of these restaurant-type markets are having a marked effect on the kinds of appetizers being prepared in Germany today.

In a sense, this chapter on appetizers can be described as borrowing—on a small scale—from nearly each and every one of the other chapters in the book. The dishes are essentially scaled-down portions so individual appetizers can be enjoyed in advance of the main entrees without taking away the diner's appetite. The more traditional appetizers have been included here, starting with the ever-present canapés, which can be prepared in as many combinations and permutations as there are breads and spreads. It's important to note that there are no official rules for canapé making. Yes, they're prepared with small squares or rounds of rye, wheat, white or other breads. And yes, a variety of pâtés, sauces, dressings and flavored butters can be spread over the bite-size breads. Then, to take them a step further, they can be topped with ingredients such as sardines, sprats, hard-cooked egg slices, cheeses, cold meats, pickled mushrooms and onions, tomatoes, green onions, horseradish, pickled beets, sliced vegetables—and everything else but the kitchen sink.

Simple vegetable plates, while always present, have recently moved to the front of the appetizer line, taking a place alongside cold cuts and cheese. Cold cuts can also include the large sausages, thinly sliced, along with sliced cold-smoked pork loin, tongue and other specialty meats, and pig's knuckles, hot or cold. There are numerous hot appetizers prepared with sausages, ham, and mushrooms. Mushroom caps are filled with a tasty mouthful of cooked chicken, turkey, liver, ham or sausage stuffing. Included are marinated smoked cheese, the ever-present pâtés of liver and chicken and herring galore, with numerous accompaniments.

Vegetable Plate with Blue Cheese Dip

Gemüseteller

Variety and presentation are guidelines to preparing effective vegetable appetizer plates. Pickled cucumbers, tomatoes, onions, shallots, leeks, celery stalks, olives, relishes, pickles, peppers, cauliflower, sliced parsley root, zucchini, yellow squash, thawed frozen green peas and cabbage of all colors can be used for making small or large vegetable snack plates.

Green, red, or yellow bell peppers can be hollowed out and filled with other vegetables such as blanched green beans or thin spears of marinated asparagus. Instead of using a traditional small glass serving dish, fill a green or red bell pepper, hollowed-out half of a small red cabbage or cucumber boats for dips.

Red, white and black radishes provide colorful garnishes. Add apple and pear slices sprinkled with lemon juice to prevent discoloration. Pineapple, cherries, and plums are other standbys. *Makes about 2 2/3 cups.*

1 lb. blue cheese, room temperature
2 (3-oz.) packages cream cheese, room temperature
1/3 cup milk
3 tablespoons white wine (Rhine or Moselle)

1/4 teaspoon ground white pepper
1/8 teaspoon onion salt
Ripe olive slices or coarsely chopped walnut pieces for garnish
Chips and crackers
Assorted vegetables (see above)

Combine blue cheese and cream cheese in a medium-size bowl, stirring with a fork. Blend milk, wine, pepper and onion salt into cheese mixture. Spoon blue-cheese dip into a small serving dish. Refrigerate 1 hour, if desired. Top with a few sliced olives or coarsely chopped walnuts. Serve with chips, crackers, celery or carrot sticks, tomato wedges, or cucumber slices.

Canapés

❖ ··· ❖

Cocktailgebäck

First, select any five of the ten spreads below if you're using only one loaf of bread. It's best to select several meat spreads and several of the nonmeat spreads to use with each loaf. If you want to use all the spreads, you'll need to use another full loaf of bread, and slice it accordingly. Keep in mind that firm, heavy loaves of bread will work the best for this recipe. They will allow you to stack and trim and sharply slice the individual portions in an eye-pleasing manner. Note that all butter or margarine should be at room temperature for easy spreading. Other options for each bread loaf are to use a half-loaf of white bread, and another half-loaf of German rye. Or a half-loaf of dark pumpernickel with a half-loaf of German rye. Or try half wheat with half white, or wheat with rye. *Each loaf of bread and 5 spreads makes 15 to 20 appetizers.*

Herring Spread (see below)
Green Spread (see below)
White-Meat Chicken Spread
* (see below)*
Dark-Meat Chicken Spread
* (see below)*
Pork Spread (see opposite)

Beef Spread (see opposite)
Veal Spread (see opposite)
Tomato Spread (see opposite)
Onion Spread (see opposite)
Egg & Anchovy Spread (see opposite)
About 1 loaf German rye bread,
* unsliced, for every 5 spreads*

HERRING SPREAD
2 hard-cooked eggs, chopped
1 oil-packed herring fillet, drained,
* chopped*
1 teaspoon minced chives

GREEN SPREAD
2 tablespoons chopped fresh parsley
* or chives*
1 1/2 tablespoons butter or
* margarine, room temperature*
1 tablespoon fresh lemon juice
1/8 teaspoon salt

WHITE-MEAT CHICKEN SPREAD
1/2 cup ground cooked chicken breast
2 tablespoons butter or margarine,
* room temperature*
1/8 teaspoon sweet paprika

DARK-MEAT CHICKEN SPREAD
1/2 cup ground cooked dark chicken
* meat*
2 tablespoons butter or margarine,
* room temperature*
1/8 teaspoon freshly ground black
* pepper*

PORK SPREAD

1/2 cup ground cooked pork
2 tablespoons butter or margarine,
 room temperature
Pinch of celery salt or garlic salt

BEEF SPREAD

1/2 cup ground cooked beef
2 tablespoons butter or margarine,
 room temperature
Dash of Maggi seasoning

VEAL SPREAD

1/2 cup ground cooked veal
2 tablespoons butter or margarine,
 room temperature
1/4 teaspoon honey

TOMATO SPREAD

1 (3-oz.) package cream cheese,
 room temperature
2 teaspoons tomato paste
1 garlic clove, crushed
Pinch of salt

ONION SPREAD

1/2 medium Vidalia or other sweet
 onion, chopped
1 medium dill pickle, chopped
1 tablespoon sour cream
1 tablespoon shredded sharp
 Cheddar cheese
Several drops red food coloring or
 1/4 teaspoon beet juice

EGG & ANCHOVY SPREAD

2 hard-cooked eggs
6 desalted anchovy fillets
 (see page 33)
2 tablespoons mayonnaise

Prepare any five of the above spreads. Using a blender or food processor fitted with the metal blade, process ingredients for each spread into a smooth paste.

Slice off ends and trim crust from top, bottom and sides of bread. Cut trimmed bread horizontally into 6 (1/2-inch-thick) slices. Remove top bread slice from stack; set aside. Place a thin layer of each of 5 spreads on 5 remaining bread slices. Stack bread layers in their original positions. Top with remaining slice, then gently press layers together. Cut stacked loaf into serving-size squares or triangles.

Note

Lightly butter crusts and sprinkle with a little garlic salt and cook until browned over medium heat or broil for croutons.

Open-Face Canapés

Öffen-Face Cocktailgebäck

Another way to make canapés is to trim the crusts from slices of white, rye, or wheat bread and cut the bread slices into squares, triangles or other bite-size shapes. Use the following spreads and toppings to create a mixed canapé platter.

Smoked Eel Canapés

Spread mayonnaise over black rye bread pieces. Sprinkle with chopped fresh dill; top with smoked eel pieces.

Caviar Canapés

Spread soft butter or margarine over bread pieces. Mash 2 hard-cooked eggs and spread them over buttered bread pieces; top with caviar.

Smoked-Salmon & Shrimp Canapés

Spread soft butter or margarine over bread pieces. Arrange smoked-salmon slices and small cooked shrimp on buttered bread pieces. Garnish with dollops of mayonnaise and ripe olive slices.

Cold Cuts & Cheese

Kalte Schnittchen & Käse

One of the most popular appetizer courses that can be found at any gathering is the cold-cut and cheese platter. The variety of German luncheon meats, sausage-type meats and cheeses is truly amazing. They are usually served accompanied by every type of dip and sauce imaginable. The presentation is important, with many of the meats thinly sliced and folded over in symmetrical patterns.

The German cheese selection, like that of the cold meats, is enormous. Popular varieties include Emmentaler, Edam, Butter Käse, Steppenkäse, Tilsit, Gouda, Esrom and smoked cheeses of various flavors and colors. Cut the assortment of cheeses into bite-size cubes and serve them with colorful cocktail picks. Arrange cheese cubes on a serving platter and surround them with an assortment of crackers. In any event, both meats and cheeses are almost always served with hard rolls, pickles, and a number of relishes and marinated vegetables such as peppers, onions and cucumbers.

Sausage Rolls

···

Wurstbrötchen

Smoked or plain frankfurters will also fit nicely into this recipe. *Makes about 6 dozen appetizers.*

3 cups all-purpose flour	*About 1 cup buttermilk (see Note)*
1 1/3 tablespoons baking powder	*6 links (about 2 oz. each) smoked*
1/4 teaspoon salt	*sausage links*
1/2 cup butter or margarine, chilled	*Grated Parmesan cheese*
2 cups (8 oz.) shredded Cheddar	
cheese	

Preheat oven to 425F (220C). Grease 2 baking sheets.

Sift flour, baking powder and salt into a large bowl. With a pastry blender, cut butter or margarine into flour mixture until it resembles coarse meal. Add Cheddar cheese and buttermilk. With your hands, quickly work mixture into a soft dough. Shape half of the dough into 1-inch balls. Slice sausage links into about 12 pieces each. Lightly press 1 sausage slice into each dough ball. Place rolls about 2 inches apart on greased baking sheets. Sprinkle with Parmesan cheese. Repeat with remaining dough. Bake 12 to 15 minutes or until lightly browned. Serve immediately. Or cool and freeze them in a airtight container for up to 1 month.

Note
If buttermilk is not available, add 1 tablespoon lemon juice or vinegar to a 1-cup measure. Add milk and let stand 10 minutes.

Mushroom & Ham Delights

Champignons & Schinken Delights

It's best to use freshly baked crescent rolls with or without poppy seeds or sesame seeds. Larger mushrooms can also be used if they're cut into bite-size pieces first. *Makes 24 to 32 servings.*

About 1/2 lb. fresh button mushrooms
1/2 cup water
1/2 teaspoon salt
4 tablespoons butter or margarine,
   room temperature

3 crescent rolls, sliced crosswise into
   1/2-inch-thick rounds
1/4 lb. sliced ham, cut into 1 1/2-inch
   squares

Place mushrooms in a medium saucepan. Add water, salt and 1 tablespoon of the butter or margarine. Bring to a boil over high heat. Reduce heat to medium-low and cook, uncovered, until tender. Drain. Discard cooking liquid. Let mushrooms cool.

Preheat oven to 375F (190C). Grease a baking sheet.

Spread remaining butter or margarine evenly on both sides of crescent roll slices. Place 1 or 2 slices ham on each roll slice. Top with 1 cooked mushroom, cap side up. Secure with a wooden pick and place on greased baking sheet. Repeat process until all roll slices, ham slices and mushrooms are used. Bake 6 to 8 minutes or until browned.

Stuffed Mushroom Caps

Gefüllte Champignons

Y ou can use smaller-size or larger-size mushrooms; just adjust the amount of stuffing mixture that goes into each cap. Mushrooms that are all the same size will make a more attractive presentation. *Makes 20 stuffed mushrooms.*

20 large (1 1/2- to 2 1/2-inch) fresh
   mushrooms
2 tablespoons butter or margarine
2 tablespoons finely chopped shallots
   or onions
1/2 cup finely chopped cooked chicken,
   turkey, liver, ham or sausage
1/4 cup shredded Swiss cheese
2 tablespoons dry bread crumbs

1 tablespoon half and half
1 egg
1 tablespoon chopped fresh parsley
1/2 teaspoon salt
1/4 teaspoon freshly grated nutmeg
1/8 teaspoon freshly ground black
   pepper
Freshly grated Parmesan cheese

Preheat oven to 400F (205C). Grease a 10-inch square baking dish.

Separate mushroom stems and caps; set caps aside. Finely chop stem pieces. Melt butter or margarine in a small skillet over medium heat. Add shallots or onion and sauté until tender. In a small bowl, combine sautéed shallots or onion, chopped mushroom stems, chopped meat, grated Swiss cheese, bread crumbs and half and half. In a small bowl, beat egg with a fork; add to stuffing mixture. Stir in parsley, salt, nutmeg and pepper until blended.

Pack about 1 heaping teaspoon stuffing mixture into each reserved mushroom cap. Arrange mushroom caps, stuffing side up, in greased dish. Sprinkle Parmesan cheese over each stuffed mushroom cap. Bake, uncovered, 20 to 25 minutes. Serve hot.

Bavarian Cheese Toast

Bayrischer Käse Toastet

Cut the toast into quarters, if desired, or leave them whole. Additional toppings may include anchovies, sliced black olives, thinly sliced zucchini, and chopped tomatoes. *Makes 12 servings.*

12 slices white or whole-wheat bread, lightly toasted

2 cups diced Westphalian, Black Forest, or other lean ham

2 cups shredded Emmentaler cheese

5 eggs

3/4 cup milk

1 teaspoon spicy brown prepared mustard

1/4 teaspoon salt

1/8 teaspoon freshly ground black pepper

1/8 teaspoon freshly grated nutmeg

1 tablespoon chopped fresh parsley

Preheat oven to 350F (175C). Lightly butter a large baking sheet with a rim.

Arrange toast in 1 layer on buttered baking sheet. If desired, toast can be trimmed to fit the baking sheet. Sprinkle ham and cheese evenly over toast. In a large bowl, beat eggs, milk, mustard, salt, pepper and nutmeg. Pour slowly over the ham and cheese. Top with parsley. Bake 20 to 30 minutes or until golden brown. Serve hot.

Variation

Try other cheeses, such as Edam, Tilsit or any of the natural smoked varieties.

Rye Cheese Toast with Garlic

Überbackenes Roggenbrot mit Käse & Knoblauch

I f you'd prefer less salt, use 1/4 teaspoon garlic powder instead of garlic salt. Of course, you can use other kinds of bread, rolls, and bagels, if desired. *Makes 24 appetizers.*

6 slices rye bread
2 tablespoons butter or margarine,
   room temperature
2 cups (8 oz.) shredded Cheddar
   cheese

1/2 teaspoon garlic salt
Sweet paprika
6 whole dill pickles, sliced lengthwise
   into 4 slices each

Preheat broiler. Toast bread lightly; remove crusts with a knife. Place toast on baking sheet. Lightly butter toast and sprinkle evenly with cheese, garlic salt and paprika. Broil until tops turn golden brown. Let cool 1 minute and slice into equal-size triangles. Serve with sliced dill pickles.

Cheese Balls

Käseballchen

Cheese balls can be eaten with a variety of sauces and dips. Favorites include hot seafood sauce or horseradish sauce. *Makes 10 cheese-ball appetizers.*

1 lb. Brie or Camembert cheese, room temperature
2 tablespoons minced shallots
About 1/4 cup all-purpose flour

2 eggs, lightly beaten
1 cup dried bread crumbs
Vegetable oil for deep-frying

In a medium bowl, mix cheese and shallots. Divide cheese mixture into 10 equal portions; form balls by rolling cheese portions in your hands. Place cheese balls on a plate; cover and refrigerate 1 hour. Place flour in a small bowl. Place beaten eggs in another small bowl and bread crumbs in a third small bowl. Roll a cheese ball in flour, then in beaten eggs. Let excess egg drip off, then roll cheese ball in bread crumbs. Repeat breading process with remaining cheese balls.

Heat vegetable oil in a medium saucepan or deep-fryer to 365F (185C). Carefully lower cheese balls into hot oil, one at a time. Fry a small number of cheese balls at a time. Cook 3 to 5 minutes or until golden brown. Remove cooked cheese balls with a slotted spoon; drain on paper towels. Serve warm.

Brie Pastry

Brie Geback

The flaky puff pastry practically melts in your mouth and nicely complements the wonderful flavor of Brie. Try Brie wheels that have herbs or other seasonings. *Makes 16 appetizers.*

1 (8-oz.) sheet frozen puff pastry, thawed

1 (8-oz.) round cold, firm Brie

2 eggs, lightly beaten

All-purpose flour

Preheat oven to 425F (220C). Line a large baking sheet with foil.

On a lightly floured work surface, roll out pastry into a 1/8-inch-thick round. Cut dough round into 16 equal triangles, beginning in center. Cut the cheese wheel into 16 equal triangles. Using your hands, roll cheese triangles into balls. Place a cheese ball on each dough triangle. Wrap cheese balls with dough and arrange dough-wrapped cheese balls on foil, 1 1/2 to 2 inches apart. Brush with beaten eggs. Bake 15 to 20 minutes or until golden brown.

Chicken Liver Pâté

Hähnchen-Leben Schädel

This versatile appetizer can serve as a canapé filling, or can be eaten by itself, sliced, with crusty bread or raw vegetable strips. *Makes 1 loaf, about 10 servings.*

1/2 lb. lean bacon

1 lb. chicken livers

1/2 lb. ground pork

3/4 cup chopped onion

1/4 lb. fresh mushrooms, chopped

1 large garlic clove, minced

2 tablespoons chopped fresh parsley

2 tablespoons sherry

2 teaspoons salt

1/4 teaspoon freshly ground pepper

1/3 teaspoon crushed dried thyme
 leaves

1/4 teaspoon freshly grated nutmeg

1/4 teaspoon ground allspice

1 cup dried bread crumbs

1/2 cup Chicken Broth (page 57)
 or chicken bouillon

1 egg, lightly beaten

Place 3 bacon slices in a large skillet; cook over medium heat until crisp. Remove cooked bacon and drain on paper towels. When cooled, crumble cooked bacon strips into skillet. Add livers, pork, onion, mushrooms, garlic, parsley, sherry, salt, pepper, thyme, nutmeg and allspice. Cook, stirring gently, over medium heat 5 to 7 minutes or until livers are cooked but not browned. Let cool.

Preheat oven to 300F (150C). In a medium bowl, combine bread crumbs and broth or bouillon. Using a blender or food processor fitted with the metal blade, process cooled liver mixture until finely chopped. Stir egg and bread crumbs into liver mixture until combined.

Set aside 3 slices of the remaining bacon. Line a 9 × 5-inch loaf pan with remaining bacon. Spoon liver mixture into bacon-lined pan. Arrange remaining 3 bacon slices on top of liver mixture and cover with foil. Set loaf pan into a large baking pan. Add 1 inch of hot water. Bake 2 hours or until pâté starts to pull away from sides of loaf pan.

Remove loaf pan from water; let pâté cool in loaf pan. Refrigerate pâté in loaf pan overnight. Turn pâté out onto a platter. Remove bacon strips. Serve as an appetizer, snack or canapé filling.

Liver Pâté in Brioche

Leber-Schädel in Brioche

If desired, trickle melted Butterkäse cheese over the individual liver-brioche portions. Butterkäse cheese doesn't really contain any butter, but it has a fresh, creamy, mild flavor that children—and adults—love. *Makes 8 to 10 servings.*

Liver Pâté (see opposite)	*2 1/4 cups all-purpose flour*
1 package active dry yeast	*1/2 teaspoon salt*
1/3 cup warm milk	*1/2 cup butter or margarine, chilled*
1 tablespoon sugar	*3 eggs*

Prepare Liver Pâté. In a small bowl, combine yeast, milk and sugar. Set aside in a warm place until mixture is frothy, about 5 minutes.

Using a food processor fitted with the steel blade, process flour, salt and butter or margarine until mixture resembles very fine crumbs. (Or, use a pastry bender to cut butter or margarine into flour and salt and mix in remaining ingredients with a large spoon.) Add yeast mixture; process until combined, about 5 seconds. Add 2 of the eggs. Process until dough forms a ball. Grease a medium bowl; place dough in bowl. Cover and let rise in a warm place until dough doubles in size, about 2 hours.

Punch dough down; knead several times. Cut off one-third of dough and set aside. Wrap remaining dough in plastic wrap and refrigerate. Roll out the one-third portion of dough into an 8- to 9-inch round. Cover and let rise in a warm place 20 minutes.

Preheat oven to 375F (190C). Bake round 15 minutes or until very lightly browned. Let cool on a wire rack.

Place pâté in center of cooked brioche round. Trim sides if uneven. Roll out remaining dough into an 11-inch round; arrange round over pâté so at least 1 inch of dough overlaps pâté and cooked brioche round. Trim off any excess dough. Tuck overhanging dough beneath bottom of cooked brioche round. Let dough rise in a warm place 20 minutes.

Lightly beat remaining egg in a small bowl. Brush dough with beaten egg. Bake 40 to 45 minutes or until top is lightly browned. Serve hot.

LIVER PÂTÉ

2 tablespoons butter or margarine
1 1/2 cups chopped onions
1 garlic clove, minced
1/2 teaspoon crushed dried thyme
  leaves
3/4 lb. calf liver

1/2 lb. ground pork
1 egg, lightly beaten
1/3 cup dry white wine
1 teaspoon salt
1/2 teaspoon freshly ground black
  pepper

Melt butter or margarine in a medium skillet over medium heat. Add onions and cook, stirring occasionally, until tender, about 10 minutes. Add garlic and thyme; cook 2 minutes. Remove from heat.

Finely chop liver with a knife or in batches in a food processor. In a medium bowl, mix chopped liver and pork, onion mixture, egg, wine, salt and pepper until well combined. Place liver mixture in a 7- or 8-inch nonstick pie pan. Place pie pan in a large baking pan and add 3/4 inch of water. Bake 1 hour or until juices are clear when pierced with a skewer. Remove from water and cool in pan; refrigerate until chilled or up to 24 hours. Turn out onto a platter.

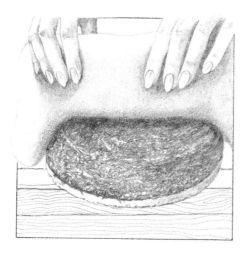

Chicken Pâté

Hähnchen Schädel

It is better to use a meat grinder rather than a food processor or blender for grinding the chicken and livers. It is easy to overprocess the mixture. A meat grinder, when used to grind the ingredients twice, will produce just the right consistency. *Makes 1 loaf, about 10 servings.*

4 cups water	*2 eggs, lightly beaten*
Salt	*1/2 teaspoon freshly grated nutmeg*
1 (2- to 2 1/2-lb.) chicken, cut up	*1/4 teaspoon ground allspice*
1/4 lb. chicken livers	*1/4 teaspoon freshly ground black*
1/4 lb. unsmoked bacon, chopped	* pepper*
2 day-old dinner rolls	

Heat water and 1/2 teaspoon salt in a large deep skillet. Add chicken, livers and bacon. Bring to a boil over medium-high heat. Cover with a tight-fitting lid, reduce heat to medium-low, and simmer 1 hour or until chicken is tender. Remove chicken, livers and bacon from cooking liquid; let cool. Reserve cooking liquid.

Preheat oven to 350F (175C). Grease a 9 × 5-inch loaf pan. Remove bones and skin from chicken and discard. Break rolls into small pieces. Soak roll pieces in reserved cooking liquid until moistened; squeeze out excess liquid. Grind cooked chicken, livers, bacon and soaked rolls into a large bowl. Grind resulting mixture a second time. Blend in eggs, 1/2 teaspoon salt, nutmeg, allspice and pepper. Spoon chicken mixture into greased loaf pan; pat smooth. Bake, uncovered, 1 hour or until pâté is firm.

Let pâté cool in pan. Cover and refrigerate in loaf pan 48 hours. Turn pâté out onto a platter.

Cocktail Puffs

Cocktail Blätterteig

There are many, many other cooked fillings you can try with these puffs, including shrimp, lobster, sausage slices, vegetable chunks, and pieces of fruit. *Makes about 36 puffs.*

1 cup beer	4 eggs
1/4 lb. butter or margarine	1 cup Chicken Pâté (page 28),
1 cup sifted all-purpose flour	Liver Pâté (page 27), sautéed
1/2 teaspoon salt	mushrooms or other filling

Prepare Chicken or Liver Pâté, sauteed mushrooms or other filling. Preheat oven to 450F (230C). Grease a baking sheet.

Combine beer and butter or margarine in a small saucepan. Place over medium-high heat until butter or margarine melts. Reduce heat to low. Add flour and salt. Cook, stirring, until mixture comes away from the sides of the pan. Remove from heat. Beat in eggs, one at a time, until dough is shiny. Using 2 teaspoons, drop the dough onto greased baking sheet in teaspoon-size balls. Bake 10 minutes. Reduce heat to 350F (175C) and bake 10 minutes longer or until browned. Let cool.

Split baked puffs halfway down the middle, forming a small pocket. Fill pocket with pâté, cooked mushrooms or other filling. Serve warm or at room temperature.

Pickled Herring

Eingelegter Hering

Herring makes the best pickled fish. The fillets should come from the larger herring available fresh at fish markets. *Makes 10 to 12 servings.*

2 cups water

1 cup vinegar

3 small onions, sliced

8 peppercorns or whole allspice
   berries

1/2 teaspoon sugar

2 bay leaves

1 1/2 lbs. herring fillets

2 tablespoons olive oil

Sliced dill pickles and carrot sticks
   for garnish

In a medium saucepan, combine water, vinegar, onions, peppercorns or allspice berries, sugar and bay leaves. Bring to a boil and boil, uncovered, over medium heat 5 minutes. Remove from heat; let cool.

Cut herring fillets into 1 1/2-inch slices, or roll whole fillets and secure with wooden picks. Arrange herring in a glass serving dish or bowl. Pour cooled brine mixture over herring. Drizzle with olive oil. Cover and refrigerate overnight. Serve with sliced pickles and carrot sticks.

Herring in Oil

Hering in Öl

After the pickled herring fillets are drained, pat them dry with paper towels before proceeding with the rest of the recipe. *Makes 10 to 12 servings.*

2 lbs. small pickled herring fillets,
   drained

1/2 cup prepared mustard

1/2 cup vegetable oil

2 bay leaves, crushed

8 black peppercorns

Lemon wedges and parsley sprigs
   for garnish

Lay fillets out flat, skin sides down. With a butter knife spread mustard evenly over inside of fillets. Roll fillets and secure with wooden picks. Arrange rolled fillets in a shallow glass dish. Drizzle oil over fillets. Add crushed bay leaves and peppercorns to oil. Cover and refrigerate overnight; turn rolled fillets 3 or 4 times. Serve slightly chilled. Garnish with lemon wedges and parsley sprigs.

Herring in Sour-Cream Marinade

Hering in Sauercrememarinade

In Germany as well as throughout much of Europe, herring is prepared and eaten with the bones in. If that doesn't appeal to you, split the herring above the backbone with a sharp knife. Then cut around the backbone and gently pull it up and out, pulling many or most of the small bones along with it. *Makes 12 to 14 servings.*

1 cup sour cream	2 lbs. fresh dressed herring, sliced
1/2 cup plain nonfat yogurt	into 1/2-inch pieces
Juice from 1/2 lemon	4 radishes, sliced
1/2 teaspoon sugar	1 lemon, cut into wedges
1/2 teaspoon white pepper	6 cherry tomatoes
1 tablespoon prepared horseradish	2 hard-cooked eggs, cut into wedges
3 onions, thinly sliced	1 apple, cored and sliced

In a medium bowl, combine sour cream, yogurt, lemon juice, sugar, white pepper and horseradish. Line a glass serving dish with half of the onion slices. Place half of the herring over onions; spoon half of the sour cream marinade over herring and onions. Top with layers of the remaining onions and herring. Spoon remaining marinade over top herring layer. Cover and refrigerate overnight. To serve, arrange radish slices, lemon wedges, tomatoes, hard-cooked eggs and apple slices around herring. Serve chilled.

German Kippers

Deutsche Bücklinge

Kippers are herring that have been split, salted, dried and cold-smoked. *Makes 4 servings.*

4 kipper fillets

1 1/2 cups plain low-fat yogurt

2 hard-cooked eggs, finely chopped

1 large tomato, peeled and finely chopped

1/2 teaspoon dry mustard

1/4 teaspoon hot-pepper sauce

1 tablespoon chopped fresh parsley

Place kippers in a medium saucepan. Cover with boiling water and let stand 5 minutes. Drain off water; let kippers cool in pan. Cut kippers into thin strips. Arrange kipper strips on 4 serving dishes.

In a medium bowl, combine yogurt, eggs, tomato, dry mustard and hot-pepper sauce. Spoon equal portion of sauce over each dish of kippers. Sprinkle with parsley.

Anchovies with Green Sauce

Sardellen mit Grüner Sosse

For this recipe, mild-flavored olives are best, because there're plenty of seasonings already in the anchovies and green sauce. *Makes 8 servings.*

2 (2-oz.) cans anchovy fillets,
   drained
1/2 cup vinegar
1/2 cup water
Pitted ripe olives
2 tablespoons minced fresh parsley
1/2 clove garlic, minced

3 hard-cooked egg yolks
1/8 teaspoon salt
1/8 teaspoon freshly ground black
   pepper
1 1/2 tablespoons vegetable oil
1 1/2 tablespoons vinegar
4 hard-cooked eggs, cut into wedges

Remove salt from anchovy fillets by placing fillets in a small bowl and adding the vinegar and water. Let fillets stand in vinegar mixture 2 hours; drain. Carefully wind each fillet around an olive and place them on a serving platter.

Using a food processor fitted with a steel blade, blend parsley, garlic, egg yolks, salt, pepper, oil and vinegar into a smooth sauce. Pour sauce over fillets and olives. Let marinate at room temperature 1 hour. Serve with hard-cooked egg wedges.

Stuffed Eggs with Herring

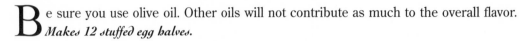

Gefüllte Eier mit Hering

Be sure you use olive oil. Other oils will not contribute as much to the overall flavor. *Makes 12 stuffed egg halves.*

6 hard-cooked eggs

1/2 cup dry bread crumbs

About 8 oz. cleaned, boned, skinned salted herring, finely chopped

1/4 cup finely chopped onion or chives

1 tablespoon olive oil

1/8 teaspoon freshly ground black pepper

Sweet paprika

Peel eggs and slice in half lengthwise. Carefully remove egg yolks. Slice a tiny piece off each egg white bottom, so stuffed egg halves will rest flat.

In a blender or food processor with a steel blade, process egg yolks, bread crumbs, herring, onion or chives, oil and pepper. Spoon egg-yolk and herring mixture into egg-white pockets. Refrigerate 30 minutes to 1 hour. Sprinkle with paprika before serving. Serve chilled.

Variation

In a blender or food processor, process egg yolks, 1 cup flaked boned smoked fish such as salmon or whitefish, 1 small day-old roll soaked in milk and squeezed, 1 small chopped onion, 2 tablespoons mayonnaise and 1 tablespoon chopped fresh parsley. Fill egg whites as above.

Stuffed Eggs with Smoked Fish

Gefüllte Eier mit Geräuchertem Fisch

You shouldn't need any salt in this recipe because of the smoked fish. *Makes 10 stuffed egg halves.*

5 hard-cooked eggs
1 tablespoon vegetable oil
2 small onions, minced
1/4 cup milk
1 day-old dinner roll

1 cup flaked, boned, smoked fish such
  as salmon or whitefish
3 tablespoons mayonnaise
2 tablespoons chopped fresh parsley
Sweet paprika

Peel eggs and slice in half lengthwise. Carefully remove egg yolks and set them aside. Heat oil in a small skillet. Add onions and sauté until tender, about 5 minutes. Pour milk into a small bowl. Add roll and let milk soak into roll, then squeeze out excess milk.

In a food processor fitted with a metal blade, process smoked fish, mayonnaise, sautéed onions, parsley, squeezed roll and egg yolks. Do not overprocess or puree; the mixture should have a consistency resembling a sturdy paste. Spoon processed mixture into egg-white halves, evenly distributing all processed mixture into the egg-white halves. Sprinkle a little paprika over stuffed eggs. Cover loosely and refrigerate 1 hour. Serve slightly chilled.

Variation
Substitute 3/4 cup chopped cooked ham for smoked fish; decrease amount of mayonnaise to 2 tablespoons.

Hard-cooked Egg Faces

Hartgekochte Eigesichter

Decorate these hard-cooked eggs into funny faces with almost anything you can think of. For adults, use anchovies, capers, tiny shrimp, pimentos, pickles and hot peppers to create moustaches, eyes, noses, ears and hair. *Makes 8 servings.*

8 hard-cooked eggs	Cucumber slices
About 3 tablespoons mayonnaise	Matchstick-size carrot sticks
Sweet paprika	Small red apple wedges and pieces
Tomato slices	Chopped chives

Slice 1/2 inch off large end of each egg. Arrange eggs standing up, cut sides down, on a serving platter. Carefully trickle about 1 teaspoon mayonnaise over each egg. Let stand 2 to 3 minutes. Sprinkle eggs with paprika. Using pieces of tomato and cucumber slices, carrot sticks, apple pieces, chopped chives or other salad or fruit accompaniments, make faces by lightly pressing vegetable pieces into mayonnaise on eggs. If eggs are to be prepared for adults, brightly colored wooden picks can also be used to fasten other edible bits to the eggs, such as pieces of ripe or green olives and different colored peppers. Avoid using the wooden picks if children will eat the eggs.

Salads

·························· ✿ ··························

Salate

*A*lthough lettuce-based salads do not have very deep roots in German cuisine, a variety of cold salad dishes have over the years spread from the western part of the country through the east with a flourish. More recently, as a result in part of the relatively new emphasis on healthy eating, salads have found their way into both home and restaurant kitchens. Instead of lettuce, German salads typically rely on cooked and raw vegetables such as potatoes, cabbage, sauerkraut, beets, beans, cucumbers, parsley roots, celery roots, cucumbers, onions, leeks and radishes.

The most plentiful and popular versions are from the potato salad family. There are cold as well as hot potato salads. There are versions that include bits of cooked sausage, smoked ham, hard-cooked eggs and cheese. Minced dill pickles or pickled herring sometime find their way into potato salads, as do diced apple or parsley root.

Many salads blend their individual ingredients together in a vinegar- or wine-based marinade, or delicious sauce. Indeed, it's sometimes difficult to tell where the salads leave off and the vegetables begin. It may only be a question of consistency. When grated and sprinkled with a vinegar-based dressing or marinade, a platter full of sliced raw and partly cooked vegetables becomes a platter of salad. Likewise when individual ingredients are mixed with a little mayonnaise and lemon juice.

Fresh herbs are also heavily relied upon to make simple salads more interesting, as are bits of crispy bacon or minced smoked ham.

Salads fit in nicely with modern German diets, which often consist of many small snacks throughout the day and evening. Indeed, salads are at the same time inexpensive, simple to make and nutritious.

German Coleslaw

Deutscher Gemüsesalat

Try different kinds of cabbages for this coleslaw: green, white, red and savoy. Make sure the cabbage is finely shredded into pieces of fairly equal size. *Makes 6 to 8 servings.*

4 cups finely shredded cabbage	1 1/2 tablespoons hot water
1/2 medium green bell pepper, minced	2 tablespoons white vinegar
1/2 cup finely chopped onion	1/4 teaspoon celery seeds
1/4 cup grated carrots	1/2 teaspoon salt
10 sliced ripe olives	Pinch of freshly ground black pepper
1 1/2 tablespoons sugar	1/4 cup olive oil

Place cabbage, bell pepper, onion, carrots and olives in a large bowl; gently mix to combine. In a small bowl, stir together sugar and hot water until sugar dissolves. Stir in vinegar, celery seeds, salt and pepper. Pour dressing over cabbage mixture; drizzle with olive oil. Toss. Cover and refrigerate 2 hours to overnight. Serve chilled; toss again before serving.

Potato Salad

Kartoffelsalat

Select tender new potatoes for the best potato salad. White or red varieties will both work. Some cooks prefer to cut the cooked potatoes into thin slices. This is fine, but thin potato slices tend to stick together and it's much more difficult to evenly coat them with the dressing. *Makes 6 to 8 servings.*

2 lbs. new potatoes	1/2 cup mayonnaise
1 teaspoon salt	1 tablespoon Dijon mustard
1/2 teaspoon ground white pepper	1 tablespoon sour cream
2 tablespoons white vinegar	Romaine or other lettuce leaves
1 small onion, chopped	2 tablespoons chopped fresh dill
1 cup diced celery	10 to 12 cherry tomatoes for garnish
2 tablespoons chopped dill pickle	

Place potatoes in a large saucepan; add water to cover. Cover pan and cook over medium heat 30 minutes or until tender. Do not overcook or potatoes will fall apart in salad. Using a slotted spoon, remove potatoes from pan; discard cooking liquid. Let potatoes cool enough so they can be safely handled.

Peel and cut warm potatoes into 1/4-inch cubes. Place potatoes in a large bowl; sprinkle with salt, white pepper and vinegar. Add onion, celery and dill pickle; gently mix.

In a small bowl, combine mayonnaise, mustard and sour cream. Gently stir into vegetable mixture. Cover and refrigerate 2 hours to overnight. Serve chilled in lettuce-lined salad bowls or arranged on lettuce-lined platter. Sprinkle with chopped dill and garnish with cherry tomatoes.

Variations
Add 1 small peeled, cored, diced apple and 1/4 cup diced cooked ham.
Substitute 1 cup diced cucumber for celery and add 1 1/2 teaspoons celery seeds.
Use 1/4 cup mayonnaise and 1/4 cup dairy sour cream instead of 1/2 cup mayonnaise.

Hot Potato Salad

Heisser Kartoffelsalat

I t's critical that the potatoes not be cooked too long. If they are, you won't be able to slice them correctly. Remember to slice the potatoes while they're still warm for the best results. Then take extra care when combining the potatoes and dressing. If slices of potatoes stick together without getting coated, an uneven, unattractive salad will result. *Makes 6 to 8 servings.*

2 lbs. small new white or red potatoes
1 bacon slice, diced
1/4 cup minced onion
1 1/2 teaspoons all-purpose flour
2 teaspoons sugar
1 teaspoon salt
1/4 teaspoon ground white pepper

1/3 cup white vinegar
1/2 cup water
2 tablespoons finely chopped fresh
* parsley*
1 teaspoon celery seeds
1/2 cup sliced radishes, room
* temperature*

Place potatoes in a large saucepan; add water to cover. Cover and cook over medium heat 30 minutes or until tender. Do not overcook or potatoes will fall apart in salad. Using a slotted spoon, remove potatoes from pan; discard cooking liquid. Let potatoes cool enough so they can be handled safely.

Peel and cut potatoes into 1/4-inch-thick slices; place in a large bowl and keep warm. In a small skillet sauté bacon over medium heat until crisp. Drain off excess bacon fat. Add onion to same skillet; sauté until onion is tender but not browned, about 10 minutes. Remove skillet from heat and set aside.

In a medium bowl, combine flour, sugar, salt, white pepper, vinegar and water; stir until smooth. Add mixture to bacon and onion; simmer over medium-low heat until slightly thickened.

Turn out potatoes into a medium, warm serving dish. Gently stir or fold hot bacon and onion dressing into potatoes, so potato slices are evenly coated with dressing. Sprinkle parsley and celery seeds over potatoes. Garnish with radish slices just before serving.

Low-Cal Potato Salad

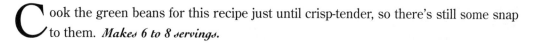

Kartoffelsalat Light

Cook the green beans for this recipe just until crisp-tender, so there's still some snap to them. *Makes 6 to 8 servings.*

2 lbs. new potatoes

1 cup (3/4-inch pieces) cooked green beans

1 (8-oz.) container plain nonfat yogurt

1 teaspoon salt

1/2 teaspoon curry powder

1/4 teaspoon garlic powder

1/4 teaspoon ground white pepper

Romaine or other lettuce leaves

2 tablespoons chopped chives

2 small red apples, cored and cut into wedges just before serving

Place potatoes in a large saucepan; add water to cover. Cover and cook over medium heat 30 minutes or until tender. Do not overcook or potatoes will fall apart in salad. Using a slotted spoon, remove potatoes from pan; discard cooking liquid. Let potatoes cool enough so they can be handled safely.

Peel and cut warm potatoes into 1/2-inch cubes; place in a large bowl. Add green beans to potatoes.

In a small bowl, combine yogurt, salt, curry powder, garlic powder and white pepper. Gently stir dressing into potatoes and beans. Cover and refrigerate 2 hours to overnight.

Serve chilled in individual lettuce-lined salad bowls, or arrange on lettuce-lined platter. Before serving, sprinkle with chopped chives and garnish with apple slices.

Cucumber Salad

Gurkensalat

Some Germans leave the skin on cucumbers—as long as the cucumbers are sliced extra thin. In any event, select thinner instead of fatter cucumbers. *Makes 6 to 8 servings.*

3 large cucumbers, peeled and thinly
    sliced
2 teaspoons salt
1 1/2 cups sour cream

1/3 teaspoon ground white pepper
1/4 cup wine vinegar
1 tablespoon minced chives

Place cucumber slices in a medium bowl. Add salt; mix lightly until salt adheres evenly to cucumber slices. Cover and refrigerate 1 hour. Drain juice from cucumber slices. In a small bowl, combine sour cream, white pepper, wine vinegar and chives. Add to cucumber slices; gently mix. Cover and refrigerate until ready to serve.

Cucumber & Dill Salad

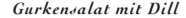

Gurkensalat mit Dill

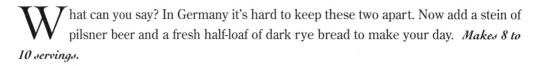

What can you say? In Germany it's hard to keep these two apart. Now add a stein of pilsner beer and a fresh half-loaf of dark rye bread to make your day. *Makes 8 to 10 servings.*

4 medium cucumbers, peeled and
    thinly sliced
2 teaspoons salt
1 tablespoon sugar
1/2 teaspoon freshly ground black
    pepper

3 tablespoons olive oil
1/2 cup light cream
1/4 cup tarragon vinegar
1/2 cup chopped fresh dill

Place cucumber slices in a medium bowl. Add salt; mix lightly until salt adheres evenly to cucumber slices. Cover and refrigerate 1 hour. Drain juice from cucumber slices. Sprinkle sugar, pepper and olive oil over cucumber slices. In a small bowl, combine light cream, vinegar and chopped dill. Add to cucumber slices; gently mix. Cover and refrigerate until ready to serve.

Tomato & Onion Salad

Tomatensalat mit Zwiebeln

Do not prepare this salad too far in advance. Tomatoes don't refrigerate well when they're in a marinade. *Makes 6 servings.*

6 medium tomatoes

1 large onion, thinly sliced

3 tablespoons olive oil

2 tablespoons wine vinegar mixed
   with 1 tablespoon water or

3 tablespoons lemon juice

1 teaspoon sugar

2/3 teaspoon oregano

1/2 teaspoon salt

1/2 teaspoon freshly ground black
   pepper

1 tablespoon chopped fresh parsley

Place a large saucepan half full of water over high heat; bring to a full boil. Using tongs, carefully drop tomatoes into boiling water. Remove tomatoes 1 minute after the last tomato was dropped in. Rinse tomatoes with cold water. Peel and cut tomatoes into thin wedges.

Place tomatoes and onion in a large bowl. In a small bowl, combine olive oil, vinegar and 1 tablespoon water or lemon juice, sugar, oregano, salt and pepper. Pour olive oil mixture over tomatoes and onions. Using a rubber spatula, gently toss to combine. Cover and refrigerate 1 to 2 hours. Before serving, garnish with chopped parsley. Serve chilled.

Beet & Horseradish Relish

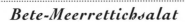

Bete-Meerrettichsalat

Here's a powerful combination of shredded cooked beets and horseradish; a little bit goes a long way. It's a must for spreading on canapés or cold sliced meats and is almost always present at holiday festivities. You'll find it not only in Germany but also in Poland and other border countries. *Makes about 3 cups.*

2/3 lb. (1 1/3 cups) grated fresh cooked or canned beets
2/3 lb. (1 1/3 cups) prepared horseradish
3 tablespoons lemon juice

1/4 teaspoon sugar
1/8 teaspoon freshly ground black pepper
Salt

Combine beets, horseradish, lemon juice, sugar and pepper in a small bowl. Add salt to taste. Cover and refrigerate overnight. Serve chilled over cold pork, veal, beef, sausage or sandwiches.

Beet Salad

Betesalat

Beets should be cooked in their skins to preserve their color, flavor and nutrients. When you cut the leaves off, cut about 3 inches above the bottom of the stem, so the beets won't bleed as they cook. Beets are done when fork tender (see Pickled Beets & Eggs, opposite). Let cool slightly before peeling and shredding. *Makes 6 to 8 servings.*

3 tablespoons olive oil
1 medium onion, chopped
1 1/2 lbs. shredded cooked beets (see opposite)
3 tablespoons vinegar or lemon juice

Sugar
Salt
Freshly ground black pepper
2 tablespoons chopped fresh parsley

Heat oil in a medium skillet. Add onion and sauté over medium heat until tender, about 5 minutes. Add beets and vinegar or lemon juice. Season with sugar, salt and pepper to taste. Gently stir over low heat 15 minutes or until heated through. Remove from heat. Let stand in skillet 15 minutes. Sprinkle with parsley to garnish. Serve warm.

Pickled Beets & Eggs

Eingelegte Bete und Eier

S mall beets are easier to handle for this recipe. Try to get beets that are similar in size to the eggs for an aesthetically pleasing combination. *Makes 8 to 10 servings.*

1 3/4 to 2 lbs. small beets

Salt

4 hard-cooked eggs

2/3 cup red wine vinegar

2/3 cup red wine

1 medium onion, thinly sliced

10 black peppercorns

6 whole cloves

2 tablespoons olive oil

Cut off beet stem ends, leaving about 3 inches of stem. Scrub beets; rinse clean with cold running water. Place whole washed beets in a large saucepan. Add salt and enough water to cover. Bring to a boil over high heat. Reduce heat to medium-low. Cover with a tight-fitting lid and cook 1 hour or until fork-tender. Remove beets from cooking liquid; discard liquid. Let beets cool enough so they can be handled safely. Peel beets. Cut beets crosswise into 1/4-inch-thick slices; place in a deep glass or ceramic bowl.

Peel hard-cooked eggs; add whole peeled eggs to beets. In a medium saucepan, combine vinegar, wine, onion, peppercorns, cloves and 1 teaspoon salt. Bring to a boil over high heat. Pour vinegar mixture over beets and eggs. Cool to room temperature. Drizzle olive oil over beets. Gently mix. Cover and refrigerate overnight. Serve slightly chilled.

Sauerkraut & Wine Salad

Sauerkraut und Weinsalat

Believe it or not, sauerkraut—in one form or another—could make an appearance in every chapter of this book. By acting as a sort of culinary base, it helps make a wide variety of salads. The one below is seasoned with red wine and caraway seeds. *Makes 6 servings.*

1 lb. sauerkraut
1 1/2 cups red or white wine
2 tablespoons vegetable oil
1 large onion, diced

1 tablespoon caraway seeds
1/4 teaspoon freshly ground black
    pepper

Rinse and drain sauerkraut; place in a medium saucepan. Add wine and cook, partially covered, over medium heat 20 minutes. Heat oil in a medium skillet. Add onion and sauté over medium heat 5 minutes or until tender. Add onion, caraway seeds and pepper to sauerkraut; stir to combine. Cook sauerkraut mixture, uncovered, 10 to 12 minutes or until most of the wine evaporates. Do not overcook; sauerkraut should be moist, not dry. Cover and let cool to room temperature, or refrigerate and serve chilled.

Sauerkraut Salad with Bacon & Mushrooms

Sauerkrautsalat mit Speck und Champignons

If you use the water instead of the vegetable broth, select larger mushrooms to make up for the difference in flavor. *Makes 8 to 10 servings.*

1 1/2 lbs. sauerkraut
2 tablespoons vegetable oil
2 large onions, chopped
3 bacon slices
6 dried mushrooms
1 cup Vegetable Broth (page 63)
   or water

1 teaspoon ground allspice
1 teaspoon salt
1/2 teaspoon freshly ground black
   pepper

Rinse and drain sauerkraut. Place sauerkraut in a large bowl. Heat oil in a medium skillet. Add onion and sauté over medium heat 10 minutes or until tender. Add sautéed onions to sauerkraut. In the same skillet, sauté bacon until crisp; drain on paper towels. Crumble cooled bacon into sauerkraut and onion mixture.

In a small saucepan, place dried mushrooms and Vegetable Broth or water. Bring to a boil over medium-high heat. Gently boil until most of the liquid evaporates and mushrooms are tender. Remove mushrooms from saucepan; let cool. Chop mushrooms. Add chopped mushrooms, allspice, salt and pepper to sauerkraut mixture. Gently stir to combine. Cover and refrigerate 1 hour to overnight. Serve chilled or at room temperature.

Sauerkraut Salad

Sauerkrautsalat

For a lip-puckering tart salad, rinse sauerkraut only once, briefly. For a more neutral-tasting flavor, rinse three or more times. *Makes 6 servings.*

1 large apple

1 tablespoon lemon juice

1 lb. sauerkraut, rinsed, drained and chopped

2 medium carrots, peeled and grated

1 medium onion, finely chopped

2 tablespoons sunflower oil

1/2 teaspoon sugar

Freshly ground black pepper to taste

Peel, core and shred apple into a large bowl. Drizzle lemon juice over shredded apple; stir. Add sauerkraut, carrots, onion, sunflower oil and sugar. Gently mix and season with pepper to taste. Cover and refrigerate 1 hour to overnight before serving. Serve chilled.

Bean & Bacon Salad

Bohnensalat mit Speck

This recipe is prepared year-round. Frozen blanched beans are also good, but they should first be cooked 10 to 15 minutes in gently boiling salted water, then allowed to cool before use. If desired, substitute yellow beans for variety. *Makes 10 to 12 servings.*

2 (16-oz.) cans cut green beans, drained, or 2 lbs. fresh green beans, cut into 1-inch pieces and cooked
1/2 cup chopped onion
1/3 cup olive oil
1/4 cup red wine vinegar
1/2 teaspoon salt
1/4 teaspoon freshly ground black pepper

1/4 teaspoon dried savory
4 hard-cooked eggs, chopped
1/4 cup mayonnaise
1 teaspoon Dijon mustard
2 teaspoons white wine vinegar
1/4 teaspoon garlic salt
5 bacon slices, crisp-cooked and crumbled
Crisp leaf lettuce
Ground sweet paprika

In a medium bowl, combine beans, onion, olive oil, red wine vinegar, salt, pepper and savory. Toss lightly. Cover and refrigerate.

In a small bowl, combine eggs, mayonnaise, mustard, white wine vinegar and garlic salt; gently mix. Before serving, drain bean mixture. Add bacon and toss. Line individual salad bowls with crisp leaf lettuce. Spoon bean mixture into lettuce-lined bowls. Top beans with a spoonful of egg mixture. Sprinkle with paprika to garnish.

Red-Cabbage Salad

Rotkohlsalat

Red cabbage was traditionally a winter vegetable that could be stored in root cellars for relatively long periods of time. It is still, even with all of the refrigeration available now, just as popular as ever. *Makes 4 to 6 servings.*

3 bacon slices
1/2 head red cabbage, shredded
1/4 cup red or white wine
2 tablespoons white vinegar
1 tablespoon sugar

2 tablespoons olive oil
1 teaspoon caraway seeds
1/2 teaspoon salt
1/4 teaspoon freshly ground black
    pepper

In a small skillet, sauté bacon over medium heat until crisp; drain on paper towels. Reserve bacon. Place cabbage in a large bowl. In a small saucepan, combine wine, vinegar and sugar. Bring to a boil over medium heat, stirring until sugar is dissolved. Pour wine mixture over cabbage. Toss with oil, caraway seeds, salt and pepper. Crumble cooled bacon over salad mixture.

Radish Salad

Rettichsalat

A picture perfect salad. The color of red, white or black radishes, when the radish slices are arranged in artistic patterns, can create special effects—edible party displays. *Makes 6 to 8 servings.*

1 lb. red radishes, thinly sliced
2 green onions, sliced
1/2 cup sour cream
1/2 teaspoon salt

Ground white pepper
Green lettuce leaves
Dill sprigs for garnish

In a medium bowl, combine radishes, green onions, sour cream and salt. Season with white pepper to taste. Serve chilled on lettuce leaves. Garnish with dill sprigs.

Variations

Use white radishes; line dish with red lettuce and garnish with several cherry tomatoes.
Use half red and half white radishes; arrange in a pattern.
Use black radishes.

Parsley Root Salad

Petersiliensalat

Parsley root, or turnip-rooted parsley, is a root vegetable frequently used in soups and salads. It's a member of the parsley family that develops a taproot similar to that of a parsnip or fat carrot. It has been used by German, Polish and Hungarian cooks for centuries as a flavoring agent. Its leaves can also be minced as a garnish. *Makes 6 to 8 servings.*

6 to 8 young parsley roots, peeled and cut into thin strips	1/3 cup white vinegar
1 medium onion, minced	2 tablespoons chopped fresh dill
1/2 cup olive oil	1/8 teaspoon white pepper
	Salt

Combine parsley roots and onion in a medium bowl. In a small bowl, combine oil, vinegar, dill and white pepper. Season with salt to taste. Pour dressing over parsley root mixture. Toss evenly to coat. Cover and refrigerate 1 hour. Serve chilled.

Variations
Substitute parsnips or celery roots if you can't find parsley root
Add 2 tart apples, peeled and cut into narrow strips.
Shred the roots and apples instead of cutting them into strips.

Soups

Suppe

Soup has always been an important but low-key component of German cuisine, one that historically has been kept on the back burners until recently. While soup continued to be a staple in the German diet, it never achieved the respect it eventually earned in neighboring France, despite individual efforts such as those of the famous French chef Escoffier, who prepared his "showcase" soups for the Kaiser and other German dignitaries. It seems the Germans were just never quite as impressed with soup as the French thought they ought to be, and pronouncements like the one made by another ranking French chef, that "No woman should marry if she cannot make soup," didn't help impress the German *frauleins,* either.

Linguists explain that the word *soup* has ties both to the German *saufen,* which means "to swallow," and the Germanic *sop,* which at one time referred to a bread that was served in hot broth to lend the broth some substance. In any sense of the word, soup was an ever-present dish found simmering in large stockpots on farmhouse and peasant stoves across the countryside. For many families the stockpot always had something in it, providing a continual source of the soluble and nutritional parts of meat scraps, leftovers, bones, vegetables, herbs and seasonings. More "fuel" than cuisine, it nourished early-to-rise and late-toiling farmers, laborers, and woodcutters. Again, emphasis was on its practical value instead of on pleasures realized by the finer points of soup making; to have eaten soup was considered infinitely more important than the enjoyment of soup while it was being eaten.

At the same time, soup was recognized as an important source of nutrients for growing children. It was available and inexpensive, and it could easily "fill up" children, leaving the more desirable foods for hard-working parents. Unfortunately, the children had other plans. They preferred sweets and more expensive meat and gravy dishes. So a concentrated effort similar to that of popularizing spinach with Popeye cartoons resulted in a kind of German advertising campaign to convince skeptical children of the importance of eating their soup. This was even reflected in popular literature of the day. Who hasn't heard of Grimm's fairy tales? Of Little Red Riding Hood, Snow White, and Sleeping Beauty? Within the framework of similar Grimm tales are found numerous references to soup as a beloved and necessary staple of honest, simple, hard-working people and their youngsters. The hugely popular German writer Heinrich Hoffman produced an often-read book of stories for children. It was full of tales with lessons to be learned. One story in particular, called "Suppenkaspar," featured a youngster who refused to eat his prescribed portions of soup. He gradually wasted away, finally dying. In the tearful conclusion a soup bowl is gently placed on his grave, in stark testimony to the folly of not eating one's soup. "Who soups long, lives long," goes an old German saying.

For a number of reasons, soups have, within the past generation of German cooks, been promoted to a higher level on the culinary scale. The overriding reason is the realization that some traditional German eating habits were simply unhealthy. A steady diet of meals featuring large quantities of meats and other ingredients prepared with lard, for instance, was found to be hazardous to one's health. So were meal after meal of dumplings swimming in gravy and pound after pound of sausages, luncheon meats and cheeses. While dishes could indeed be prepared using somewhat less fat, the portion sizes also had to be reduced. To stay within the boundaries of modern nutritional guidelines, soups became one of the logical supplements, along with more vegetables, fruits and grains. Calories are used sparingly in many soups. Even the typical butter or vegetable oil used to sauté meats, onions, mushrooms or other vegetables, when divided among the many portions a soup provides, adds up to surprisingly few calories per serving.

What's more, Germans have discovered that they actually *like* soups. Certainly, there are soups to suit the taste and needs of almost everyone, from the most robust workers or athletes to the fussiest of connoisseurs. Modern Germans have come to appreciate the eating as well as the "have eaten" when it comes to soups. They know that soups can be at the same time aromatic, tasty and satisfying. Chilled soups can cool diners on a sweltering July mid-afternoon, while hot soups will warm the coldest February evenings. Too, soups stimulate the appetite and provide social encouragement and opportunity. They allow time for small talk between appetizers and dessert. They're attractive and bring variety to the table. As such, they fit in well with both casual and formal entertaining and celebrations.

The German cook has also found soups to be extremely kind to the family budget. During times when jobs are getting scarce and taxes and living expenses are rising faster than the head of the household's ability to earn, the food budget takes up a major part of the typical German family's disposable income. Soups make the most of less-expensive ingredients. Spare, even overripe or older vegetables, leftover and inexpensive cuts of meat, that pork-roast or beef-roast bone, may all find their way into the soup pot to create additional, bonus courses for the table. It's an efficient way of "recycling" or extending many edible ingredients that could otherwise be wasted.

Another important reason why modern German cooks like more soup with their meals is that the preparation of soup can be fairly effortless. Few tricky techniques are ever involved; if you can boil water, you can make soup. Today, blenders and food processors will mince, chop, grate, shred and slice ingredients. After a few onions or celery stalks or mushrooms or chunks of meat are chopped and sautéed, the stove and the cooking pot will do most of the rest. Plus an increasing variety of relatively inexpensive products such as dried bouillon, canned stocks, and instant prepackaged soup broths and bases are readily available in grocery stores. This makes it even easier for working parents who may not have as much time as they'd like to prepare a tasty broth which could later be used as the basis of a soup.

More good news is that it isn't necessary to follow instructions to the letter in all cases. Certainly, use the recipes as starting points—just as German household cooks do—but later feel free to experiment with a little more garlic if you desire, or a little less salt. Analyze your likes and dislikes, then tailor the soup that way, by making incremental changes until you get it to taste just the way you want. Soup is, after all, the result of foods, seasonings, liquids and heat, all blended together in a pleasant manner. Plus you never have to make the same soup twice if you don't want to. There can be lots of trial and error. Of course, you'll always want to be able to duplicate a successful recipe; if you change things, make notations in the margins so you'll be able to remember what you did later on.

With soup, you can start from scratch, using water, vegetables, meats, bones and seasonings, cooking it slowly for hours. Or you can start with the liquid portion—a stock or broth prepared in a large quantity weeks before. Or you can substitute store-bought bouillon, making allowances for the salt content in commercially prepared products.

There's no arguing that good broth or stock is the basis of a good soup. A good broth is easy to make. Seven are included in this chapter and can be made in quantity and frozen until needed, thus saving energy and time. It's the modern way of providing old-fashioned soups. By using prepared broths as building blocks for your soup, you'll find the soup-making process less labor intensive and you won't be easily discouraged by the lengthy cooking times some soups need when starting from scratch.

For healthier broths, make sure you remove as much fat as possible, preferably when it congeals after being refrigerated. Congealed fat can simply be lifted off and thrown away as a solid. Other calorie-savers include using half-and-half instead of heavy cream and cutting down on butter or margarine and vegetable oil by using nonstick sprays and nonstick skillets and pans.

Most soups require a certain amount of simmering time. To simmer, it's advisable to first bring the soup to a boil, then turn the heat down low—just hot enough so the soup cooks with occasional tiny bubbles rising to the surface. If you can hear the soup boil, it's almost always too hot. Too much liquid could evaporate and the ingredients at the bottom of the pot could burn. Check soups that require long simmering times frequently. A soup going just right at first may cook too quickly in another hour, after the stove heats up or the temperature of the day rises ten or fifteen degrees.

Another simple and frequently used German soup technique is the thickening of soup with a "roux," which combines butter or margarine and flour into a smooth paste. Make sure the flour is well blended and slightly cooked before a little of whatever soup you are thickening is added. That liquid should be added slowly and stirred vigorously and continuously so the resulting mixture is smooth and not full of lumps.

There are over thirty soups and broths featured in this chapter. Some can be served as the entree of a meal. Goulash Soup (see page 67), for instance, consists of lean chunks of beef, onions, celery, potatoes and carrots all simmered together in a beef or vegetable broth that may be fortified with tomato juice or Burgundy wine and further seasoned by numerous herbs and spices. Vegetable-meat soups are wonderful ways to extend veal or beef or ham in a healthy and tasty manner. There are German and Eastern European soups such as borscht, cabbage soup and sauerkraut soup. Legumes play a major role in a number of German soups. Lentil soups—in which split peas can also be substituted—are popular year-round because they're made with dried ingredients that store well. The bean soup in this chapter provides enough nutrients to satisfy the most demanding requirements. Potato soup is another dish served and relished from one end of the country to the other.

Soups. They're far more than the sum of their ingredients. They can also provide sustenance beyond pure physical nourishment. What of the memories they may evoke? The grandmother patiently tending a simmering pot on a firebrick stove, or a parent or close friend painstakingly preparing chicken soup when you were ill? There are certain "one-of-a-kind" soups, made by a loved one, the aromas and tastes of which bring back floods of memories. Indeed, one of the soups in this chapter may one day do the same for you.

Chicken Broth

Hühnerbrühe

If one soup, one broth could be called "the mother of all others," then this is it. Chicken broth, often with dumplings or noodles, is the soup that appears most frequently in both German homes and restaurants. It has always been a favorite of farmers who find that older, tougher chickens lend themselves nicely to producing more flavorful broths and soups than do younger birds. This broth is the "starting point" for many, many other soups, sauces and combination dishes. *Makes about 3 quarts.*

2 (3-lb.) chickens, cut up, or 6 lbs. chicken backs and wings

About 5 qts. water

2 large onions, halved

1 large onion, char-burned (see below)

1 leek, trimmed and cut into large pieces

1 celery root, quartered

1 parsley root, quartered, or 1 tablespoon chopped fresh parsley

1 head savoy cabbage, quartered

6 allspice berries

5 whole cloves

1 large bunch fresh thyme

1 bay leaf

2 teaspoons salt

10 black peppercorns

Rinse chicken; remove and discard excess fat. Place chicken and enough water to cover in a stockpot. Bring to a boil over medium-high heat. Reduce heat to medium-low, add remaining ingredients and cook, partially covered, 2 to 2 1/2 hours, skimming foam from surface until surface is clear.

Strain broth into a large bowl. Discard cooked vegetables. Let strained chicken cool. Remove chicken meat from bones; reserve for other use. Discard bones and skin. Cool broth, uncovered. Pour into quart or pint containers with tight-fitting lids. Refrigerate until fat congeals. Lift fat off broth with a fork; discard fat. Use immediately or cover and refrigerate up to 2 days or freeze up to 3 months. Bring broth to a full boil before using.

Note

To char-burn onion: Using a gas stove, hold peeled onion with metal tongs, over the open flame until slightly charred. Using an electric stove, place onions under the broiler, or halve them and char the flat sides in an old skillet.

Beef Broth

Rindfleischbrühe

The typical German household cook is not particular when preparing or describing his or her broths or stocks. While restaurants may take great pains to clarify their broths, you needn't. This recipe produces a delicious broth which can be enjoyed by itself or with noodles, dumplings or potatoes, or it can be turned into a wide variety of nourishing hot soups. Remember, you don't always need to exclusively use beef for this broth. Combinations with chicken, pork or other meats will also work. *Makes about 3 quarts.*

5 qts. water
4 lbs. meaty bones and beef scraps
1 large onion, char-burned
  (see Note, page 57)
2 large carrots, quartered
1 parsley root, quartered, or
  1 tablespoon chopped fresh parsley

1 celery root, quartered
1 medium leek, trimmed and cut
  into pieces
1/2 head savoy cabbage, quartered
12 black peppercorns
Salt

Place water, bones and beef in a stockpot. Bring to a boil over medium-high heat. Skim foam from surface until surface is clear. Reduce heat to medium. Cook, uncovered, 30 minutes. Add onion, carrots, parsley root, celery root, leek, cabbage and peppercorns. Reduce heat to low, partially cover and simmer 2 to 2 1/2 hours.

Season broth with salt to taste; strain into a large bowl. Discard beef scraps, bones and cooked vegetables. Cool broth, uncovered. Pour into quart or pint containers with tight-fitting lids. Refrigerate until fat congeals. Lift fat off with a fork; discard fat. Cover; refrigerate up to 2 days or freeze up to 3 months. Bring broth to a full boil before using.

Dark Beef Broth

Dunkle Rindfleischbrühe

This version will result in a darker broth that's excellent for both soups and gravies. *Makes about 3 1/2 quarts.*

2 lbs. chuck roast or other inexpensive cut of beef	1/2 cup chopped celery or celery root
3 lbs. shin and marrow bones, cracked	2 parsley roots, quartered, or 2 tablespoons chopped fresh parsley
2 large onions, quartered	2 bay leaves
5 qts. water	2 tablespoons salt
1/2 cup sliced carrots	10 peppercorns

Preheat oven to 450F (230C). Place beef, bones and onions in a large roasting pan. Roast, uncovered, 1 hour. Remove from oven and let cool 20 minutes. Place roasted meat, bones and onions, carrots, celery or celery root, parsley roots or parsley, bay leaves, salt and peppercorns in a large stockpot. Add water. Bring to a boil over medium-high heat. Use a strainer or slotted spoon to skim off foam as it rises. Reduce heat to low, cover and simmer 3 hours.

Carefully remove beef and reserve for soup or other use. Cool broth, uncovered. Strain broth and pour into quart or pint containers with tight-fitting lids. Discard cooked vegetables. Refrigerate broth until fat congeals. Lift fat off with a fork; discard fat. Cover; refrigerate up to 2 days or freeze up to 3 months. Bring broth to a full boil before using.

Veal Broth

Kalbsbrühe

Since veal is such a lean meat, there's very little fat to remove after cooking. Again, if you don't have enough veal scraps for a full broth recipe, feel free to supplement with beef or even chicken. The bones are split to extract every possible bit of flavor from the marrow. *Makes about 2 1/2 quarts.*

4 1/2 to 5 lbs. meaty veal bones, cleaved or sawed to expose marrow	2 celery roots, halved
3 1/2 quarts water	4 large carrots, halved
2 parsley roots, halved, or 2 tablespoons chopped fresh parsley	1 large onion, quartered
2 leeks, trimmed and cut into large chunks	1 small green cabbage, quartered
	14 black peppercorns

In a large stockpot, bring to a boil enough water to cover veal bones. Add veal bones; bring water back to a boil. Drain; discard water. Add the 3 1/2 quarts water. Cover; bring to a boil over medium heat. Skim foam from surface until surface is clear. Cook 30 minutes. Add parsley roots, leeks, celery roots, carrots, onion, cabbage and peppercorns. Bring mixture to a boil. Reduce heat, cover and cook 1 1/2 hours. Simmer, uncovered, 10 minutes.

Strain broth into a large bowl; reserve veal for another use. Discard cooked vegetables. Cool broth, uncovered. Pour into quart or pint containers with tight-fitting lids. Refrigerate until fat congeals. Lift fat off with a fork; discard fat. Cover; refrigerate up to 2 days or freeze up to 3 months. Bring broth to a full boil before using.

Ham Broth

Schinkenbrühe

This broth is exceptionally good in bean and vegetable soups containing ham. Since the salt content of ham can vary widely, use less salt than you think you should. More can be added toward the end of cooking time, if needed. *Makes about 3 quarts.*

3 to 3 1/2 lbs. smoked ham with bone, trimmed of fat

3 celery stalks with leaves, cut into large chunks

4 medium carrots, quartered

2 parsley roots, quartered, or 2 tablespoons chopped fresh parsley

1 leek, trimmed and cut into large chunks

12 black peppercorns

1 bay leaf

Up to 1 teaspoon salt, if needed

1/2 teaspoon brown sugar

4 quarts water

Place all ingredients in a stockpot. Cover with a tight-fitting lid. Simmer over low heat 2 1/2 hours. Strain; reserve ham for another use. Discard vegetables. Cool broth, uncovered. Pour into quart or pint containers with tight-fitting lids. Refrigerate up to 2 days or freeze up to 3 months. Bring broth to a full boil before using.

Meat Broth

Fleischbrühe

Because German families often tend to accumulate small portions of leftover meats in their refrigerators, meat broths are one way to see that those leftovers won't go to waste. Pieces of lean sliced luncheon meats such as corned beef and ham can also be included. *Makes about 5 quarts.*

8 to 9 lbs. meaty bones and meat
    scraps from beef, pork and veal or
    a combination
8 qts. water
2 medium onions, char-burned,
    (see Note, page 57)
2 parsley roots, quartered, or 2
    tablespoons chopped fresh parsley

4 medium carrots, quartered
4 celery stalks with leaves, cut
    into chunks
2 leeks, trimmed and cut into chunks
18 black peppercorns
4 whole cloves
1 bay leaf
2 tablespoons salt

Preheat oven to 375F (190C). Place bones and meat in a large roasting pan. Roast until browned. Place water, roasted bones and meat in a large stockpot. Cover; bring to a boil. Skim foam from surface until surface is clear. Reduce heat to medium. Cook, uncovered, 1 hour. Add onions, parsley roots, carrots, celery, leeks, peppercorns, cloves, bay leaf and salt. Cover; bring to a boil. Reduce heat to low, cover and simmer 3 hours.

    Strain broth into a large bowl. Discard meat scraps, bones and cooked vegetables. Cool broth, uncovered. Pour into quart or pint containers with tight-fitting lids. Refrigerate until fat congeals. Lift fat off with a fork; discard fat. Cover; refrigerate up to 2 days or freeze up to 3 months. Bring broth to a full boil before using.

Note
Remember, for a healthier lower-fat product, prepare meat broth with time enough in advance to let it chill in the refrigerator, so fat can be removed.

Vegetable Broth

Gemüsebrühe

Due to the delicate nature of vegetables, they'll lose both flavor and nutrients if over-cooked. And while older or tougher birds and less-expensive cuts of meat may be fine for meat broths, vegetable broths will only be as good as their ingredients: strive for healthy, fresh vegetables that could just as easily be eaten raw or prepared as side dishes. The onion skins in this recipe will help add color to the broth. *Makes about 3 quarts.*

2 tablespoons butter or margarine
2 large yellow or red onions, peeled
    and skins reserved for broth and
    chopped
5 qts. water
4 medium carrots, sliced
2 parsley roots, quartered, or 2
    tablespoons chopped fresh parsley
1 celery root, quartered
2 medium new potatoes, quartered
1 large tomato, quartered

1 leek, trimmed and cut into
    large chunks
3 small celery stalks with leaves,
    cut into chunks
1 small head savoy cabbage,
    quartered
3 tablespoons chopped fresh dill or
    1 tablespoon dill weed
12 black peppercorns
2 bay leaves
Salt to taste

Melt butter or margarine in a medium skillet. Add onions; sauté over medium heat until tender but not browned, about 10 minutes. In a large stockpot, combine sautéed onions, onion skins, water, carrots, parsley roots, celery root, potatoes, tomato, leek, celery and cabbage. Bring to a boil over high heat. Reduce heat to low. Add dill, peppercorns and bay leaves. Season with salt to taste. Partially cover; simmer about 1 hour.

Strain broth into a large bowl. Discard cooked vegetables. Cool broth, uncovered. Pour into quart or pint containers with tight-fitting lids. Refrigerate up to 2 days or freeze up to 3 months. Bring broth to a full boil before using.

Fish Broth

Fischbrühe

Fish is much more delicate than beef, pork, chicken or even veal. Cooking times for fish broth are considerably less than cooking times for other broths. In Germany and the rest of Europe, it's traditional to include fish heads for a more flavorful broth. *Makes about 2 quarts.*

2 1/2 lbs. fresh fish, cleaned and
    dressed
2 qts. water
1 cup dry white wine
1 large onion, chopped
3 carrots, chopped
2 celery stalks with leaves, chopped
1 garlic clove

5 peppercorns
2 bay leaves
3 parsley sprigs or 1 parsley root,
    quartered
3 tablespoons white tarragon vinegar
    or lemon juice
Salt

In a large stockpot, combine fish, water, wine, onion, carrots, celery, garlic, peppercorns, bay leaves, parsley or parsley root and vinegar or lemon juice. Cook, partially covered, over medium heat 30 minutes or until fish is easily removed from bones. Strain into a large bowl; discard solids. Return broth to stockpot. Season with salt to taste. Simmer over low heat 10 minutes.

Oxtail Soup

Ochsenschwanzsuppe

Oxtails may be found behind butcher counters at most large markets. Beef may be substituted, if desired; the end result will closely approximate that of the original. *Makes 8 servings.*

2 tablespoons vegetable oil
1 1/2 lbs. oxtail, cut into 2-inch
   lengths, or beef, cut into
   3/4-inch cubes
1/4 cup all-purpose flour
1/2 cup diced onion
2 quarts Meat Broth (page 62)
1/3 cup diced carrot
1/2 cup diced celery
3 thyme sprigs

3 parsley sprigs
2 bay leaves
1 teaspoon salt
1/4 teaspoon freshly ground
   black pepper
3 small potatoes, peeled and diced
1/2 cup chopped tomatoes
1 tablespoon Maggi seasoning
1 tablespoon lemon juice

Heat oil in a large skillet over medium-high heat. Place oxtail or beef pieces in a large bowl. Sprinkle with flour; mix lightly until flour adheres evenly to oxtail or beef pieces. Place oxtail or beef in heated oil and cook 10 minutes, turning to brown on all sides. Reduce heat to medium. Add onion; sauté until onion is tender, about 5 minutes.

Bring broth to a simmer in a large saucepan over high heat. Add oxtail or beef and onion. Reduce heat to medium-low, cover and simmer until oxtail meat falls away from bones or beef is tender, 2 1/2 to 3 hours. Let cool slightly; carefully remove bones. Add carrot, celery, thyme, parsley, bay leaves, salt and pepper. Simmer, covered, over low heat 30 minutes. Add potatoes; simmer 15 minutes or until potatoes are tender. Discard bay leaves and herb sprigs. Add tomatoes, Maggi seasoning and lemon juice. Heat and serve.

Vegetable-Veal Soup

Gemuse-Kalbssuppe

Because veal is so lacking in fat, it's easily dried out and burned. While you won't have to worry about the veal drying out in soup, it still shouldn't be allowed to burn. While sautéing, keep it moving over the skillet for even cooking. *Makes 8 to 10 servings.*

3 tablespoons butter or margarine
1 cup diced onion
1 cup diced leeks, white part only
3 garlic cloves, minced
1 cup halved baby carrots
1 1/2 lbs. lean veal, cut into
   small cubes

2 1/2 qts. Veal Broth (page 60) or
   Chicken Broth (page 57)
1/2 teaspoon ground white pepper
2 bay leaves
1 cup half and half
2 tablespoons chopped fresh parsley

Melt butter or margarine in a large skillet over medium heat. Add onion, leeks, garlic and carrots. Cook, uncovered, 10 to 12 minutes, stirring several times. Add veal; cook, stirring, 8 minutes.

In a large saucepan, bring broth, white pepper and bay leaves to a boil. Add cooked vegetables and veal. Cover; bring to a boil. Reduce heat to low; simmer 40 minutes. Discard bay leaves. Add half and half and parsley. Heat until hot, but do not boil. Serve hot.

Goulash Soup

Gulaschsuppe

I t's a good idea to prepare this soup in advance and let it rest in the refrigerator overnight for more flavor. *Makes 8 to 10 servings.*

2 tablespoons vegetable oil
2 lbs. lean boneless beef, cut into
    1 1/2-inch cubes
3 onions, finely chopped
2 tablespoons all-purpose flour
2 tablespoons ground sweet
    Hungarian paprika
2 garlic cloves, minced
2 celery stalks, finely chopped
1 1/2 qts. Beef Broth (page 58) or
    Vegetable Broth (page 63)

3 cups water or tomato juice, or
    1 1/2 cups water and 1 1/2 cups
    Burgundy wine
3 bay leaves
1 1/2 teaspoons salt
3/4 teaspoon Tabasco sauce
1/4 cup tomato paste
1/4 cup cider vinegar
2 teaspoons dried thyme, crumbled
1 1/2 cups diced peeled potatoes
1 1/2 cups baby carrots

Heat oil in a large skillet over medium-high heat. Add meat; sauté 10 minutes or until browned on all sides. Add onions; cook 3 more minutes. Stir in flour, paprika, garlic and celery. Cook, stirring, 2 minutes.

Bring broth, water or tomato juice, or water and wine to a simmer in a large saucepan over high heat. Add beef mixture, bay leaves, salt, Tabasco sauce, tomato paste, vinegar and thyme. Reduce heat to low. Cover with a tight-fitting lid; simmer 2 hours. Add potatoes and carrots; simmer 30 minutes or until carrots are tender. Discard bay leaves.

Variations

Substitute or add the following vegetables: 1 cup chopped green beans, 1 cup lima beans or 2 cups tomatoes or stewed tomatoes.

Garnish with either 2 tablespoons chopped green bell pepper or 2 tablespoons chopped fresh parsley.

Creamy Vegetable-Ham Soup

Gemüse-Schinkencremesuppe

Brussels sprouts are members of the cabbage family that have to fight for a place amongst their larger cabbage cousins. Brussels sprouts go well with ham and other vegetables in this aromatic and attractive soup. *Makes 6 to 8 servings.*

2 tablespoons butter or margarine
1 medium onion, chopped
3 cups diced ham
2 quarts Chicken Broth (page 57)
2 medium carrots, chopped
1/2 cup fresh or frozen green peas

1/2 cup chopped fresh green beans
1/2 cup whole-kernel corn
1/2 cup chopped Brussels sprouts
2 cups milk
1/4 teaspoon ground white pepper
2 tablespoons chopped fresh parsley

Melt butter or margarine in a small skillet over medium heat. Add onion and ham; sauté 6 to 8 minutes, until onion is tender and ham is browned. In a large saucepan, bring broth to a boil. Add sautéed onion and ham, carrots, peas, green beans, corn and Brussels sprouts. Cover and bring to a boil. Reduce heat to low; cook 30 minutes.

Stir milk into broth and vegetables. Heat until hot, but do not boil. Add white pepper to taste. Garnish with parsley. Serve hot.

Beet Soup

Borscht

This traditional soup covers a lot of ground: from Eastern Europe all the way across what was formerly the Soviet Union. It's a refreshing combination of meat and beet flavors. Vegetarians make it with vegetable broth instead of beef broth. *Makes 8 servings.*

2 lbs. fresh beets
1 1/2 tablespoons salt
2 1/2 qts. Meat Broth (page 62) or
*   Beef Broth (page 58)*
3 tablespoons white vinegar
1/4 teaspoon freshly ground
*   black pepper*

Lemon juice
Sugar
2 tablespoons chopped fresh dill or
*   parsley for garnish*

Scrub and rinse beets clean; rinse with cold water. Leave roots, 1 to 2 inches of stem and skin intact. Place whole washed beets in a large saucepan. Add salt and enough cold water to cover. Bring to a boil over high heat. Cover with a tight-fitting lid; reduce heat to medium-low. Cook 1 hour or until tender. Remove beets from liquid. Let cool, then peel.

Bring broth to a simmer in a large saucepan over high heat. Slice or grate cooked beets; add to broth. Reduce heat to low. Simmer, uncovered, 30 minutes. Stir vinegar and pepper into beet mixture. Season with lemon juice and sugar to taste. Simmer over low heat 1 hour; do not boil. Strain into a serving tureen. Serve steaming hot. Garnish with dill or parsley.

Cabbage Soup

Weisskohlsuppe

Cabbage is a wonderful source of vitamin C. German cooks tend to save the water they cook cabbage and other vegetables in so it can be used later in soups and sauces instead of plain water. You can substitute other kinds of cabbage in this recipe. *Makes 8 servings.*

3 cups chopped fresh green cabbage
1 large onion, chopped
3 cups water
7 cups Chicken Broth (page 57) or
    Veal Broth (page 60)
3/4 cup sour cream

1 1/2 tablespoons all-purpose flour
1 1/2 tablespoons Maggi seasoning
Salt
1/8 teaspoon ground white pepper
2 tablespoons chopped fresh dill or
    parsley for garnish

Place cabbage, onion and water in a large saucepan. Cook, uncovered, over medium heat 15 to 20 minutes or until tender.

In a large saucepan, bring broth to a boil. In a small bowl, combine sour cream and flour until smooth. Stir 1 cup hot broth into sour-cream mixture. Return mixture to saucepan. Bring to a boil, uncovered, over medium-high heat, stirring occasionally. Add cabbage mixture to broth. Reduce heat to low and simmer, uncovered, 10 minutes. Add Maggi seasoning. Season with salt and white pepper to taste. Simmer 5 minutes. Serve steaming hot. Garnish with dill or parsley.

Sauerkraut Soup

Sauerkrautsuppe

Since sauerkraut is simply shredded raw cabbage that's been pickled in salt, it should be prepared in non-metal cookware. A slow cooker is ideal, but any glass or enameled cookware will work equally well. *Makes 12 servings.*

1 1/2 lbs. sauerkraut

1 (2 1/2- to 3-lb.) ham bone

10 black peppercorns

2 bay leaves

4 qts. water or 2 qts. water and 2 qts. Ham Broth (page 61)

8 medium potatoes, peeled and diced

1/4 lb. bacon, diced

2 medium onions, chopped

2 tablespoons all-purpose flour

Place sauerkraut, ham bone, peppercorns, bay leaves and water or water and broth in a Dutch oven. Cover; bring to a boil. Uncover; cook over medium heat 1 1/2 hours. Carefully remove ham bone; let cool. Slice any lean ham from the bone; return meat to cooked sauerkraut. In a medium saucepan, cook potatoes with enough water to cover until tender; drain well. Add potatoes to sauerkraut mixture.

In a small skillet, fry bacon over medium heat until crisp. Remove bacon and drain on paper towels. Reserve 2 tablespoons bacon drippings. Add bacon to sauerkraut mixture. In reserved drippings, sauté onions, stirring, until golden brown, about 15 minutes. Stir in flour. Ladle 1 cup sauerkraut broth into onion mixture; stir to combine. Stir resulting mixture into soup. Bring to a boil. Remove and discard bay leaves. Serve hot.

Cream of Cauliflower Soup

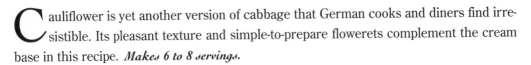

Blumenkohlcremesuppe

Cauliflower is yet another version of cabbage that German cooks and diners find irresistible. Its pleasant texture and simple-to-prepare flowerets complement the cream base in this recipe. *Makes 6 to 8 servings.*

1 large cauliflower	2 cups milk or half and half
1/2 lemon	Dash of nutmeg
4 cups Chicken Broth (page 57)	Ground sweet paprika
1/4 cup butter or margarine	Salt to taste
3 tablespoons chopped onion	1/2 cup (2 oz.) shredded Emmentaler
3/4 cup minced celery	cheese
1/4 cup all-purpose flour	

Rinse cauliflower; remove and discard tough stem end and leaves. Place cauliflower in cold salted water, head down for 10 minutes. Drain cauliflower and separate flowerets. Place cauliflower in a medium saucepan with 1 inch of water; add lemon (to keep cauliflower white). Bring water and cauliflower to a boil over medium-high heat. Cover, reduce heat to medium and cook 10 minutes. Drain, reserving cauliflower cooking water and about one-third of the flowerets. Discard lemon. Puree remaining cauliflower in a food processor or blender, or using a wooden spoon press cauliflower through a sieve; set aside.

Bring broth to a simmer in a large saucepan over high heat. In a small skillet, melt butter or margarine. Add onion and celery; sauté over medium heat 5 minutes or until onions turn a light golden color. Add flour; stir over medium heat until combined. When flour mixture starts to bubble, stir in 1 cup hot broth. Stir thinned flour mixture into remaining broth; bring to a boil. Add pureed or sieved cauliflower and cauliflower cooking water; stir to combine. In a small saucepan, heat milk or half and half until almost boiling; add to broth mixture. Add reserved cauliflower flowerets, nutmeg, paprika and salt. Simmer 5 minutes over medium heat; do not boil. Sprinkle with cheese to garnish. Serve hot.

Lentil Soup

Linsensuppe

This is a simple version—despite its many ingredients—of a family of bean-and-pea soups found in every German home and restaurant. You can easily substitute whole dried peas, yellow or green split peas and other types of small dried beans. Remember that larger dried beans may need longer soaking and cooking times. *Makes 12 to 15 servings.*

4 qts. Beef Broth (page 58)

10 black peppercorns

2 bay leaves

1/2 lb. uncooked ham bone

2 tablespoons butter or margarine

1/2 lb. smoked ham, sliced and chopped

1 celery stalk, chopped

1 medium onion, chopped

1 large carrot, thinly sliced

1 small leek, chopped

2 cups dried lentils, rinsed and drained

4 medium potatoes, peeled and cubed

5 bacon slices, diced

2 tablespoons all-purpose flour

Heat broth, peppercorns and bay leaves in a large stockpot. Add ham bone. Partially cover; cook over medium-low heat about 30 minutes. In a medium skillet, melt butter or margarine over medium heat. Add smoked ham; sauté 5 to 8 minutes or until browned. Add ham to broth. Add celery, onion, carrot and leek to ham drippings in skillet; sauté over medium heat 2 to 3 minutes. Add sautéed vegetables and lentils to broth. Simmer, partially covered, over low heat 1 1/2 hours. Add potatoes; simmer 30 minutes.

Fry bacon in a small skillet. Using a slotted spoon, add cooked bacon to soup. Stir flour into bacon drippings. Cook over medium heat, stirring with a wire whisk. Add 1 cup of broth from stockpot to flour mixture, stirring with whisk. Add flour mixture to soup, stirring to combine. Bring soup to a boil and cook 10 minutes, stirring occasionally. Remove bay leaves, peppercorns and ham bone. Serve hot.

Bean Soup

Bohnensuppe

To the saying "Man or woman cannot live by bread alone," add "but he or she can with bean soup," for a brand-new maxim. This bean soup can be considered an entire meal unto itself. *Makes 8 to 10 servings.*

2 cups (about 1 lb.) dried navy or
    baby lima beans
3 to 4 lbs. ham bones
2 1/2 to 3 qts. water
5 black peppercorns
1 bay leaf
1 teaspoon salt
1 parsley root, quartered (optional)
4 medium carrots, chopped

3 medium onions, chopped
2 celery stalks, chopped
4 medium potatoes, peeled and diced
1/4 teaspoon garlic salt
1 chicken bouillon cube
1/4 lb. bacon, diced
2 tablespoons vegetable oil or
    bacon drippings
2 tablespoons all-purpose flour

In a medium saucepan, cover beans with boiling water; let soak overnight. Over medium heat, cook beans in same water about 1 hour or until almost tender. Skim off and discard bean skins that float. Drain water.

Meanwhile, place ham bones in a stockpot. Add 2 1/2 to 3 quarts water, peppercorns, bay leaf, salt and parsley root, if using. Boil over medium-high heat, uncovered, 2 hours. Remove bones. Add carrots, onions and celery. Cover and cook over medium heat until vegetables are tender, about 30 minutes.

Place potatoes in a medium saucepan. Cover with cold water. Boil 20 minutes; drain. Add cooked potatoes, beans, garlic salt and bouillon cube to soup; bring to a boil. In a small skillet, fry bacon over medium heat until crisp. Using a slotted spoon, add bacon to soup. Drain off all but 2 tablespoons bacon drippings. Stir flour into bacon drippings with a whisk; cook over medium heat until golden, 2 to 3 minutes. Ladle 1 cup broth from soup into flour mixture; whisk to combine. Add flour mixture to soup, stirring to combine. Bring to a boil, stirring occasionally. Remove bay leaves and peppercorns. Serve hot.

Variation
Substitute 2 quarts Ham Broth (page 61) for 2 quarts water above. If necessary, use more water to achieve desired consistency.

Potato Soup

Kartoffelsuppe

Germans, who have always been conscious of the importance of strong, healthy bodies, are paying increasing attention to retaining as much nutritional value as possible from their cooking ingredients. With potatoes it means peeling potatoes right before they'll be cooked—instead of peeling them in advance and letting them sit in water. *Makes 8 to 10 servings.*

8 medium potatoes, peeled and cut
    into 1/2-inch cubes
3 medium carrots, thinly sliced
3 celery stalks, thinly sliced
1 large onion, chopped
2 qts. water
2 3/4 cups Meat Broth (page 62)
    or Vegetable Broth (page 63)

2 tablespoons butter or margarine
2 tablespoons all-purpose flour
1 teaspoon salt
1/3 teaspoon ground white pepper
1 1/2 cups milk
2 tablespoons chopped fresh parsley

Combine potatoes, carrots, celery, onion, water and broth in a large saucepan. Cover with a tight-fitting lid. Cook over medium heat 30 minutes or until vegetables are tender.

In a small saucepan, melt butter or margarine over medium heat. Stir in flour, salt and white pepper. Cook, stirring constantly, until mixture bubbles. Slowly add 1/4 cup of the milk, stirring until smooth. Add remaining milk, stirring until smooth. Bring to a boil, stirring constantly. Stir into hot broth mixture. Bring to a simmer over medium heat. Reduce heat to low and simmer 10 minutes. Serve hot, garnished with parsley.

Potato-Bacon Soup

Kartoffelsuppe mit Speck

This traditional potato soup is made from scratch. The quality of potatoes used here is especially important. Family cooks are known to make a number of different versions by merely switching the kinds of potatoes. Sometimes, if red potatoes are used, the skins are carefully scrubbed and left on. *Makes 4 servings.*

4 tablespoons butter or margarine

6 medium potatoes, peeled and
    coarsely diced

About 1 1/2 cups diced celery root

2 medium carrots, diced

About 1 1/2 qts. water

1 leek, trimmed and finely sliced

1 medium onion, diced

1 cup half and half

1/2 teaspoon salt (optional)

1/4 teaspoon freshly ground
    black pepper

1/4 teaspoon ground nutmeg

6 lean bacon slices, diced

Garlic croutons

1 tablespoon chopped fresh parsley

Heat 3 tablespoons of the butter or margarine in a large saucepan over medium-low heat. Add potatoes, celery root and carrots. Sauté, stirring, 10 minutes. Do not brown or burn. Add water, cover with a tight-fitting lid, and simmer over low heat 35 to 40 minutes or until all vegetables are tender. Ladle about half of cooked vegetables from saucepan into a sieve; press through sieve or puree in a blender or food processor fitted with the steel blade.

Melt remaining 1 tablespoon butter or margarine in a small skillet over medium heat. Add leek and onion; sauté until tender, about 5 minutes. Using a slotted spoon, add leek and onion to soup mixture. Add bacon to skillet; fry over medium heat until crisp. Drain on paper towels. Meanwhile, stir pureed vegetables and half and half into soup. Season with salt, if using, pepper and nutmeg. Simmer until hot, but do not boil. To serve, ladle hot soup into individual serving bowls. Top with bacon, croutons and chopped parsley.

Spinach Soup

Spinatsuppe

Spinach, a popular ingredient in Germany, finds its way into soups, salads, casseroles, egg dishes and various fillings. If possible, use the water in which the spinach for Creamed Spinach (page 119) was cooked for additional flavor and nutrients. *Makes 6 servings.*

5 medium potatoes, peeled and cut into 1/4-inch cubes	1/2 teaspoon salt
4 bacon slices, diced	1/8 teaspoon freshly ground black pepper
1 tablespoon all-purpose flour	1 lb. fresh spinach, chopped
4 cups water	1/2 cup sour cream
2 cups milk	1 tablespoon Maggi seasoning
2 garlic cloves, crushed	

Place potatoes in a medium saucepan. Add water to cover. Bring to a boil over high heat. Reduce heat to medium; cook 20 minutes or until almost tender. Drain; set aside.

In a small skillet, fry bacon over medium heat until crisp. Carefully drain off all but about 2 tablespoons bacon drippings. Stir flour into bacon; cook, stirring, 2 to 3 minutes or until flour evenly coats bacon. Add bacon mixture to a medium saucepan. Stir water, milk, garlic, salt and pepper into bacon mixture. Add spinach; bring to a boil over medium heat. Reduce heat to low; simmer, partially covered, stirring occasionally, 10 minutes. Add cooked potatoes. Combine sour cream and Maggi seasoning in a small bowl. Stir into spinach mixture. Simmer 15 minutes. Serve hot.

Variation

Substitute sorrel for spinach. Sorrel is a tangy, leafy green. Sorrel soup is sure to bring an initial expression of surprise to those unfamiliar with its "sour" characteristics. But it's a soup that can grow on you. Also, if sorrel or spinach is not available, kale may be substituted with favorable results.

Onion-Wine Soup

Zwiebel-Weinsuppe

This soup is closer to French onion than some German cooks like to admit. If desired, toasted rye bread may be substituted for the traditional French bread. Be sure to serve it steaming hot. If the individual portions sit out, they'll quickly lose their heat. *Makes 6 servings.*

3 tablespoons butter or margarine
2 large onions, thinly sliced
7 cups Beef Broth (page 58)
1/8 teaspoon freshly ground
   black pepper
1 1/2 cups dry red wine

6 slices French bread, toasted
1/3 cup (1 1/2 oz.) freshly grated
   Parmesan cheese
1/2 cup (2 oz.) shredded Gruyère
   cheese

Melt butter or margarine in a large saucepan over medium heat. Add onions; sauté until golden brown. Add broth; bring to boil. Reduce heat to low and simmer, uncovered, 25 minutes. Add pepper and wine to onion mixture. Simmer 10 minutes.

Preheat oven to 400F (205C). Divide soup equally among 6 ovenproof crocks or bowls; float 1 slice toasted bread in each. Combine cheeses in a small bowl and sprinkle equal amount over each slice of toast. Bake 5 to 7 minutes or until cheese melts and slightly browns. Serve immediately, steaming hot.

Mushroom Soup

Champignonsuppe

This recipe is open to a wide variety of different mushrooms. Mushroom gathering in Germany is an activity that could be equated to strawberry picking in the United States. The Germans know their mushrooms, and there are numerous varieties beyond the commercially grown white ones. Try some of the different kinds that are available in large vegetable markets to prepare this aromatic and delicious soup. *Makes 6 servings.*

2 tablespoons butter or margarine
1 lb. fresh mushrooms, thinly sliced
2 shallots, minced
2 celery stalks, chopped
1 leek, trimmed, with greens, chopped
2 tablespoons all-purpose flour
5 cups Chicken Broth (page 57)

1 tablespoon lemon juice
1 bay leaf
2 cups half and half
1/4 teaspoon ground nutmeg
1/8 teaspoon ground white pepper
Salt
2 tablespoons chopped fresh parsley

Melt butter or margarine in a large saucepan over medium heat. Add mushrooms, shallots, celery and leek; sauté until shallots are translucent and tender. Stir flour into mushroom mixture until combined. Slowly add broth, stirring. Add lemon juice and bay leaf. Reduce heat to low; simmer, partially covered, 45 minutes. Stir in half and half. Add nutmeg and white pepper. Season with salt to taste. Simmer 10 minutes. Remove and discard bay leaf. Before serving, sprinkle with parsley. Serve hot.

Vegetable Soup

Gemüsesuppe

If fresh vegetables are out of season or unavailable, frozen ones make acceptable substitutes. *Makes 6 to 8 servings.*

1/4 cup butter or margarine
1 cup minced onion
1 cup thinly sliced leeks
1/4 cup sliced carrots
1/2 cup chopped celery
2 qts. Chicken Broth (page 57)
1/2 cup whole-kernel corn

1/2 cup sliced fresh green beans
1/2 cup fresh or frozen green peas
1 cup cooked noodles
1 cup (4 oz.) shredded Gruyère or
Swiss cheese
2 tablespoons chopped chives

Melt butter or margarine in a large skillet over medium heat. Add onion, leeks, carrots and celery. Cook, uncovered, 10 to 12 minutes, stirring several times. In a large saucepan, bring broth to a boil. Add cooked vegetables, corn, green beans and peas. Cover; bring to a boil. Reduce heat to low; cook 30 minutes. Add noodles and cheese. Cook, uncovered, until cheese melts. Garnish with chopped chives.

Vegetable & Barley Soup

Gemüse und Gerstensuppe

This soup is often associated with cold winter days, when it supplies the warmth and nourishment needed in between outdoor activities such as skiing, sledding and sleigh riding, ice fishing, climbing and hiking. Barley grits have the same reputation as they do in the United States—that of providing "stick-to-your-ribs" satisfaction. Vegetable soups are where the German cook can get creative. He or she will use whatever is available from the garden, from a neighbor's garden or from the previous day's salad—even trimmings from preparations of another day's meals. This is the soup that will handle the odds and ends of ingredients. Use the recipe as a guideline, but feel free to improvise! *Makes 8 to 10 servings.*

1/4 cup butter or margarine	1 (16-oz.) can tomatoes
1 large onion, diced	1 cup barley grits
2 celery stalks, diced	1 teaspoon salt
2 large carrots, diced	1 teaspoon dried oregano
2 1/2 qts. Vegetable Broth (page 63)	1/2 teaspoon freshly ground black pepper
2 1/2 cups cubed zucchini	1 bay leaf
1 1/2 cups cauliflower flowerets	4 whole cloves
1 medium potato, peeled and diced	3 parsley sprigs
1 cup cut fresh green beans	Chopped fresh dill

Melt butter or margarine in a large skillet over medium heat. Add onion, celery and carrots; sauté 5 to 7 minutes or until onion is tender. Heat broth in a large saucepan; add sautéed vegetables. Stir in zucchini, cauliflower, potato, green beans, tomatoes and barley. Cover; bring to a boil. Reduce heat to low; cook 15 minutes. Add salt, oregano, pepper, bay leaf, cloves and parsley. Cover and simmer over low heat 20 minutes or until barley and vegetables are tender. Remove bay leaves and cloves. Serve hot, garnished with chopped fresh dill.

Note
If whole spices and herbs are tied in cheesecloth before adding to a soup, they are easy to remove before serving.

Cheese Soup

Käsesuppe

This soup is best if made the day before and then reheated. Try first with chicken broth and then later with beef broth to compare flavors. An unlimited combination of different cheeses can also be employed, including certain hot-pepper cheeses that can give it a peppery character. *Makes 4 to 6 servings.*

2 tablespoons butter or margarine
1 large onion, finely chopped
1 leek, chopped
1 tablespoon all-purpose flour
2 cups Chicken Broth (page 57)
    or Beef Broth (page 58)
2 cups half and half or milk

3/4 cup (3 oz.) shredded Cheddar
    cheese
1/2 teaspoon ground nutmeg
Dash ground white pepper
About 2 tablespoons chopped fresh
    parsley
Croutons

Melt butter or margarine in a large saucepan over medium heat. Add onion and leek; sauté until onion is tender, about 10 minutes. Stir flour into onion and leek. Slowly add broth, stirring until combined. Bring broth mixture to a boil. Reduce heat to low; simmer 30 minutes. Stir half and half or milk into broth mixture. Bring to a boil. Strain through a sieve into another saucepan. Discard onion and leek. Add cheese, nutmeg and white pepper. Cook over low heat, uncovered, stirring until cheese melts. Sprinkle with parsley and croutons before serving. Serve hot.

Variation
Add 3 tablespoons each cooked chopped carrot, celery and parsley with cheese.

Beer Soup

Biersuppe

If you prefer, cut the toasted bread into bite-size cubes. It will be easier to eat. You'll be surprised at how "unlike" beer that beer can taste when prepared this way. *Makes 4 servings.*

6 cups light beer	1/2 teaspoon salt
2 egg yolks	4 slices French or dark bread, toasted
1 cup sour cream	1 cup (4 oz.) Emmentaler or Swiss
1 teaspoon cornstarch	cheese
1 teaspoon sugar	

Place beer in a medium saucepan; cover and bring to a boil over medium heat. In a medium bowl, beat egg yolks. Beat sour cream, cornstarch, sugar and salt into egg yolks. Transfer egg-yolk mixture to a medium saucepan. Slowly add hot beer to egg mixture, stirring constantly. Continue to stir over low heat until thoroughly heated but not boiling. Warm individual serving bowls. Place a piece of toast in each warmed bowl; sprinkle each piece of toast with cheese. Pour hot soup over toast and cheese. Serve hot.

Cold Rhubarb Soup

Kalte Rhabarbesuppe

Commercially grown rhubarb is usually nice and tender and ready for cooking. But the outdoors or "wild" varieties are often tougher and the stalks may require peeling before use. Select the youngest, most tender shoots. *Makes 4 servings.*

1 1/2 lbs. rhubarb	1 cup sugar
2 qts. plus 1/4 cup water	1/2 cup whipping cream
1/4 cup cornstarch	1/2 cup sliced fresh strawberries

Trim rhubarb; discard any tough fibers. Cut stalks into bite-size pieces. Combine rhubarb and 2 quarts water in a large saucepan. Bring to a boil over medium-high heat. Reduce heat to medium. Cook, stirring occasionally, 30 minutes. Strain rhubarb, reserving rhubarb liquid. Return rhubarb liquid to saucepan; bring to a boil over medium heat.

In a small bowl, blend cornstarch with 1/4 cup water, stirring until smooth. Pour cornstarch mixture and sugar into cooking rhubarb liquid, stirring continuously. Cook 6 to 10 minutes, or until slightly thickened. Remove from heat; let cool. Cover with a tight-fitting lid and refrigerate several hours to overnight. In a small bowl, beat cream until stiff peaks form. To serve, spoon whipped cream and sliced strawberries over individual portions of chilled soup.

Chilled Peach & Pear Soup

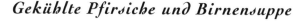

Gekühlte Pfirsiche und Birnensuppe

Use only ripe, fresh fruit. Fruit that's "green" or unripe will result in a very uneven texture. The amounts of fruit can vary, too. If you don't have enough of one, more of the other will do. *Makes 6 to 8 servings.*

1 lb. ripe fresh peaches	About 1/2 cup sugar
1 lb. ripe fresh pears	1/2 teaspoon grated orange peel
1 qt. water	2 tablespoons cornstarch
2 cups red or rose wine	1/2 cup whipping cream (optional)
1 cinnamon stick	

Rinse peaches and pears; remove pits from peaches and cores from pears. Cut peaches and plums into quarters. Place quartered fruit, water, wine and cinnamon stick in a large saucepan. Partially cover and cook over low heat about 15 minutes or until fruit is soft. Add sugar and orange peel. Remove and discard cinnamon stick. Push fruit mixture through a sieve or blend in a blender or food processor fitted with the steel blade.

In a small bowl, combine cornstarch with 2 tablespoons of the cooled blended fruits. Return mixture to the soup. Cook over medium heat 2 to 3 minutes or until fruit soup is slightly thickened. In a small bowl, whip cream, if using, until soft peaks form. Ladle chilled soup into individual bowls. Garnish with spoonfuls of whipped cream, if desired.

Variations
Serve soup hot instead of chilled.

Substitute pitted cherries, strawberries, raspberries or plums for peaches and pears.

Fruit Soup

Früchtesuppe

Here's a fruit soup specially made for those hot summer days, with a twist of cinnamon to give it some bite. If desired, white grape juice can be substituted for the white wine. Serve in frosted goblets for a festive presentation. *Makes 6 servings.*

1/4 lb. prunes	About 1/2 cup sugar
5 cups water	Lemon juice
2 lbs. tart apples	1/2 cup white wine
1 cinnamon stick	2 tablespoons white raisins
2 tablespoons potato flour	Ground cloves or cinnamon
2 cups half and half	

Wash prunes and place in a medium saucepan; add the water. Refrigerate and let prunes soak overnight. Cover and cook prunes in the same water over medium-low heat about 1 hour or until prunes are very soft. Let prunes cool; remove pits. Puree pitted prunes and cooking water in a blender or food processor fitted with the metal blade.

Peel, core and slice apples. In a small saucepan, cook apples over medium heat 20 minutes or until soft. Puree cooked apples. Combine prune and apple purees in a large saucepan. Add cinnamon stick. Mix potato flour with half and half; add to pureed prunes and apples. Bring to a boil and add sugar. Reduce heat to medium-low. Stir wine into fruit puree. Add raisins. Partially cover; heat thoroughly. Serve hot or refrigerate 2 hours and serve chilled, sprinkled with ground cloves or cinnamon, if desired.

Variation
Serve over cooked noodles.

Noodles & Dumplings

Nudeln und Knüdel

At one time or another, who has not seen or conjured up in his or her mind the image of a happy, plump, red-faced Bavarian sitting down before a platter heaped with dumplings in sauce, a stein of frothy beer to the right and bowls of sausage, sauerkraut and noodles to the left? What spaghetti and pasta are to Italy, what potatoes are to Ireland, what pierogies are to Poland, noodles and dumplings are to Germany.

While noodles and noodle "dough-wares," or *Teigwaren,* represent numerous lines of noodles and dumplings, most individual noodles are made from essentially the same doughs in slightly different configurations. For noodles, sometimes the dough is rolled and cut into strips, like the conventional noodles familiar to Western tastes. Other times the dough is rolled and cut into tiny squares, diamonds or other shapes, the exact thickness and size of which are totally up to the household cook of the day. Or the noodle dough can be forced through the holes in a colander or sieve into boiling water or broth, where the tiny squiggles of dough get cooked almost on contact.

Indeed, noodles—in all of their many forms—are so easy to make that children in German households are frequently delegated the task and do just as well as their parents would. Dumplings, on the other hand, are a different story.

Dumplings have been the subject of probably the greatest amount of culinary debate throughout Germany. Why? Because there are so many varieties and so many ways to prepare each variety. And each variety can be made in different sizes and in different consistencies, too. All of this means that dumplings can be tricky to make. The end result depends on a number of variables, such as how much moisture is in the flour to begin with, how strong the potato starch is in the potatoes, how fresh the eggs are, how fast the pan conducts heat, how close in size the dumplings are made and how firmly—or loosely—they're formed. No doubt, there is an art to dumpling making. But luckily, it's an art that can be quickly learned as long as a few basic concepts and rules are understood and followed.

Until you get a feel for dumpling making, use the recipes as guidelines, but be aware you may have to fine-tune the steps a bit to achieve the results you want. A few general guidelines include:

- Never prepare all of the dumplings in advance and then cook them. Why? Because what if the consistency is wrong, or off just slightly? Then you won't be able to adjust the dough; it'll be too late. Instead, make a single dumpling first. Cook it. Watch how it reacts. See how long it takes to cook. Does it suddenly fall apart in the water or broth? Or does it float almost immediately? It's like that first pancake. Breakfast chefs know that they should try a test pancake before filling up the pan or grill. Same with dumplings. Run a test first, then make adjustments to the dough if necessary.

- The water or broth should be boiling rapidly when the dumplings are dropped in, but the heat should be controlled so the liquid will not regain such a rapid boil while the dumplings are cooking.

- Cook dumplings in small batches. Too many dumplings dropped in all at once will cause several problems. They will lower the temperature of the water or broth too quickly and they may crowd each other, sticking together and preventing parts of the dumplings from being cooked. Drop the dumplings in, one after another. A pan of boiling water or broth might accept five or six large dumplings, or ten to twelve smaller ones.

- Once more, drop dumplings into boiling liquid; cook them, gently stirring so they don't stick together; then remove them with a slotted spoon to a colander where they can drain, shaking them a little so they again won't stick to each other. Then bring the liquid to a full boil again and drop in the next batch.

- If the dumpling dough is too sticky to handle, try dipping your hands in luke-warm water, then shaking off the excess water before shaping each or every few dumplings.

- Some cooks like to add anywhere from 1/2 teaspoon to 1 1/2 teaspoons baking powder to the dumpling mixture to produce lighter, puffier dumplings.

- Dumplings are best served shortly after they're cooked. They won't improve with age; on the contrary, they'll likely deteriorate by absorbing moisture or drying out.

- Although it's best to prepare only as many dumplings as you're likely to consume at a sitting, larger dumplings can be served as leftovers, reheated in a microwave oven or sliced in half and sautéed in a little butter sprinkled with minced chives or parsley.

Noodles

Spätzle

This version of spätzle is made from dough soft enough to be pushed through the medium-large holes of a colander. But that's too time consuming and messy to be practical. It's better to just cut off bits of dough with a sharp knife, making the spätzle as large or as small as you want. *Makes about 6 servings.*

About 2 cups all-purpose flour	*1/2 cup milk*
1 teaspoon salt	*Soups or broths or butter or*
1/2 teaspoon ground nutmeg	*margarine, fresh herbs, Parmesan*
3 eggs, lightly beaten	*cheese or bread crumbs to serve*

Sift flour, salt and nutmeg into a medium bowl. Pour eggs and milk into center of flour mixture. Beat several minutes with a wooden spoon. Dough should be soft and slightly sticky, yet elastic. Add more flour if dough is too soft.

Bring 5 to 6 inches of water to a boil in a large pot. Put the dough on a plate held to the side of the pot. Being careful you're not burned by the pot or from steam rising from the boiling water, cut pieces or strips of dough and slide the dough pieces or "strings" into the boiling water. Cook only as many noodles as will fit on the boiling water's surface, or they will cook together and not keep separate. Gently boil 6 to 8 minutes or until noodles are fully cooked. Remove from water with a slotted spoon or strainer. Repeat until all dough is cooked. Serve in soups or broths or sauté in butter or margarine seasoned with salt and pepper. Fresh herbs, Parmesan cheese or bread crumbs may also be cooked with these noodles.

Noodle Squares

Nudelquadrate

These noodles are favorites with children. Noodle squares are simple to make, can be prepared in advance and take only minutes to cook. *Makes 4 to 6 servings.*

1 egg, lightly beaten
2/3 cup all-purpose flour
1/4 teaspoon salt

Salted water, soup or broth
Butter or margarine (optional)
to serve

Combine egg, flour and salt in a small bowl. Using your hands, work mixture into a stiff dough, kneading at least 10 minutes. Cover and let stand 30 minutes.

On a lightly floured surface, roll dough very thin. Let rolled dough dry until dough is no longer sticky. Cut dough into 3-inch-wide strips. Dust strips with flour and place strips one on top of the other. Cut crosswise into 1/3 × 3-inch strips. Next, cut 9 (1/3-inch) squares from each 3-inch strip. Spread noodle squares out to dry. Let dry several hours.

Bring salted water, soup or broth to a boil in a large saucepan. Drop handfuls of noodle squares into boiling liquid. Gently boil 5 to 7 minutes or until noodle squares are cooked through. If serving plain, strain noodles and cook in butter or margarine seasoned with salt and pepper, if desired.

Cheese Noodles

Käsenudeln

Try other cheeses such as Cheddar, Jarlsberg and Parmesan. *Makes 4 to 6 servings.*

2 tablespoons butter or margarine
2 small onions, sliced
3/4 cup (3 oz.) shredded Emmentaler
   cheese

1 teaspoon dry mustard
About 3 cups cooked Noodles (page
   91), cooled
3 tablespoons chopped chives

Preheat oven to 350F (175C). Melt butter or margarine in a skillet over medium-high heat. Add onions; sauté 5 minutes or until tender. In a medium bowl, toss cheese with dry mustard. Add sautéed onions and noodles; mix well. Place noodle mixture in a casserole dish; bake, uncovered, 30 minutes or until slightly browned on top. Garnish with chives before serving. Serve hot.

Homemade Noodles

Hausgemachte Nudeln

Alas, many people, even in Germany, too often rely upon commercially made noodles. It's easy to forget just how good homemade noodles are. There's no beating their flavor or texture and the cook can custom-cut whatever size noodles he or she wants. *Makes 6 to 8 servings.*

2 1/2 cups all-purpose flour
2 eggs, lightly beaten
About 1/3 cup cold water

Soups or broths or butter or
margarine or vegetables or meats
to serve

Combine flour, eggs and water in a medium bowl. Using your hands, work flour mixture into a stiff dough. Use more or less water, depending on dryness of flour. Knead dough until bubbles begin to form under surface of dough. On a lightly floured surface, roll out dough to about 1/8-inch thickness. Sprinkle a little flour over rolled dough, then let dough dry 15 to 20 minutes.

Roll dough, jelly-roll style, and cut crosswise into thin noodle strips. Bring 5 to 6 inches of salted water to a boil in a large pot over medium-high heat. Drop handfuls of uncooked noodles into boiling water; cook 20 minutes or until noodles are cooked through, stirring to prevent sticking. Pour noodles into a colander to drain. Rinse noodles with hot water. Serve in soups or broths, or sauté plain in melted butter or margarine, or with vegetables or meats.

 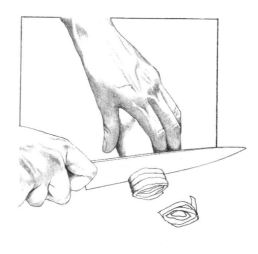

Pancake Strips

Eierkuchenstreifen

Place handfuls of these light delicacies in soup bowls, then ladle hot chicken or beef broth over them. *Makes 8 to 10 servings.*

3 eggs	*1 1/2 cups all-purpose flour*
1 cup water	*1/2 teaspoon salt*
1 cup milk	*Butter or margarine*

In a large bowl, beat eggs about 1 minute. Add water, milk, flour and salt. Beat into a smooth batter. Grease a crepe pan or 7-inch skillet with butter or margarine. Heat greased pan or skillet over medium heat. Pour a little less than 1/4 cup batter onto center of hot pan or skillet. Tip skillet so batter is evenly distributed. Cook over medium heat until lightly golden. Turn over and cook briefly until golden. Do not brown. Remove from skillet and place on a platter.

Repeat process until all batter is used, greasing skillet as necessary. When crepes are cool enough to handle, roll each one, jelly-roll style, and cut crosswise into thin strips.

Potato Dumplings

Kartoffelknödel

When cooking potato dumplings, use the first dumpling as a test. See how the dough reacts and how long it takes to cook, then you'll be able to make adjustments to the dumpling consistency or the cooking time to achieve desired results. *Makes 65 to 70 dumplings, 6 to 8 servings.*

8 medium potatoes, cooked in skins,
   still warm
1 1/2 to 2 cups all-purpose flour
2 eggs, lightly beaten
1 teaspoon salt

1/4 teaspoon white pepper
About 3 qts. Beef Broth (page 58)
   or beef bouillon
Dill Sauce (page 135) or Mushroom
   Sauce (page 131) (optional)

Peel and grate warm potatoes into a large bowl. Stir about 1 1/2 cups of the flour, eggs, salt and white pepper into potatoes. Using your hands, work potato mixture into a stiff dough. Dust your hands with flour, then shape 1 heaping teaspoon dough into a 1- to 1 1/4-inch ball. Repeat with remaining dough. If dumplings are too soft and won't hold together, add a little more flour.

Bring broth or bouillon to a boil in a large saucepan. Drop dumplings into boiling broth or bouillon one at a time so boiling liquid will not cool down too much. Cook dumplings in small batches, about 3 minutes each batch, or until dumplings float and are cooked through. Serve in broth or in a soup or remove with a slotted spoon and serve with sauce.

Variations

Place a deep indentation in center of uncooked dumplings with your thumb, so dumpling resembles a small, thick bowl. These indented dumplings will take a little less time to cook, because they won't have a true center.

Mix 2 tablespoons finely chopped marjoram, 1 tablespoon finely chopped thyme and 2 tablespoons finely chopped parsley into dough.

Potato-Bread Dumplings

Kartoffel-Semmelknödel

Serve hot with Mushroom Sauce (page 131), other sauces or alongside Rheinischer Sauerbraten (page 197). To reheat dumplings, slice in half and sauté in butter or margarine. *Makes about 16 dumplings, 6 to 8 servings.*

3 slices white bread

2 tablespoons butter or margarine

9 medium potatoes (about 3 lbs.), peeled

3 egg yolks, beaten

3 tablespoons cornstarch

3 tablespoons uncooked semolina or Cream of Wheat cereal

1 teaspoon salt

1/2 teaspoon ground white pepper

1/4 teaspoon ground nutmeg

1/4 cup all-purpose flour

Butter or margarine, melted, herbs or sauce to serve

Cut bread into 1/2-inch cubes. Heat butter or margarine in a medium skillet over medium heat. Add bread; sauté, stirring often, until golden brown. Drain sautéed croutons on paper towels.

Place potatoes in a large saucepan; add salted water to cover. Bring to a boil over medium-high heat. Reduce heat to medium. Cover with a tight-fitting lid; cook 20 minutes or until fork tender. Drain and mash potatoes. Add egg yolks, cornstarch, semolina, salt, pepper and nutmeg. Stir to combine.

Using your hands, shape the potato mixture into dumplings about the size of table-tennis balls, pressing one or more croutons into the center of each dumpling. Place flour on a dinner plate; roll dumplings in flour until dumplings are evenly coated.

In a large saucepan, bring 2 quarts salted water to a boil. Using a slotted spoon, gently lower dumplings into boiling water. Cover and reduce heat to medium-low. Simmer dumplings 15 minutes or until cooked through; do not allow water to boil. Remove cooked dumplings with a slotted spoon. Serve hot with melted butter and herbs, or practically any sauce.

Semolina Dumplings

Weizengriessknödel

Semolina is a creamy colored, large-grained wheat flour that's used commercially to manufacture all kinds of pasta. It "holds together" a lot better than regular all-purpose flour does. *Makes 4 servings.*

2 tablespoons butter or margarine	1/2 teaspoon salt
1 cup milk	1/2 teaspoon freshly ground pepper
1/2 cup uncooked semolina or Cream	About 1 1/2 qts. Beef Broth (page
of Wheat cereal	58) or bouillon
2 eggs, separated	Fresh chopped herbs (optional)

Melt butter or margarine in top half of a double boiler. Add milk and heat until hot. Slowly stir in semolina; cook, stirring constantly, until thick and smooth. Remove from heat and let cool. Stir egg yolks into cooled semolina mixture. In a medium bowl, beat egg whites until stiff but not dry. Fold egg whites into semolina mixture. Season with salt and pepper. Cover and let semolina mixture stand about 1 hour or until room temperature.

Bring broth or bouillon to a boil in a large saucepan. Wet your hands and shape tablespoon-size dumplings or use a wooden spoon dipped in water and drop dumplings one at a time into boiling broth or bouillon. Cook 10 minutes or until cooked through. Remove dumplings with a slotted spoon. Serve in broth or plain, garnished with chopped fresh herbs, if desired.

Liver Dumplings

Leberknödel

Be prepared to use more or less flour, as needed. Before processing or chopping the liver, remove all tough connective tissues and membranes. *Makes 8 to 10 servings.*

1 tablespoon butter or margarine
1 medium onion, minced
1/4 cup chopped fresh parsley
1 lb. calf liver or chicken livers
3/4 cup all-purpose flour
1 egg, lightly beaten
1/2 teaspoon salt

1/4 teaspoon ground nutmeg
1/8 teaspoon ground marjoram
1/8 teaspoon freshly ground black
   pepper
1 qt. Chicken Broth (page 57)
   or chicken bouillon
Additional broth to serve

Melt butter or margarine in a small skillet over medium-high heat. Add onion and parsley; sauté until onion is tender, about 5 minutes. Remove from heat; let cool. Rinse liver under cold running water and remove tough skin and fiber, if any are present. Grind or process liver in a food processor or chop very fine. Using your hands, combine liver, sautéed onion and parsley, flour, egg, salt, nutmeg, marjoram and pepper in a medium bowl.

Shape the liver mixture into 1-inch balls. Bring broth or bouillon to a boil in a medium saucepan. Gently drop dumplings into boiling broth, about 10 dumplings at a time; simmer 5 to 6 minutes or until dumplings are cooked through. Remove cooked dumplings with a slotted spoon. Repeat process with remaining dumplings. Serve dumplings with fresh hot broth or bouillon.

Meat-Filled Dumplings

Fleischgefüllte Knödel

A half-teaspoon of meat filling turns these potato dumplings into flavorful morsels that add character to any hot broth or cream soup. *Makes 6 to 8 servings.*

Meat Filling (see below)
1/2 cup grated raw potato, lightly
   pressed and drained in a strainer
2 lbs. boiled potatoes, cooled, peeled
   and diced

3/4 cup all-purpose flour
1/2 teaspoon salt
2 eggs, lightly beaten
Soup or broth to serve

MEAT FILLING

1/2 lb. cooked lean beef, veal or pork,
   cut into pieces (about 2 cups)
1 tablespoon butter or margarine
1 small onion, minced
1/2 tablespoon chopped fresh parsley
1/2 tablespoon minced fresh
   marjoram

1 1/2 to 2 tablespoons dried bread
   crumbs
1/4 teaspoon salt
1/8 teaspoon freshly ground
   black pepper
2 tablespoons beef or chicken broth

Prepare filling. Combine grated potato, boiled potatoes, flour, salt and eggs in a large bowl. Mix into a stiff dough. Using your hands, shape 1 tablespoon potato mixture into a flat round. Place 1/2 teaspoon meat filling in center. Roll potato mixture in a ball around filling. Repeat process until all potato mixture is used.

Bring 5 to 6 inches of water to a boil in a large pot over medium-high heat. Drop stuffed dumplings into boiling water. Boil until potatoes are cooked and dumplings float, 8 to 10 minutes. Carefully remove dumplings with a slotted spoon. Serve hot in soups or broths.

Meat Filling

Using a grinder or a food processor fitted with a metal blade, grind meat. Do not puree or process too fine. Melt butter or margarine in a medium skillet over medium heat. Add onion; sauté until tender, about 5 minutes. Let onion cool.

In a medium bowl, combine meat, onion, parsley, marjoram, bread crumbs, salt, pepper and broth. Leftover meat filling, if any, can be frozen in small freezer bags up to 3 months.

German Ravioli

Maultaschen

These German raviolis can be prepared with a wide variety of fillings. Use your imagination or borrow any of the other fillings you find in this book or in others. Leftover cooked pork and beef from roasts make exceptionally tasty fillings. *Makes 6 servings.*

Meat Filling (see below)
4 cups all-purpose flour
2 eggs
5 tablespoons sour cream
3 tablespoons vegetable oil

1/8 teaspoon salt
About 3/4 cup water
Broth, melted butter, sautéed onions,
*   Tomato Sauce (page 114) or*
*   other sauce to serve*

MEAT FILLING
1 lb. cooked pork, lamb, veal or beef,
*   cut into pieces (about 4 cups)*
2 tablespoons butter or margarine
1 medium onion, chopped

2 eggs, beaten
1/2 teaspoon salt
1/2 teaspoon freshly ground
*   black pepper*

Prepare filling. Lightly flour 2 baking sheets. Sift flour into a large bowl or onto a work surface; make a well in the center. Break eggs into well. Add sour cream, oil and salt. Blend ingredients with your fingertips. Gradually add water, working and kneading mixture into a smooth, pliable dough. Divide dough in half.

On a lightly floured surface, roll out half of dough into a rectangular sheet about 1/16 inch thick. Mark rolled dough into 3 1/2- to 4-inch squares without cutting dough. Place about 1 teaspoon of filling in the center of each square. Brush edges of each square with water, so edges will stick together to form a good seal. On another lightly floured surface, roll out remaining half of dough into a large, thin rectangle of the same size and thickness. Carefully place dough rectangle over dough squares with filling. With your fingers, press down on top dough layer between dollops of filling, so edges of squares will adhere to top layer of rolled dough, forming tight seals. Use a fluted pastry cutter to cut finished raviolis into squares. Place raviolis on lightly floured baking sheets.

Bring a large pot of salted water to a boil, using 1/2 teaspoon salt per 2 quarts water. Drop about 6 raviolis into boiling water, one at a time; stir gently to prevent them from sticking to the bottom. When water returns to a boil, add 6 more raviolis; stir carefully. Cover with a tight-fitting lid; cook 4 to 5 minutes or until they float. Gently remove raviolis from pot; drain in a colander or strainer. Rinse with hot water. Repeat until all raviolis are cooked. Serve hot in broth or by themselves, topped with melted butter, sautéed onions, Tomato Sauce (page 114) or other sauce.

Meat Filling

Using a grinder or food processor fitted with the metal blade, grind meat. Do not puree or process too fine. Melt butter or margarine in a large skillet over medium heat. Add onion; sauté until tender, about 5 minutes. Stir in meat and eggs. Sauté over medium heat about 5 minutes. Season with salt and pepper. Let cool. *Makes about 4 cups filling.*

Plum Dumplings

Pflaumenknödel

Select only ripe prunes plum or plums of any small variety. Remember to remove the pits and leave sugar cubes in their place! *Makes 4 to 6 servings.*

2 eggs, lightly beaten	Sugar cubes
3/4 cup half and half or milk	Up to 1/2 cup melted butter or
3 cups all-purpose flour	margarine
1/8 teaspoon salt	3/4 cup powdered sugar
1 lb. small prune plums	

In a large bowl, combine eggs and half and half or milk; beat until frothy. Gradually stir flour and salt into egg mixture to make a stiff dough. On a lightly floured surface, knead dough about 10 minutes or until dough is smooth and elastic. Roll out dough to 1/2-inch thickness. Cut dough into 3-inch squares. Combine dough trimmings; reroll and cut into 3-inch squares. Repeat until all dough is used.

Remove pits from plums by slicing each fruit halfway around pit edge and pulling out pit. Carefully replace each pit with a small sugar cube or half of a larger sugar cube. Place a sugar-cube–filled plum on center of a dough square. Tightly fold dough square completely around plum, crimping dough edges together to prevent water from seeping into the dumpling. Repeat with remaining plums and squares.

Bring 5 inches of water to a boil in a large pot over medium-high heat. Place 4 or 5 dumplings at a time in boiling water; cook 9 to 10 minutes, turning at least once, or until dough is cooked through. Using a slotted spoon, gently transfer cooked dumplings to a colander; rinse with hot water. Repeat with remaining dumplings. Drain dumplings well; arrange on a heated platter. Spoon melted butter or margarine over dumplings. Sift powdered sugar over dumplings. Serve hot or warm.

Variation
Substitute small apricots for plums.

Sweet Dumplings

······································

Süsse Knödel

One of the simplest dumpling recipes. Serve hot or cold with accompanying cherry sauce. Cherry liquid drained from the frozen cherries can be used for part or all of the cherry juice in this recipe. If you use fresh tart cherries, you'll need to obtain additional cherry juice. *Makes 40 to 50 dumplings with cherry sauce, 6 to 8 servings.*

1/2 cup butter or margarine	1/4 teaspoon salt1 cup water
1 cup water	2 eggs
2 cups all-purpose flour	Cherry sauce (see below)
2 tablespoons sugar	

CHERRY SAUCE

1/3 cup sugar	3 1/2 cups frozen pitted tart red
3 tablespoons cornstarch	cherries thawed and drained,
1/8 teaspoon salt	reserving juice, or pitted fresh
1/2 teaspoon ground cinnamon	tart cherries
1 1/2 cups cherry juice or water	2 tablespoons lemon juice
	2 tablespoons butter

Melt butter or margarine in a medium saucepan over medium heat. Add 1 cup water; bring to a boil. Stir flour, sugar and salt into boiling water mixture. Reduce heat to low; cook, stirring constantly, until dough mixture easily comes away from the sides of pan. Remove saucepan from heat; cool. Beat in 1 egg at a time, mixing to form a shiny dough.

Bring 5 or 6 inches of water to a boil in a large pot over medium-high heat. Drop a rounded, oval half teaspoon of dough mixture at a time into boiling water. Cook small numbers of dumplings in batches so dumplings are not crowded and won't stick together. Cook each batch about 10 minutes or until dumplings rise to the surface. Remove dumplings with a slotted spoon. Place in a colander; rinse with cool water. Prepare sauce. Serve sauce over dumplings.

Cherry Sauce

Combine sugar, cornstarch, salt and cinnamon in a large saucepan over medium heat. Gradually stir cherry juice into sugar mixture. Cook, stirring constantly, over medium heat until thickened. Stir cherries, lemon juice and butter into cherries. Bring to a boil and cook, stirring constantly, until hot. Use hot or chilled.

Vegetables

Gemüse

*V*egetables make up another class of ingredients in Germany which have come into
their own. Much in the same way that soups have edged their way onto menus and
demanded more attention alongside traditional meats and other main entrees, so too have
vegetables begun to receive more interest at mealtimes. Of course, as a meal component
they are nothing new to farmers and villagers who have raised their own vegetables for centuries. It's just that nutritionists and the medical community are now saying that vegetables
are believed to be helpful in preventing certain diseases and should be included in a healthy
diet.

The presentation of vegetables has always varied throughout Germany, but they
have generally been on the simple side. Top German chefs create works of art with ingredients, including vegetables. But they're the exceptions. Most home kitchens and restaurants feature vegetables prepared in very direct manners. On one hand, there's the simple

vegetable plate: a centerpiece in the middle of a large serving tray or platter, perhaps accompanied by a hollowed-out small red cabbage serving as a bowl for Hollandaise Sauce or, with the addition of a few tablespoons of prepared mustard, a spicy mustard sauce for dipping the surrounding multicolored strips of peppers, julienned carrots and celery, strips of celery root or parsley root, sweet onions, white and green asparagus from a tangy marinade, crispy green and yellow beans that have been lightly blanched in water with a touch of olive oil, pickled beets, mushrooms (both fresh and pickled), turnips and radishes. The raw-vegetable arrangements are directly related to what's available at the market and in gardens and in some cases, within root cellars. Pickles and radishes and other sauces and dips may round out the selections. The vegetable plates are quick to prepare and healthy to eat—nothing is lost in the cooking—plus leftovers will keep to be finished the following day, or to be used in preparing broths or soups. The German cook wastes not. Even the water in which vegetables are cooked often gets saved as a nutritional solution that can be used to make broth or soup stocks.

The next level of vegetable preparation features a number of quick-cook methods, including steaming, cooking in salted water or lightly sautéing in a little oil or butter that may be further seasoned with salt and pepper and a sprinkling of bread crumbs. Green beans, asparagus, cauliflower and mushrooms come to mind here.

As for favorite German vegetables, asparagus ranks near the top of the list in many recipe books. The most sought-after strains are the early, delicate ivory-colored spears that sprout from the ground in late April or early May, signifying the arrival of spring on the banks of the Rhine River. Asparagus is often cooked with butter and salt or butter and sugar or butter and bread crumbs, chopped hazelnuts or slivered almonds, then topped with any of a host of sauces and paired up with aromatic slices of Westphalian ham or small new potatoes quickly boiled, then sautéed in butter and chopped parsley. Leftover pieces of asparagus find their way into soups and omelets or are even chopped into small pieces and served in salads. German cooks take extra care not to overcook asparagus because it will become soft and stringy when too well done. Proper cooking leaves asparagus spears knife-point tender, but still firm to the bite. True to the German way of using everything, the tough ends and skin trimmings are rinsed and used to make soup stock or broth. Wise cooks know where the tender edible portion meets the more fibrous, tough section of stalk. A natural break occurs where the edible section can be snapped off with your fingers. To cut asparagus spears with a knife will invariably waste edible portions or include the tough stems with the tender upper parts.

The all-time winning vegetables, however, hail from the cabbage family. From one end of the country to the other, cabbage reigns. There are literally hundreds of recipes which call for cabbage in some form or another. The German words for cabbage mostly end with *kohl*. There's red cabbage or *Rotkohl*. There's white cabbage or *Weisskohl*. Brussels sprouts are called rose cabbage or *Rosenkohl,* partly due to their resemblance to rosebuds and partly to the pinkish hue they sometimes exhibit. Cauliflower, another member of the cabbage family, is known as *Blumenkohl,* meaning "flowering cabbage." Then there's winter cabbage, which is called *Winterkohl.*

Red cabbage is one of the most popular cabbages. It's plentiful, tasty and stores well. It's especially abundant during winter, when it accompanies or is included with many meat and game dishes.

When cabbage is shredded it becomes a *Kraut,* which literally means a vegetable or fruit that has been rendered into a puree or concentrated form. Taken one step further, when pickled or marinated, it becomes, of course, *Sauerkraut.* Although sauerkraut is enormously popular all over Eastern Europe and Russia, its center of influence must be in Germany. Sauerkraut is considered a fall and winter dish by some, but is served year-round, especially in the south. It frequently accompanies, provides an edible bed for or surrounds roast pork, chunks of pork and ham, sausages and wild game—from pheasant to rabbit to venison. It's found as a main ingredient in casseroles, too.

Western diners may know sauerkraut as the lukewarm, neutral-tasting, stringy, mushy accompaniment served with hot dogs. But to the typical German, properly cooked kraut is prepared so it's not dripping with juices yet is still juicy when eaten. Sauerkraut is often seasoned with sautéed onions, apple slices or caraway seeds, and wine goes with it very well. Sauerkraut is a main ingredient in numerous condiments and relishes, salads and other vegetable dishes—both hot and cold.

All sauerkraut is not equal. It should be tasted before being added to a recipe. If necessary, strong kraut may be rinsed with cold water once or twice to tone down its strength. Freshly barreled sauerkraut found in butcher shops and delicatessens in large crocks or barrels is generally of the highest quality. Sauerkraut sold in cans and bags may also be tasty, but may need additional rinsing before use to soften its tartness.

Sauerkraut, especially when cooked with vinegar or wine, should be prepared in glass or enameled cookware. Its salt brine has a high degree of acid content that will react with certain metals to produce an unsavory combination. Again, do not overcook the sauerkraut. If it's too soft, it will lose much of its appeal.

Another relative of the cabbage family is the kohlrabi, whose name means "half-cabbage, half-turnip." Given the German fondness for both cabbage and root vegetables, it's an ideal combination. Even the leaves are edible, cooked as greens, chopped and sautéed in a little water and butter. The only part of the kohlrabi that's not eaten is the hard outer skin that surrounds the white inner meat. Kohlrabi is becoming more available to Western cooks, with the trend toward large supermarkets trying to outdo each other when it comes to offering vegetable and fruit selections. The smaller bulbs are more tender; the larger ones need more peeling to expose the edible insides. For the kohlrabi in this chapter, select younger fruit for stuffing.

Throughout the German countryside, many vegetables are grown in small backyard gardens. Due to modern-day methods of transportation, though, vegetables which used to be available only in season, including tomatoes, cucumbers, eggplants and peppers, are now offered year-round. Onions, carrots, potatoes and other root vegetables are still stored in earthen cellars in rural areas to provide fresh vegetables during the winter.

Potatoes are an ever-present accompaniment that sometime serve as the main focus for a meal. They're so popular that they've got their own chapter in this book (pages 125–138).

Carrots are served simply, cooked in a little salted water until tender, often diced and mixed with green peas and served with melted butter and chopped parsley. Sometimes, though, they're served in a white sauce that's sweetened a little extra with a teaspoon or so of sugar. Whole carrots are cooked and glazed by sautéing them slowly in a combination of butter and sugar until the sugar attains a light caramel color and evenly adheres to the carrot, giving it a glossy texture.

Wild mushrooms are commonly gathered by knowledgeable individuals who are familiar with local edible specimens and who have passed down those skills over the years. The stout *boletus,* tasty morels and a host of others are available, but so too are white cultivated mushrooms. Although the latter range in flavor somewhere just below center of the mushroom pecking order, they're prized for their appearance and they make fine stuffed mushrooms with their round, bowllike caps.

It's no coincidence that a list of sauces used to top vegetables, meats and noodles and dumplings reads like an inventory of vegetables in a German market. Along with tasty broth bases, vegetables, herbs and various seasonings yield a wide variety of sauces. There are sour sauces and sweet sauces to spice up the blandest fare and sauces combining the best of both sweet and sour flavors, such as Cumberland Sauce (page 176), which is delicious over poultry or ham.

Years ago, heavy, strong-tasting sauces were used to "cover up" slightly spoiled or tasteless dishes. Sauces today are used far more sparingly and their flavors are more subtle and less likely to overpower what they're topping.

Asparagus

Spargel

Although Germans are partial to white asparagus, white asparagus is really the same variety as the green—it's just that white asparagus has soil piled up around its developing spears, so no sunlight reaches through to turn the upper portions of the spears green. Asparagus season in Germany is traditionally from early May through late June, when restaurants and vegetable markets all across the country feature asparagus specials. *Makes 6 servings.*

2 lbs. asparagus	1/4 teaspoon sugar
Water	Béchamel Sauce (page 108) and
1/2 teaspoon salt	other toppings

Rinse asparagus in cold water. With your fingers, snap off hard bottom ends; discard. Boil 1 inch of water, salt and sugar in a large skillet over medium-high heat. Add cleaned asparagus, spreading spears out evenly over the bottom of the pan. Cover with a tight-fitting lid. Cook 5 to 6 minutes. Remove from heat; drain cooking water immediately. Serve hot or warm with hot Béchamel Sauce.

Variations
Alternate toppings for asparagus include:

Melted butter or margarine	Chopped or slivered almonds or
Dill Sauce (page 135)	hazelnuts sautéed in butter or
Mustard Sauce (page 216)	margarine
Bread crumbs sautéed in butter or	
margarine	

Béchamel Sauce

Taste this sauce while slowly adding the lemon juice. If you prefer, use less lemon juice. Serve hot over meat, potatoes, vegetables or dumplings. *Makes about 2 cups sauce.*

2 tablespoons butter or margarine
2 1/2 tablespoons all-purpose flour
1 3/4 cups milk
1/2 teaspoon salt

1/8 teaspoon ground nutmeg
Pinch of ground white pepper
1 tablespoon Maggi seasoning
Juice of 1 lemon

Melt butter or margarine in a medium saucepan over low heat. Slowly stir in flour until smooth. Stir until bubbles begin to form. Gradually add milk, stirring constantly. Bring to a simmer. Stir in salt, nutmeg, white pepper and Maggi seasoning. Cook 6 to 7 minutes over medium heat until thickened. Stir lemon juice to taste into sauce.

Asparagus Vinaigrette

Spargelvinaigrette

The combination of wine vinegar and Dijon mustard gives the warm, crunchy asparagus spears just the right amount of tangy flavor. It's really a pleasant half-vegetable, half-salad that goes especially well with sausage or roast pork. *Makes 4 to 6 servings.*

24 asparagus spears
1/4 cup wine vinegar
2 teaspoons Dijon mustard
1/2 teaspoon sugar
1/2 teaspoon salt
1/8 teaspoon freshly ground
* black pepper*

1/4 cup vegetable oil
3 teaspoons finely chopped shallots
* or green onions*
2 teaspoons chopped fresh parsley

Rinse asparagus in cold water. With your fingers, snap off hard ends; discard. Cut asparagus into 1 1/2-inch pieces. In a large skillet, bring 1/2 inch salted water to a boil. Add asparagus. Cover with a tight-fitting lid; bring to a boil. Reduce heat to medium-low. Cook 7 minutes or until crisp-tender; do not overcook. Drain and place in a deep, medium serving bowl; keep warm.

In a large bowl, combine vinegar, mustard, sugar, salt, pepper and oil. Vigorously stir vinegar mixture with a wire whisk. Add shallots. Pour resulting marinade into a small saucepan; heat to lukewarm. Pour warm marinade over cooked asparagus; sprinkle with parsley. Serve warm.

Variation

In a medium nonreactive saucepan, combine 1/2 cup vinegar, 1/4 cup vegetable oil, 2 finely chopped hard-cooked eggs, 3 tablespoons chopped fresh parsley, 1 tablespoon diced green bell pepper, 1 tablespoon chopped chives, 1/2 teaspoon ground sweet paprika and 1/8 teaspoon freshly ground black pepper. Heat until hot and pour over asparagus. Serve warm.

Asparagus under Crust

Überbackener Spargel

Asparagus is rich in phosphorus, vitamin A and oxalic acid. Its shape and nutritional properties have caused asparagus lovers to view this "undeveloped fern" as an aphrodisiac. The crust in this recipe is not your traditional bakery crust, but a zesty cooked topping of bread crumbs and Parmesan cheese. *Makes 6 to 8 servings.*

2 lbs. asparagus	1/4 cup dried bread crumbs
1 cup chopped ham, Canadian bacon or smoked pork loin	5 tablespoons grated Parmesan cheese
1/4 cup half and half	1/4 teaspoon ground nutmeg
2 tablespoons butter or margarine	

Preheat oven to 425F (220C). Rinse asparagus in cold water. With your fingers, snap off hard ends; discard. Cut asparagus into 2-inch pieces. In a large skillet, bring 1/2 inch salted water to a boil. Add asparagus. Cover with a tight-fitting lid; bring to a boil. Reduce heat to medium-low. Cook 7 minutes or until crisp-tender; do not overcook. Drain and place in a medium, shallow baking dish. Sprinkle ham, Canadian bacon or smoked pork loin over asparagus. Pour half and half over top. Dab bits of butter or margarine over asparagus. Sprinkle bread crumbs, Parmesan cheese and nutmeg over asparagus and meat. Bake, uncovered, 15 minutes or until crust is golden brown.

Baked Eggplant au Gratin

Gebackene Aubergine

Most eggplant dishes in Germany, including this one, probably hail from Italy or France. Middle Eastern immigrants in the larger German cities have also of late been introducing more eggplant and other nontraditional vegetables. Try not to break through the eggplant skin when scooping out the pulp. *Makes 4 servings.*

1 large eggplant	*1 small onion, minced*
2 tablespoons butter or margarine	*1 egg, lightly beaten*
2 tablespoons all-purpose flour	*1 cup (4 oz.) shredded Gruyère or*
1 cup milk	*Swiss cheese*
1 tablespoon olive oil	*1/4 teaspoon ground nutmeg*

Preheat oven to 400F (205C). Cut eggplant in half lengthwise; place on baking sheet and bake 20 minutes. Let cool. Scoop out the pulp from eggplant, leaving skin intact, and chop pulp into about 2 cups. In a small saucepan, melt butter or margarine over medium heat; stir in flour. Using a wire whisk, stir milk into flour mixture. Cook over medium-low heat, whisking until smooth; set aside.

In a small skillet, heat oil over medium heat. Add onion; sauté 5 minutes or until tender. To the flour mixture, add chopped eggplant pulp, onion, egg, 3/4 of the cheese and the nutmeg. Gently mix well. Place eggplant shells side by side in a shallow baking dish just large enough to hold them. Carefully spoon eggplant mixture into shells; sprinkle remaining cheese over filling. Broil, 6 to 8 inches from heat, 4 minutes or until cheese melts and starts to brown. Serve immediately.

Glazed Carrots

Karotten in Aspik

Glazed carrots make ideal garnishes for meats. They add both color and flavor when arranged around beef roasts and pot roasts. Be careful to only caramelize the sugar—avoid burning it. *Makes 4 to 6 servings.*

3 cups small carrots	1 1/2 tablespoons granulated sugar
Salted water	1/4 teaspoon ground cinnamon
1/4 cup butter or margarine	1 1/2 cups carrot cooking juices

Place carrots in a medium saucepan; add salted water to cover. Bring to a boil over medium-high heat. Reduce heat to medium-low. Cover and cook 20 minutes or until almost tender. Drain and reserve 1 1/2 cups cooking juices. Melt butter or margarine in a medium skillet over medium heat. When butter or margarine is hot, stir in sugar and cinnamon; sauté until sugar turns golden caramel, without burning. Stir carrot cooking juices into caramelized sugar mixture. Add carrots; cover and simmer over low heat 10 minutes. Serve hot.

Green Beans

Grüne Bohnen

The cheese, seasonings and tomato sauce contrast nicely with the fresh, mild flavor of green beans. Beans can be found in most home gardens. They're a simple-to-grow, nutritious, low-cal vegetable that can be eaten hot or cold, cooked or raw. *Makes 6 servings.*

1 1/2 lbs. fresh green beans, French-cut	Pinch of ground paprika
1/2 teaspoon sugar	Pinch of garlic powder
1/4 lb. bacon, diced	Pinch of chili powder
1/4 teaspoon salt	1 cup (4 oz.) shredded Gouda or provolone cheese
1/8 teaspoon freshly ground black pepper	Tomato Sauce (page 114)

Preheat oven to 425F (220C). In a medium saucepan, bring 2 inches salted water to a boil. Add sliced beans and sugar. Bring to a boil over medium heat. Reduce heat to low. Cover beans with a tight-fitting lid and simmer 5 minutes or until almost tender. Drain beans; set aside. In a small skillet, sauté bacon over medium heat until crisp. Drain on paper towels.

Lightly grease a medium baking dish. Combine bacon, beans, seasonings and one-half of the shredded cheese in the prepared baking dish. Sprinkle remaining cheese over bean mixture. Bake, uncovered, 5 to 7 minutes or until cheese melts and lightly browns. Serve with hot Tomato Sauce.

Tomato Sauce

Tomatesosse

This attractive sauce is also good over stuffed peppers, stuffed cabbage leaves and meat loaves. *Makes about 3 1/4 cups.*

1 cup Meat Broth (page 62)
2 cups Béchamel Sauce (page 108)
2 1/2 tablespoons tomato paste

1 1/4 teaspoons sugar
1/2 teaspoon ground sweet paprika

Combine broth, Béchamel Sauce and tomato paste in a medium saucepan. Stir in sugar and paprika. Cook over medium heat 5 minutes, stirring constantly. Be careful not to burn sauce.

Onion Pie

Zwiebelpastete

Afriend of my mother taught me to put onions in the freezer for about an hour before slicing so you won't cry as much. Then, to make the slicing easier, first cut onion in half lengthwise through the middle, from the stem end to the root end. Lay onion halves flat and simply cut across the rings. *Makes 6 to 8 servings.*

1/2 cup butter or margarine, room
    temperature
2 tablespoons milk
1 cup all-purpose flour
1/8 teaspoon sugar
1/8 teaspoon salt
3 bacon slices, diced
2 large sweet onions, sliced
1/2 cup Chicken Broth (page 57)
    or chicken bouillon

1/2 cup sour cream
1 egg, lightly beaten
1 tablespoon chopped fresh chives
Salt
Freshly ground black pepper
1 egg yolk, beaten
1/4 teaspoon caraway seeds
Ground sweet paprika

Preheat oven to 350F (175C). In a medium bowl, combine butter or margarine, milk, flour, sugar and salt into a soft dough. Using your hands, form dough into a ball. Roll out to about 1/4-inch thickness on a lightly floured surface. Grease a 10-inch pie pan. Line pie pan with rolled dough; crimp edges. Line dough with foil. Fill with dried beans or pie weights. Bake 12 to 14 minutes or until lightly browned. Remove foil and beans or weights and set pie crust aside.

In a large skillet, sauté bacon over medium heat until crisp. Remove bacon and drain on paper towels; reserve. Drain off all bacon drippings except 1 tablespoon. Add onions to skillet. Sauté over medium heat, 5 minutes, stirring occasionally. Add broth or bouillon. Sauté 5 more minutes or until onions are tender and cooking juices are absorbed; remove from heat.

In a small bowl, combine sour cream, egg and chives; stir into onions. Add bacon pieces and season with salt and pepper. Increase oven temperature to 375F (190C). Evenly pour onion mixture into baked pie crust. Brush beaten egg yolk over onion mixture or trickle egg yolk over onion mixture with a small spoon. Sprinkle with caraway seeds and paprika. Bake 15 to 20 minutes or until onion mixture begins to brown. Remove from oven; let cool slightly. Cut into wedges. Serve warm.

Dried-Mushroom Cutlets

Getrocknete Champignonschnitzel

As throughout much of Europe, a favorite way to store and preserve mushrooms in Germany is to dry them. Fresh mushrooms, store-bought or wild-gathered, are strung together so they're not touching one another and hung in a place where there's almost continuous low-heat temperatures and lots of circulating air to remove moisture. In front of a window near the stove is a frequently used spot for drying mushrooms. *Makes 16 cutlets or 8 servings.*

2 oz. dried mushrooms	1/4 teaspoon freshly ground
1/2 cup milk	black pepper
2 large hard rolls, slightly stale	1 teaspoon chopped fresh parsley
2 tablespoons butter or margarine	Vegetable oil
1 small onion, diced	1/4 cup all-purpose flour
3 eggs	1/2 cup dried bread crumbs
1/2 teaspoon salt	Potato Sauce (opposite)

Rinse dried mushrooms in cold running water. Place mushrooms in a medium saucepan and add enough water to cover. Cover with a tight-fitting lid and cook over medium-low heat 30 to 40 minutes or until almost tender. Drain and discard cooking juices. Let cooked mushrooms cool. Squeeze excess juice from cooled mushrooms with your hands. Discard juices. Set mushrooms aside.

Place milk in a medium bowl. Break rolls apart with your hands and add to milk. Let milk soak into rolls; set aside. Melt butter or margarine in a small skillet over medium heat. Add onion; sauté until tender, about 5 minutes. With a meat grinder, grind mushrooms and soaked rolls into a medium bowl. Add sautéed onion, 2 of the eggs, salt, pepper and parsley. Work with your hands until combined. On a work surface, shape mushroom mixture into 16 (1-inch-thick) oval cutlets about 1 3/4 × 3 inches.

Heat 1/2 inch oil in a large skillet. Place flour in a pie pan. Beat remaining egg in a small, shallow bowl. Place bread crumbs in a pie pan. Carefully roll 1 mushroom cutlet in flour until all sides are evenly coated with flour. Dip floured cutlet in egg, turning once. Roll cutlet in bread crumbs, pressing crumbs evenly into cutlet on all sides. Repeat process with remaining cutlets. Place half the cutlets in heated oil. Fry over medium heat about 15 minutes, turning once, or until both sides become browned. Drain on paper towels; keep warm. Fry remaining cutlets. Serve hot, topped with warm Potato Sauce.

Potato Sauce

Kartoffelsosse

Potato Sauce can also be served over vegetables or sausage. *Makes about 2 cups sauce.*

3 tablespoons butter or margarine

1 medium onion, diced

2 tablespoons all-purpose flour

1 3/4 cups Chicken Broth (page
   57) or Veal Broth (page 60)

6 whole allspice berries

1 bay leaf, crushed

2 medium new potatoes, peeled
   and diced

1/2 tablespoon lemon juice

1/2 teaspoon salt

1/8 teaspoon ground white pepper

Melt butter or margarine in a medium skillet over medium-low heat. Add onion; cook until tender, about 5 minutes. Stir in flour. Cook, stirring, until bubbly. Add broth, allspice and bay leaf. Simmer, uncovered, over low heat 15 minutes. Strain cooking liquid into a small saucepan, discarding onion.

Add potatoes to strained cooking liquid. Cook, uncovered, over medium-low heat, stirring occasionally, 10 to 12 minutes or until potatoes are almost tender. Do not overcook. Stir lemon juice into potato sauce. Season with salt and pepper. Serve hot or warm.

Mixed Vegetable Casserole

Mischgemüse

Zucchini is as easy to grow in Germany as it is in Italy or the United States. The subtle flavors of the zucchini and eggplant are what separates this vegetable casserole from the rest. *Makes 10 to 12 servings.*

2 tablespoons vegetable oil	2 cups cauliflower flowerets
1 medium eggplant	4 medium tomatoes, peeled and
1 1/2 cups cubed zucchini	chopped
2 tablespoons butter or margarine	1 cup fresh or frozen green peas
2 medium onions, quartered	3/4 cup (2 1/4 oz.) grated Parmesan
1 cup thinly sliced carrots	cheese
1 1/2 cups (1 1/2-inch pieces) green	2 tablespoons chopped fresh parsley
beans	

Preheat oven to 350F (175C). Heat oil in a large skillet over medium-high heat. Cut eggplant in half lengthwise and remove pulp with a sharp knife. Cut pulp into cubes; add to hot oil. Sauté eggplant pulp, stirring occasionally, 6 minutes or until browned. Remove eggplant and place in a large casserole dish.

Place zucchini in skillet with eggplant drippings; sauté 4 minutes or until almost tender. Spoon zucchini into casserole dish with eggplant. Melt butter or margarine in same skillet. Add onions, carrots, beans and cauliflower; sauté until onions are tender and rest of vegetables are slightly browned, about 10 minutes. Spoon sautéed onion, carrots, beans and cauliflower into eggplant and zucchini. To same skillet, add tomatoes; sauté, turning several times with a spatula, until browned. Add tomatoes and peas to casserole dish; gently mix. Sprinkle with Parmesan cheese and parsley. Bake, covered, 20 minutes. Serve hot.

Creamed Spinach

Spinat

Reserve the spinach cooking juices for preparing Spinach Soup (page 77). *Makes 6 servings.*

1 lb. fresh spinach

2 tablespoons butter or margarine

1 tablespoon all-purpose flour

1 cup milk

1 egg, lightly beaten

1/8 teaspoon ground nutmeg

Salt to taste

Rinse spinach leaves under running cold water. Remove large stems. Place spinach in a large saucepan. Add 1 cup water. Bring to a boil over medium-high heat. Reduce heat to low. Simmer, uncovered, 10 minutes; drain. Let cool. With a meat grinder or food processor, finely chop spinach.

Melt butter or margarine in a large skillet over medium heat. Add flour; cook, stirring, until bubbly. Stir in milk. Bring to a boil. Stir in spinach; simmer over low heat until liquid evaporates to about 2 tablespoons. Gently stir egg into spinach. Season with nutmeg and salt. Serve warm.

Simmered Cabbage

Weisskohl

Cabbage is to Germany what the potato is to Ireland. As Irishmen or women use numerous terms to describe potatoes, so do Germans refer to a litany of cabbage adjectives. Simply, there's no vegetable more popular than cabbage throughout Germany and anyone who thinks otherwise may be affectionately called a *Kohlkopf*—a blockhead or "cabbage head." *Makes 8 to 10 servings.*

2 cups Chicken Broth (page 57)
 or Ham Broth (page 61)
1 (2- to 2 1/2-lb.) head savoy or
 green cabbage, shredded
2 medium carrots, shredded
2 tablespoons butter or margarine
1 medium onion, chopped
1 1/2 teaspoons all-purpose flour

5 dried mushrooms
1 cup water
2 tablespoons lemon juice or vinegar
1 teaspoon sugar
1 teaspoon garlic salt
1/8 teaspoon freshly ground black
 pepper

In a large saucepan, combine broth, cabbage and carrots. Cover and simmer 30 minutes over medium-low heat. Melt 1 tablespoon of the butter or margarine in a small skillet over medium heat. Add onion; sauté until tender, about 10 minutes. Stir onion into cabbage mixture. Melt remaining butter or margarine in same skillet. Add flour; stir over medium heat until flour becomes golden-brown. Stir 1/2 cup simmering broth into flour mixture. Add to cabbage mixture.

In a small saucepan, place dried mushrooms and 1 cup water. Bring to a boil over medium-high heat. Gently boil until most of the liquid evaporates and mushrooms are tender. Remove mushrooms from saucepan; let cool. Chop mushrooms; stir into cabbage mixture. Simmer 5 minutes, stirring frequently. Stir lemon juice or vinegar into cabbage mixture. Season with sugar, garlic salt and pepper. Serve hot.

Sweet & Sour Savoy Cabbage

Süss-Saurer Wirsingkohl

Savoy cabbage has crinkled green leaves and loosely formed heads. When preparing cabbage, discard any wilted or browned outer leaves. Cut the cabbage in half, from stem to top, then cut each half in two, from stem to top. Cut hard core off each quarter-cabbage. Shred cabbage by carefully cutting quarter-cabbage lengthwise. *Makes 6 servings.*

2 cups Meat Broth (page 62) or
  water
1 medium savoy cabbage, shredded
1/2 cup shredded carrots
1 apple, peeled, cored and chopped
2 tablespoons vinegar or lemon juice

2 tablespoons vegetable oil
1 tablespoon sugar
1/2 teaspoon salt
1/2 teaspoon freshly ground black
  pepper

In a large saucepan, bring broth or water to a boil. Add cabbage and carrots. Simmer, partially covered, over medium-low heat 1 1/2 hours or until cabbage is tender. Add more liquid if needed as cabbage cooks. Add apple, vinegar or lemon juice, oil, sugar, salt and pepper. Cook, uncovered, 15 to 20 minutes or until desired consistency is reached. Serve hot.

Sweet & Sour Red Cabbage

Süss-Saurer Rotkohl

It's important to sauté red cabbage in hot oil or fat before further simmering or cooking, or the red color may turn light pink. The color change will not affect the flavor, but the dark purple color red cabbage attains when cooked in hot fat is considered more attractive than the lighter alternative. *Makes 6 to 8 servings.*

3 tablespoons vegetable oil	1/2 cup water
1 medium red cabbage, shredded	1/4 cup red wine vinegar
2 tablespoons vinegar or lemon juice	1 teaspoon salt
6 bacon slices, diced	1/8 teaspoon freshly ground black
1/4 cup packed brown sugar	pepper
2 tablespoons all-purpose flour	1 small onion, diced

Heat oil in a nonstick or porcelain saucepan over medium heat. Add cabbage; sauté 10 minutes, stirring frequently. Add vinegar or lemon juice. Add about 1 cup water and bring to a boil over medium-high heat. Reduce heat to medium; cook 10 more minutes or until crisp-tender. Drain; place cabbage in a large serving dish or bowl and keep warm.

In a small skillet, sauté bacon over medium heat until crisp; pour off all but 1 tablespoon bacon drippings. Remove one-third of the bacon pieces and drain on paper towels; reserve. Stir brown sugar and flour into bacon and drippings in skillet. Add 1/2 cup water, red wine vinegar, salt, pepper and onion. Cook over medium heat 7 to 8 minutes or until onions are tender and mixture thickens. Stir bacon and sauce mixture into cabbage. Sprinkle remaining bacon bits over cabbage. Serve warm.

Red Cabbage & Apples

Rotkohl und Äpfel

You'll find a dish similar to this one in restaurants all over the world. The cabbage and apples will become more flavorful if prepared and refrigerated for several hours before mealtime. Simply reheat when ready to serve. A medium cabbage weighs about 2 pounds. *Makes 6 to 8 servings.*

3 tablespoons butter or margarine	3 tablespoons cider vinegar
1 large onion, finely chopped	2 teaspoons sugar
1 medium red cabbage, shredded	1 teaspoon salt
3 firm apples, peeled, cored and shredded	1/2 teaspoon ground nutmeg
3/4 cup water	1/8 teaspoon freshly ground black pepper
1/2 cup red wine	2 tablespoons lemon juice

Melt butter or margarine in a large saucepan over medium heat. Add onion; cook until tender, about 10 minutes. Add cabbage and apples; cook 10 minutes, stirring three times. Add water, red wine, cider vinegar, sugar, salt, nutmeg and pepper. Cover and cook over low heat 30 minutes or until cabbage is tender. Before serving, stir lemon juice into cabbage mixture. If the cabbage is too dry, add a small amount of hot water. Serve hot.

Stuffed Kohlrabi

Kohlrabi mit Fleischfüllung

Y ou should be able to find kohlrabi in any supermarket or ethnic market, but if you can't, you can grow it yourself. Many major seed manufacturers sell small packets of seeds that can be grown in practically any garden. *Makes 4 servings.*

8 young kohlrabi (about 1 1/2 lbs.)	*1/2 tablespoon brown sugar*
1/2 lb. bulk sausage or ground veal,	*2 tablespoons minced fresh parsley*
beef, pork or turkey	*1 3/4 cups Chicken Broth (page*
1/2 cup cooked long-grain rice	*57) or chicken bouillon*
1 egg, lightly beaten	*2 tablespoons butter or margarine*
1 teaspoon salt	*2 tablespoons all-purpose flour*
1/4 teaspoon freshly ground black	*1 cup milk*
pepper	

Preheat oven to 375F (190C). Lightly grease a baking dish large enough to hold kohlrabi. Peel thin layer of skin from the kohlrabi. Cut off about 1/2 inch of kohlrabi tops and set tops aside. With a teaspoon, hollow out kohlrabi carefully, removing pulp so round bowls with 1/2-inch-thick sides remain. Save spooned-out kohlrabi pulp for use in making soup broth or stock.

In a medium bowl, mix sausage or meat, rice, egg, salt, pepper, brown sugar and parsley. Spoon stuffing mixture into the hollow kohlrabi bottoms; cover with kohlrabi tops and secure tops with wooden picks. Arrange stuffed kohlrabi in greased baking dish. Pour broth into dish. Cover with foil and bake 30 minutes.

Melt butter or margarine in a small saucepan over low heat. Stir in flour until blended. Cook, stirring, until flour mixture turns a light golden color. Slowly add milk; cook, stirring constantly, until mixture begins to boil and thicken. Pour milk mixture into kohlrabi juices. Carefully tip baking dish slightly back and forth so milk mixture combines with kohlrabi juices. Bake, uncovered, 10 to 15 minutes or until sauce begins to boil. Serve hot with sauce spooned over stuffed kohlrabi.

Potatoes

Kartoffel

*I*n the sixteenth century, voyaging Spaniards brought potatoes home to Europe. During the Thirty Years' War, Spanish mercenaries eventually carried potatoes into Germany, where bags of the strange tubers fell into the hands of German peasants who, not knowing any better, tried eating raw potatoes, without peeling them. The peasants became sick and for years after associated illness and disease with the "foreign poison" introduced by the Spanish; it didn't help that those were times when various plagues were scourging the countryside as well.

It was only when numerous grain crops failed in Germany in the middle of the eighteenth century that large numbers of farmers started turning to the potato as a potential source of food—many farmers, in fact, had no choice in the matter. Frederick the Great actually ordered his Silesian subjects to grow potatoes—or else! Around the same time, potatoes were being fed simultaneously to pigs and to French prisoners in Germany. Even though farmers were being told to grow the hardy spuds, the popular belief was still that potatoes carried leprosy and that no civilized individual would stoop so low as to consume earthy roots that were obviously meant for barnyard animals and prisoners. These beliefs were contradicted, however, by Prussian prisoners of war who, in turn, had successfully been fed potatoes by their French captors.

Soon German peasants were growing potatoes themselves, making all sorts of potato noodles and dumplings out of the starch-rich tubers and preparing potato flour, which was mixed with other gluten-rich flour for breadmaking.

People once thought of potatoes as fattening, but now it's known that potatoes are a healthy, low-calorie vegetable and an efficient and inexpensive source of energy, full of vitamins, minerals and dietary fiber that's conveniently available year-round.

In Germany today, potatoes are an ever-present accompaniment that sometime serve as the main focus for a meal. They're sliced, grated, mashed, fried and rendered into dumplings, home fries, casseroles and baked dishes and provide a ready source for the famous German Potato Pancakes served hot with applesauce or sour cream or beef goulash. The popularity of simple fried potatoes is evident to anyone visiting any part of the country. The major fast-food restaurants that have taken hold in the cities serve shoestring-style French fries. Mashed potatoes are often recooked or baked in a buttered casserole dish and topped with bread crumbs or sautéed onions or chopped chives or parsley, so the top is cooked to a slightly crisp golden brown.

Potatoes are also used frequently in soup and stews as well as in German potato salads, which, as mentioned in the second chapter, cold, hot and sour, have successfully made the journey across the Atlantic and have been served at Western picnics and buffets for years. Frequently used as side dishes with meat, boiled potatoes are served with a little butter, with skins or without, sprinkled with minced parsley, dill, chives or caraway seeds or topped lightly with dill or onion or practically any other hot white sauce.

Potato Tips

- Keep stored potatoes away from sources of light, warmth and dampness. Dampness will encourage rot and light or warm storage temperatures will produce green patches or spots on potatoes.

- Store potatoes in a cool, dark place with good air circulation. Do not keep them in the refrigerator, either; it's too cold for them.

- Because potatoes are available all the time, buy them in small quantities, even if it means paying a bit more for them in the long run. You'll have less waste because all of your stock will be usable.

- To save as much of the nutrients as possible, peel potatoes only when you're ready to cook them.

- When boiling potatoes, use only as much lightly salted water as is needed to cover them. The less water used, the better, because fewer vitamins will be lost during cooking.

- Whenever possible, include the potato skins as part of the recipe for maximum nutrition.

Boiled Potatoes with Dill

Gekochte Kartoffeln

Boiled potatoes frequently accompany all sorts of meat dishes. They can be served with gravies, sauces, seasoned butters, sautéed onions or bread crumbs or with bits of crispy bacon or smoked ham. It's very important to dry them out after they have been cooked, so the potatoes won't become soft and mushy from a little bit of leftover cooking water. *Makes 6 to 8 servings.*

About 4 lbs. potatoes	*About 1/4 cup butter or margarine*
Cold salted water	*1 to 2 tablespoons minced dill,*
Salt	*parsley or chives*

If using small new potatoes, do not peel. If using large new potatoes, peel, if desired, then cut potatoes into quarters. If using other potatoes, peel as thinly as possible just before cooking, removing potato blemishes and eyes. Place potatoes in a large saucepan and cover with cold salted water, using as little water as possible to cover. Turn heat to medium-high; bring to a boil. Reduce heat to medium-low or to whatever heat will keep the water at a low boil. Cook 15 to 25 minutes or until potatoes are fork tender.

If potatoes of different sizes are cooking in the same pan, the smaller potatoes should be removed sooner because they'll be done quicker. Drain the cooking water by pouring potatoes and water through a colander. Return cooked potatoes to the empty pan and place them back over low heat, leaving the pan lid off and shaking the pan a few times so the water will evaporate until the potatoes are thoroughly dry. Make sure the potatoes do not burn. Season with salt to taste. Add butter or margarine and minced dill, parsley or chives to potatoes. Toss gently to combine. Serve potatoes hot.

Mashed Potatoes

....

Kartoffelpuree

Although any kind of potatoes can be mashed, russet varieties are preferred by many. Whether you mash the potatoes completely so no small pieces or bits remain or if you mash them so a few solid bits are present is a matter of choice. An excellent topping for mashed potatoes is Dried Mushroom Sauce. *Makes 4 to 6 servings.*

Dried Mushroom Sauce (opposite)
(optional)
1 1/4 lbs. peeled russet baking
  potatoes, cut into 1-inch-thick
  pieces

1/2 cup plus 1 tablespoon hot milk
Salt
Ground white pepper
Dash of nutmeg
1/4 cup butter or margarine

Prepare sauce, if using. Place potatoes in a medium saucepan; add cold salted water to cover. Place potatoes over medium-high heat; bring to a boil. Reduce heat to medium; boil potatoes 15 to 20 minutes or until fork tender. Drain potatoes in a colander and return potatoes to cooking pan. Let cool 1 minute. Use a potato masher to mash potatoes, using firm up-and-down strokes. Mash the potatoes until smooth. Blend hot milk into mashed potatoes, stirring with a wire whisk. Season to taste with salt, white pepper and nutmeg. Fold butter or margarine into potatoes. Serve hot with Dried-Mushroom Sauce, if desired.

Dried Mushroom Sauce

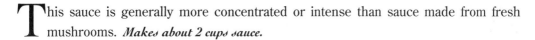

Schwammersosse

This sauce is generally more concentrated or intense than sauce made from fresh mushrooms. *Makes about 2 cups sauce.*

1 1/2 oz. dried mushrooms
2 tablespoons butter or margarine
1 medium onion, diced
1 cup sour cream

1 tablespoon all-purpose flour
Salt to taste
Freshly ground black pepper to taste

Break apart any large mushrooms with your fingers. Place mushrooms in a medium saucepan. Add 2 cups water or enough water to cover. Let stand at room temperature 1 hour. Simmer mushrooms in their soaking liquid, uncovered, over low heat 45 minutes or until almost tender. Drain; reserve cooking juices. Let cooked mushrooms cool. Chop mushrooms. Melt butter or margarine in a small skillet over medium heat. Add onion. Sauté until tender, about 5 minutes; set aside.

Blend sour cream and flour in a medium saucepan. Stir mushroom cooking juices into sour-cream mixture. Bring to a boil over medium heat. Reduce heat to low. Add chopped mushrooms, onion, salt and pepper. Simmer, uncovered, 10 minutes. Serve hot.

Onion Sauce

Zwiebelsosse

Rich with onion flavor, this sauce can be served with veal, lamb or vegetables. *Makes about 2 cups.*

2 tablespoons butter or margarine
6 medium onions, finely chopped
3/4 cup Chicken Broth (page 57)
   or Beef Broth (page 58)

2 1/2 tablespoons all-purpose flour
1/2 cup half and half
3/4 teaspoon sugar
Salt

Melt butter or margarine in a medium skillet. Add onions; sauté until tender, about 15 minutes. Using a spoon, press cooked onions and juices through a sturdy strainer into a medium bowl. Stir in broth. In a small bowl, blend flour and half and half; stir into strained onion mixture. Add sugar. Return to skillet; cook over low heat, stirring constantly, until mixture bubbles and thickens. Season with salt to taste. Serve warm.

Potato Pancakes

Kartoffelnpuffer

I t's not uncommon to see young children running through market squares carrying a crispy potato pancake in one hand and a toy or ball in the other. Potato pancakes are one of the most versatile foods in Germany. They're eaten for breakfast, lunch, snacks, dinner and supper and have been likened to "German fast-food." Potato pancakes are served hot with Bavarian Goulash or Mushroom Sauce, or spiced with a little applesauce and cinnamon. *Makes 30 to 35 pancakes.*

8 large new potatoes (about
* 3 1/2 lbs.)*
1 medium onion
1 egg, beaten
3 tablespoons all-purpose flour
1 teaspoon salt
1/4 teaspoon freshly ground black
* pepper*

1/8 teaspoon garlic powder
Vegetable oil
Bavarian Goulash (page 198),
* Veal Goulash (page 186) or*
* Mushroom Sauce (opposite)*
* to serve*

Preheat oven to 350F (175C). Using a hand grater or food processor fitted with a shredding blade, shred potatoes to make about 5 cups. Squeeze potatoes to remove liquid, reserving liquid in a small bowl. Place potatoes in a large bowl. Depending on age and type of potatoes used, up to 1 cup juice may be obtained. Finely grate onion. Stir together shredded potatoes, onion, egg, flour, salt, pepper and garlic powder. Discard top portion of reserved

potato juice, leaving juice about 1/2 inch deep or about 1/4 cup. This bottom juice contains the heavier potato starch. Stir juice into potato mixture.

In a large skillet, heat about 3 tablespoons oil over medium-high heat. Drop 1 heaping tablespoon potato mixture into skillet. Smooth out into a 3- to 3 1/2-inch round pancake. Place as many as possible in the skillet. Cook over medium-high heat until browned and crisp on bottom, about 3 minutes. Turn and cook other side until brown and crisp. Remove from skillet and drain on paper towels. When drained, transfer to a heatproof serving plate; keep hot in oven. Repeat with remaining potato mixture, adding oil to skillet as necessary. Serve hot with Bavarian Goulash, Veal Goulash or Mushroom Sauce, if desired.

Mushroom Sauce
Champignonsosse

This versatile sauce can be used with Potato Pancakes (opposite) or various meat dishes. *Makes about 5 cups.*

2 tablespoons butter or margarine
1 1/4 lbs. fresh mushrooms, thinly
   sliced
1 medium onion, chopped
2 tablespoons all-purpose flour
2 1/4 cups Chicken Broth (page
   57) or Beef Broth (page 58)

1/4 teaspoon salt
1/4 teaspoon freshly ground black
   pepper
1 cup sour cream

Melt butter or margarine in a large saucepan over low heat. Add mushrooms and onion. Cover with a tight-fitting lid; simmer 15 minutes, stirring occasionally. Stir flour into mushroom mixture until blended. Add broth; cover and simmer over low heat 30 minutes. Season with salt and pepper. Stir sour cream until blended; add to mushroom mixture, a little at a time, stirring until smooth. Cook over medium-low heat 3 minutes; do not boil.

Heaven & Earth

Himmel und Erde

Combining the best from above and below for your table: what a way to describe this special recipe! *Makes 8 to 10 servings.*

10 medium new potatoes (about
  3 1/2 lbs.)
About 1 1/4 lbs. firm apples
1 1/2 tablespoons honey
2 teaspoons salt
1/2 teaspoon freshly ground black
  pepper

2 1/4 cups cold water
1/2 lb. smoked bacon, diced
2 medium onions, peeled and sliced
  into 1/4-inch-thick rings, separated
1 1/2 tablespoons lemon juice

Peel and quarter potatoes, then cut potato quarters into 1/2-inch-thick slices. Peel and core apples, then cut into 6 wedges per apple. Combine honey, 1 teaspoon of the salt, the pepper and cold water in a large skillet. Add potatoes and apples; bring to a boil over medium-high heat. Cover with a tight-fitting lid; reduce heat to medium. Simmer, without stirring, about 20 minutes or until potatoes are tender; do not overcook.

In medium skillet, sauté bacon over medium heat until crisp. Drain bacon on paper towels. Drain all but 2 tablespoons bacon drippings from skillet. Add onion rings to remaining bacon drippings; sauté over medium heat 10 minutes or until tender and lightly browned. Stir remaining 1 teaspoon salt and lemon juice into cooked potatoes and apples. Spoon potatoes and apples into a heated serving dish. Top with cooked onion rings and bacon. Serve hot.

Sour Potatoes

Saure Kartoffeln

The tricky part of this recipe is to evenly coat cooked potato slices with sauce without breaking slices apart. This is easier done if the potatoes are not cooked too long to begin with. *Makes 6 to 8 servings.*

8 medium new potatoes (about 3 1/2 lbs.)	3 tablespoons cider vinegar or dry white wine
3 cups cold water	Salt
1 teaspoon salt	Freshly ground black pepper
1/2 lb. lean bacon	Sausages, pork roast or cold cuts
3 tablespoons all-purpose flour	to serve

Peel potatoes and cut into 1/4-inch-thick slices. In a large saucepan, combine potatoes, water and salt. Bring to a full boil over medium-high heat. Boil 12 to 15 minutes or until tender; do not overcook. Drain potatoes in a colander or sieve placed over a large bowl; reserve the cooking water. Return cooked potatoes to saucepan. Cover potatoes with a tight-fitting lid and keep warm.

In a medium skillet, sauté bacon over medium heat until crisp. Carefully drain off all but about 2 tablespoons bacon drippings. Stir flour into bacon and drippings. Reduce heat to low. Cook, stirring constantly, until flour turns a light golden color. Do not let flour burn. Slowly stir reserved cooking water into bacon and flour mixture. Increase heat to high. Boil, stirring constantly, until sauce is smooth and thick. Reduce heat to low. Stir vinegar or wine into sauce. Simmer, covered, 10 minutes. Pour hot sour sauce over potatoes. Gently mix sauce and potatoes until potatoes are evenly coated. Season with salt and pepper. Transfer potatoes to a heated serving dish or bowl. Serve hot with sausages, pork roast or cold cuts.

Potatoes in Wine & Basil Sauce

Kartoffeln mit Wein und Basilkumsosse

This low-fat dish can be spiced up by using any of an assortment of herb vinegars or different varieties of basil. *Makes 4 servings.*

1 1/2 lbs. new potatoes
2 garlic cloves, minced
1/2 cup chopped chives
1 1/2 cups dry white wine
1/4 cup basil or tarragon vinegar
3/4 teaspoon dried basil or
   1 1/2 tablespoons fresh basil

Freshly ground black pepper
2 teaspoons Dijon mustard
2 tablespoons chopped fresh basil
   leaves or parsley

Wash potatoes and cut lengthwise into quarters. Place potatoes, garlic, chives, wine, vinegar, basil and pepper in a medium saucepan. Bring to a boil over medium heat. Reduce heat to medium-low; cover with a tight-fitting lid. Cook slowly, 15 to 20 minutes or until potatoes are tender. Remove potatoes with a slotted spoon; place on a platter and keep warm. Continue to cook the sauce, uncovered, until it has reduced and thickened. Stir mustard and basil or parsley into sauce. Cook 5 more minutes. Spoon hot sauce over potatoes and serve immediately.

Potato & Tomato Bake

Gebackende Kartoffeln und Tomaten

You say "tomato," I say "potato." This unusual recipe combines the two with fresh bell peppers, cheese and Dill Sauce. *Makes 8 to 10 servings.*

Dill Sauce (see below)

6 large ripe tomatoes

2 green bell peppers

2 red bell peppers

8 medium new potatoes (about
   3 1/2 lbs.)

2 teaspoons salt

1 teaspoon freshly ground black
   pepper

1/2 teaspoon dried-leaf marjoram

3 cups (12 oz.) shredded Emmentaler
   cheese

2 tablespoons cold butter or
   margarine, cut in small pieces

2 tablespoons chopped fresh parsley

DILL SAUCE

2 tablespoons butter or margarine

2 1/2 tablespoons all-purpose flour

1 1/4 cups Meat Broth (page 62)

1 cup sour cream

1/4 cup chopped fresh dill

Salt

Prepare Dill Sauce; keep warm. Boil 6 inches of water in a large pot over high heat. Drop tomatoes into boiling water 3 to 4 minutes; remove tomatoes and peel. Cut peeled tomatoes in half lengthwise. Cut peeled tomato halves into 1/2-inch-thick slices. Cut bell peppers in half lengthwise, then cut lengthwise again into thin strips. Peel potatoes and cut crosswise into thin slices; season with salt, pepper and marjoram.

Preheat oven to 400F (205C). Lightly grease a 2- to 2 1/2-quart casserole dish. Arrange half of sliced potatoes in greased dish. Add bell pepper strips. Evenly top pepper strips with shredded cheese. Gently pour Dill Sauce over cheese and bell pepper. Top with pieces of butter or margarine; sprinkle with parsley. Bake, uncovered, about 1 hour and 15 minutes or until potatoes are tender. Serve hot.

Dill Sauce

Melt butter or margarine in a small skillet over medium heat. Stir in flour; cook until bubbly. Slowly stir in broth; bring to a boil. Cook, stirring constantly, until thickened. Stir in sour cream and dill. Season with salt to taste. *Makes about 2 cups sauce.*

Stuffed Potato Shells

....

Gefüllte Kartoffeln

Be careful when scooping out the potato flesh from potato bottoms; it's easy to poke through the bottoms if too much force is used. Let the round bottom of the spoon do the work: use the spoon handle like a small lever and lift the potato flesh inward away from the skin. *Makes 8 servings.*

8 large russet potatoes
1 cup low-fat cottage cheese
1/4 cup milk
2 eggs
2 tablespoons butter or margarine
1 cup chopped cooked ham or sausage

2 tablespoons chopped chives
1 teaspoon salt
1 teaspoon freshly ground black
   pepper
Ground sweet paprika

Preheat oven to 350F (175C). Rinse and scrub potatoes. Puncture top of each potato once with a fork. Bake potatoes 50 minutes to 1 hour or until tender. Let potatoes cool slightly. Cut about 1/2-inch-thick top from each potato. Using a teaspoon, scoop out baked potato flesh from tops of potatoes. Scoop enough potato flesh from bottoms to leave 1/2-inch-thick potato shells.

Using a food processor fitted with the steel blade, process potato flesh, cottage cheese, milk, eggs and butter or margarine. Transfer potato mixture to a medium bowl. Fold ham or sausage and chives into potato mixture. Season with salt and pepper. Fill potato shells with potato mixture. Sprinkle with paprika. Place stuffed potatoes on an oven rack. Bake 20 minutes or until tops become lightly browned. Serve hot.

Potato & Cheese Fans

Kartoffel und Käsefacher

It may take you a while to slice the fan sections of these potatoes, but the effect will be worth it. Potato & Cheese Fans are an ideal party and formal-dinner vegetable side dish. For safety's sake, consider wearing a cut-resistant glove on the hand that will be holding the potatoes steady while your other hand wields the knife. *Makes 8 servings.*

8 medium baking potatoes	2 cups (8 oz.) shredded Emmentaler
Salt	cheese
Freshly ground black pepper	1/2 cup (2 oz.) shredded sharp
2 tablespoons butter or margarine,	Cheddar cheese
room temperature	2 tablespoons chopped fresh parsley

Preheat oven to 400F (205C). Peel potatoes. Using a thin-bladed sharp knife, carefully cut potatoes lengthwise into thin slices from the top down, not cutting entirely through potato bottoms. When finished, each potato should be sliced in a fanlike manner. Sprinkle with salt and pepper. Grease a baking dish. Arrange potatoes, fan sides up, in greased dish. Place dabs of butter or margarine on tops of potatoes. Bake potatoes, uncovered, 30 minutes or until bottoms are tender and top sections are getting crispy. Sprinkle shredded Emmentaler cheese over potatoes. Top with shredded Cheddar cheese. Sprinkle parsley over cheese. Bake 8 to 10 minutes or until cheese melts and becomes lightly browned. Serve hot.

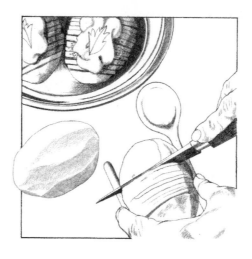

Sweet-Potato Croquettes

....

Süss-Kartoffel Kroketten

The trick here is to achieve the right consistency so the croquettes hold together during cooking. *Makes 6 to 8 servings.*

2 lbs. medium sweet potatoes	2 to 3 eggs
2 tablespoons butter or margarine	All-purpose flour
1/2 teaspoon salt	2 cups dry bread crumbs
1/2 teaspoon ground nutmeg	Vegetable oil for deep-frying

Rinse sweet potatoes under cold running water. Place potatoes in a large saucepan; cover with salted water. Bring to a boil over medium-high heat; reduce heat to medium-low. Cover with a tight-fitting lid; simmer 30 minutes or until potatoes are tender. Drain potatoes; let cool. Melt butter or margarine in a medium saucepan over low heat. Peel, mash and press potatoes through a sieve into pan with melted butter or margarine. Cook, stirring several times, 5 to 7 minutes or until heated through. Cool slightly. Stir salt, nutmeg and 1 of the eggs into cooked sweet-potato mixture; blend well.

Dust your hands with flour, then shape potato mixture into 2 × 1 1/2-inch oval croquettes. Pour bread crumbs into a pie pan. Lightly beat 1 egg in a small bowl. Dip 1 floured croquette in beaten egg, then roll in bread crumbs. Lightly press croquette into crumbs so crumbs adhere evenly all over croquette. Place breaded croquette on a rack; let stand at room temperature 15 to 20 minutes. Repeat process with remaining croquettes, using another lightly beaten egg for dipping floured croquettes, if required.

Heat oil for deep-frying to 360F (180C) in a medium saucepan or deep-fryer. Gently drop breaded croquettes, one at a time, into hot oil. Cook in batches of 4 to 5 croquettes, so croquettes are not crowded. Stir to make sure they don't stick to the bottom of the pan or to each other. Cook 2 to 3 minutes or until croquettes float and turn a golden-brown color. Remove croquettes with a slotted spoon; drain on paper towels. Serve hot, plain or with Onion Sauce (page 129), Béchamel Sauce (page 108) or Dill Sauce (page 135).

Eggs

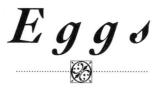

Eier

Consider the age-old question of which came first: the chicken or the egg? In this book, it's the egg. In Germany, eggs are everyday fare. They're inexpensive, have always been—even in the most difficult times—readily available and are easy to prepare. They even come in their own convenient packages.

The most popular way to prepare them is fried, sunny side up. Also called "mirror" eggs, they're frequently accompanied by fried ham, sausage or lightly sautéed plain onion rings.

Requests for fried eggs are closely followed by those for scrambled eggs. Scrambled eggs or "stirred" eggs are most always flavored with additional ingredients such as minced fresh parsley, chives, dill or other herbs; grated cheese; chopped bacon, ham, or sausage; or various chopped vegetables from onions, zucchini and red peppers, to mushrooms. Seafood isn't left out, either. Bits of lobster, shrimp and smoked fish have all found their way into servings of German scrambled eggs.

For breakfast hard-cooked eggs (or soft-cooked eggs) served in dainty porcelain egg cups, topped off with a tiny stocking "cap" are featured. Breakfasts would also not be complete without hard rolls, butter and steaming hot tea. At other times during the day or night, hard-cooked eggs are served peeled, covered with cheese sauce, mushroom sauce or tomato sauce and sprinkled with chopped dill or other fresh herbs.

French-style omelets provide occasional variety and are filled with asparagus, Westphalian ham, bacon, mushrooms, cheese and practically any fresh or leftover ingredients. Soufflé omelets feature stiffly beaten egg whites combined with yolks and other flavorings and cooked either on top of the stove or baked in an oven. Sweet soufflés make popular desserts and when flour is added to the soufflé batter, spongy cakes, crepes and sweet, thin pancakes can result.

Poached eggs are served topped with cheese, tomato sauce and even anchovies. Eggs are cooked slowly in sauce for a few minutes or sauces can be spooned over the eggs just before serving. Eggs are also used to thicken sauces, to garnish all kinds of salads and main dishes, to make egg salads, to stuff as appetizers with any of a huge assortment of fillings, to fortify beverages and to help bind meats, fish and vegetables into hearty casseroles. Even raw egg yolks, whipped with a little red wine, are used to cure *Katzenjammers*—particularly strong German hangovers.

German household cooks recognize the efficiency of using eggs in all kinds of recipes. Too, raising chickens enables farmers and families in rural areas to enjoy fresh eggs without depleting their flocks. Although eggs have received their share of bad press during recent years, the medical community has backed off somewhat, with latest indications that healthy individuals can moderately consume a few eggs per week as long as the person's cholesterol level is under control. On average, the typical German eats five or six eggs per week.

Germans, as most Europeans and some Americans, prefer eggs that are not pure white. Instead, brown, tan and mottled eggs are considered "healthier," even though nutritionally there is no difference.

Scrambled Eggs with Ham

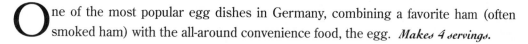

Rübreier mit Schinken

Ohne of the most popular egg dishes in Germany, combining a favorite ham (often smoked ham) with the all-around convenience food, the egg. *Makes 4 servings.*

1 tablespoon vegetable oil

2 medium tomatoes, sliced

8 eggs

2 tablespoons skim milk

1/2 teaspoon salt

1/8 teaspoon white pepper

1 tablespoon butter or margarine

1 cup chopped cooked ham

1 tablespoon finely chopped fresh
  chives

Rub oil over the bottom of a large skillet. Place skillet over medium heat; add tomato slices. Sauté over medium heat until both sides are lightly browned. Remove skillet from heat.

In a large bowl, combine eggs, milk, salt and pepper. Using a wooden spoon or wire whisk, beat until frothy. Melt butter or margarine in a medium skillet over low heat. Pour egg mixture into heated skillet. Add ham and chives. Cook, gently stirring and scraping eggs from the sides and bottom of skillet. Remove from heat when eggs are still soft, since they'll continue to cook until removed from the skillet. Serve with several sautéed tomato slices.

Variations
Add 2 tablespoons sour cream with the ham and chives for a tangy flavor.

When the eggs and ham are almost done, stir in 1 cup low-fat cottage cheese or 1 (3-oz.) package cream cheese.

Scrambled Eggs with Mushrooms

Rühreier mit Champignons

Any mushrooms will work here, even, in a pinch, canned sliced varieties. *Makes 4 servings.*

1 tablespoon butter or margarine

1 1/2 cups sliced fresh mushrooms

1 tablespoon lemon juice

1/2 teaspoon salt

1/8 teaspoon ground white pepper

1 teaspoon all-purpose flour

8 eggs

2 tablespoons skim milk or half
  and half

1 tablespoon chopped fresh parsley

Cayenne pepper (optional)

Melt butter or margarine in a medium skillet over low heat. Add mushrooms, lemon juice, salt and pepper. Sprinkle with flour. Cook, stirring occasionally, 10 minutes or until mushrooms are cooked through and tender.

In a large bowl, combine eggs and skim milk or half and half; vigorously beat with a wooden spoon or wire whisk. Pour beaten eggs over mushrooms; cook until firm, gently stirring and scraping eggs from sides and bottom of skillet. Serve immediately, garnished with parsley and cayenne pepper, if desired.

Variations
Sauté 1/4 cup chopped sweet red onion with mushrooms.
Add 1 1/2 cups coarsely flaked crabmeat or chopped cooked lobster instead of mushrooms.

Fried Eggs with Anchovies

Spiegeleier mit Anchovis

You won't need any salt to season these eggs; the anchovy fillets provide all the seasoning that's needed. *Makes 4 servings.*

Butter or margarine, room
  temperature
4 slices white or rye bread

8 eggs
8 anchovy fillets

Spread butter or margarine on one side of bread slices. Heat a large skillet over medium heat. Add bread, buttered sides down. Cook about 1 minute or until lightly browned. Turn bread slices over and cook 1 minute. In a skillet with a nonstick surface, fry eggs sunny side up over medium heat. Place 2 fried eggs on each slice of bread. Cut anchovies in half lengthwise. Arrange sliced anchovy fillets in the shape of a cross over each egg yolk. Serve hot.

Omelet

Omelett

Some novice cooks try to make extra-large omelets by doubling the number of eggs a recipe calls for. Unfortunately, that almost always results in a shaggy-looking omelet with an outside that's too well done and an inside not done enough. Stick to the four-eggs-per-omelet rule and you'll come out ahead. *Makes 2 or 3 servings.*

4 eggs	*1/8 teaspoon freshly ground black*
1/4 cup skim milk	*pepper*
1/2 teaspoon salt	*2 tablespoons butter or margarine*

Combine eggs, milk, salt and pepper in a medium bowl. Using a fork or wire whisk, vigorously beat egg mixture; set aside. Melt butter or margarine in a large, heavy skillet over medium-high heat. Evenly spread melted butter or margarine over bottom of skillet by tilting skillet. Pour egg mixture into hot skillet and reduce heat to medium. While omelet cooks, carefully lift its edges with a spatula so uncooked egg mixture can flow underneath cooked eggs. Increase the heat slightly. Fold the cooking eggs over to form a half circle. Brown each side. Serve hot, slicing omelet in 2 or 3 equal portions.

Variations

Before omelet is folded over, top cooking egg mixture with an even sprinkling of 2 tablespoons chopped fresh herbs such as parsley, chives, tarragon, dill or chervil.

Or, instead of chopped fresh herbs, use 3 tablespoons minced fresh red or green bell pepper, 2 tablespoons grated Parmesan cheese or 1/2 cup cooked vegetables cut in small pieces such as asparagus tips, zucchini, onions or mushrooms.

Note

If more servings are desired, repeat entire recipe while keeping first omelet warm. Caution: Do not attempt to make larger omelets in this manner by simply doubling or tripling ingredient amounts; larger omelets cooked this way are difficult to handle and may not stay together.

Berlin-Style Hard-Cooked Eggs

Berliner Eier

The trick here is to evenly crack and loosen the egg shells without having them fall off. It's not difficult but it may take a little practice to get the hang of it. *Makes 8 servings.*

1 1/4 qts. water	8 eggs, room temperature
1/3 cup salt	1/4 cup white wine
1 tablespoon garlic salt	2 tablespoons vegetable oil
2 bay leaves	1 1/2 tablespoons vinegar
1 1/4 teaspoons black peppercorns	1 tablespoon prepared mustard
1/2 small leek, cut in half	Salt

In a medium saucepan, combine water, 1/3 cup salt, garlic salt, bay leaves, peppercorns and leek. Cook, uncovered, 30 minutes over medium-low heat. Let cool 10 minutes. Remove and discard leek and bay leaves. Place eggs in slightly cooled cooking water; cover with a tight fitting lid. Simmer 8 to 10 minutes over low heat. Immediately transfer eggs into a medium bowl of cold water to stop the cooking process. Cool cooking liquid. Change cold water 3 times, at 1-minute intervals.

Wrap a cooled hard-cooked egg in a clean cloth; roll egg against a flat, hard surface, applying enough downward pressure to crack and loosen shell all over egg. Do not peel shell, however. Repeat process until shells of all eggs have been cracked (but not removed). Place cracked eggs into cooled cooking water. Cover and refrigerate 2 to 3 days.

In a small bowl, combine wine, oil, vinegar and mustard. Season with salt to taste. Drain eggs. Serve eggs in their cracked shells, to be peeled individually as eaten, with each person instructed to cut shelled egg in half, remove halves of yolk, spoon mustard sauce into each egg-white well, replace yolk halves lightly over the mustard sauce and eat.

Farmer's Broiled Omelet

Bauernfrüfstuck

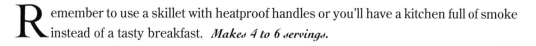

Remember to use a skillet with heatproof handles or you'll have a kitchen full of smoke instead of a tasty breakfast. *Makes 4 to 6 servings.*

6 eggs

3/4 cup (3 oz.) shredded Emmentaler cheese

2 tablespoons butter or margarine

1 medium onion, diced

8 oz. fresh mushrooms, chopped

1 cup chopped cooked ham

3 large cooked potatoes, peeled and diced

1/2 cup frozen or fresh green peas

1/4 teaspoon freshly ground black pepper

Ground sweet paprika

Combine eggs and cheese in a large bowl. Using a wire whisk, vigorously beat egg mixture. Melt butter or margarine in a large, heavy skillet with an ovenproof handle over medium heat. Add onion, mushrooms and ham; sauté until onion is tender and mushrooms are cooked through, about 10 minutes. Add potatoes and peas, gently stirring until mixed; cook 2 more minutes. Preheat broiler. Pour egg mixture evenly over sautéed vegetables and ham. Reduce heat and cook until eggs are set, loosening egg mixture from sides and bottom of skillet with a spatula. Place skillet beneath broiler 1 to 2 minutes or until top of egg mixture browns. Serve hot from skillet.

Egg Cutlets

Eieschnitzel

Mushroom or Horseradish Sauces are not the only sauces you can use with this dish. Dill Sauce (page 135) and Mustard Sauce (page 216) are equally good. *Makes 12 to 14 cutlets.*

2 medium day-old hard rolls
3/4 cup milk
1 1/2 tablespoons minced onion
1 tablespoon chopped fresh parsley
3 tablespoons finely chopped green
    bell pepper
1/4 cup butter or margarine, room
    temperature

6 hard-cooked eggs, finely chopped
1 extra-large egg, slightly beaten
1 teaspoon salt
1/2 teaspoon freshly ground black
    pepper
About 3/4 cup dry bread crumbs
Mushroom Sauce (page 131) or
    Horseradish Sauce (page 172)

In a small bowl, soak rolls in milk. Squeeze excess milk from rolls. Discard milk. In a medium bowl, combine onion, parsley, bell pepper and 1 tablespoon butter or margarine. Add chopped eggs, raw egg, salt, pepper and soaked rolls. Using your hands, work egg mixture, forming cutlets about 1 inch thick × 3 inches. Don't make them any larger or they'll tend to break apart while handling and cooking.

Place bread crumbs on a large plate. Carefully press egg cutlets into bread crumbs so all sides are evenly coated. Let breaded cutlets stand at room temperature 8 to 10 minutes. Melt remaining 3 tablespoons butter or margarine in a large skillet over medium heat. Carefully add egg cutlets; cook 2 to 2 1/2 minutes on each side or until both sides are browned. Serve hot with Mushroom Sauce or Horseradish Sauce.

Eggs in Spinach

Eier in Spinat

You can use fresh spinach too, but make sure you chop it by hand. Attempting to use a food processor to do the chopping may process it too finely for this recipe. It needs to "hold together" enough to support the eggs before they're cooked. *Makes 4 servings.*

1 tablespoon butter or margarine
1 tablespoon vegetable oil
1 small onion, chopped
2 (10-oz.) packages frozen chopped
   spinach
1 1/4 cups whipping cream
1/2 teaspoon salt

1/4 teaspoon freshly ground black
   pepper
1/4 teaspoon ground nutmeg
4 eggs
3/4 cup (3 oz.) shredded Cheddar
   cheese

Preheat oven to 350F (175C). Heat butter or margarine and oil in a large skillet over medium-low heat. Add onion; sauté until tender, about 5 minutes. Add frozen spinach. Simmer until thawed, turning once. Pour whipping cream over thawed spinach. Cook 6 to 8 minutes, gently stirring several times. Season spinach with salt, pepper and nutmeg. Spoon cooked spinach mixture into a shallow casserole baking dish. Make 4 wells in the spinach, one near each corner, by indenting the spinach with the bottom of a small soup ladle. Break 1 egg into each well. Sprinkle cheese over the top, but not on egg yolks. Bake, uncovered, 10 to 12 minutes or until cheese is slightly browned and egg whites are fully cooked. Serve immediately.

Gruyère Cheese Soufflé

Greyerzerlauf

Also try Edam, Emmentaler and Butter Kase for equally mild-flavored soufflés. *Makes 6 to 8 servings.*

3 tablespoons butter or margarine
6 tablespoons all-purpose flour
1 cup hot milk
1/2 teaspoon salt
1/8 teaspoon freshly ground white
   pepper

1/8 teaspoon nutmeg
5 eggs, separated
1/8 teaspoon cream of tartar
1 1/4 cups (5 oz.) shredded Gruyère
   cheese

Preheat oven to 400F (205C). Grease a 2-quart soufflé dish, then lightly dust inside of greased dish with flour. Melt 3 tablespoons butter or margarine in a medium saucepan over low heat. Add 6 tablespoons flour. Cook until bubbly, stirring constantly. Add milk, salt, pepper and nutmeg, stirring vigorously. Bring to a boil and simmer over low heat 1 minute or until thickened. Remove from heat; add egg yolks, one at a time, stirring to blend.

In a large bowl, beat egg whites with cream of tartar until stiff but not dry. Fold half of the egg whites into egg mixture until combined. Fold in the remaining egg whites. Add cheese. Stir to combine but do not overmix. Pour egg mixture into prepared soufflé dish. Smooth top lightly with a spatula. Bake 20 to 25 minutes or until golden brown and puffed up about 2 inches above the dish rim. Serve immediately.

Variation

Instead of Gruyère cheese, add 1 1/2 cups cooked asparagus tips cut in small pieces, 1/3 cup grated Parmesan cheese, 2 tablespoons chopped fresh parsley, 2 tablespoons chopped chives and 1 tablespoon chopped fresh dill.

Poultry

·······❧·······

Geflügel

*T*here's no doubt about it: members of the poultry family are the unsung heroes and heroines of German household kitchens. While pork, veal and beef get a lot of credit within traditional German cuisine, and sausage is widely publicized, chicken is often ignored, especially by the finer restaurants and cooking publications of the day. Perhaps chickens are considered too commonplace to be talked about. Even though most adjoining countries have installed chicken toward the head of their own national and regional cuisines—in Poland, Czechoslovakia, France, and the Netherlands, for example—in Germany, chicken barely makes it into the cookbooks. Yet, ironically enough, huge numbers of chickens are consumed in Germany. Consider that during the sixteen-day Octoberfest in Munich, over 750,000 roasted chickens are eaten, and loved.

As always, for the Germans there are logical reasons for this. Chickens are relatively inexpensive to buy, live or butchered. And they're simple to raise: they need little other than sheltered space in a barn, feed, and water. Throughout much of rural Germany, and especially in the eastern part of the country, where families have become more reliant on what they have grown and raised for themselves, chickens have been an almost automatic farm animal, providing a steady source of eggs, meat, and flavor for broths and soups. A chicken grows quickly, maturing into a bird that can feed a family of five in little more than a few months' time. Plus chickens are not seasonal birds: they can be kept year-round, and killed whenever needed. The household isn't faced with storing a large quantity of meat, as is required when a pig or steer is butchered. Chickens are kept until needed and, when needed, are consumed in their entirety, with no worries as to how to store leftovers. This meant a lot in years past, when refrigeration and home freezers were scarce.

The methods of preparation have largely come from Eastern Europe, and more recently, the Middle East. Roasted chicken, with or without vegetables and mushrooms, cooked and basted with seasoned wine or sour-cream mixtures, is on practically every home cook's recipe list. As is fried, sautéed, and various versions of simmered chicken.

Lightly sautéed chicken livers and onions are often cooked with a broth-based sauce seasoned with a little sherry and herbs, and sometimes mushrooms, and served hot over rice or noodles.

Cornish hens are available, fresh or frozen, and are also baked with fresh squash, tomatoes, and other vegetables.

Turkey is just now gaining prominence in Germany, largely due to its nutritional values: its flesh contains less fat and more meat than its traditional counterpart—the German goose. While Americans traditionally favor turkeys for large holiday feasts such as Thanksgiving and Christmas, similar celebrations at German tables feature stuffed young geese.

The eating of goose at holiday and traditional celebrations has a long history in Germany. In ancient times roast goose was offered for grain and other harvests that had been gathered in during late fall. This was a natural ritual because geese hatch in spring and are at their prime eight or nine months later. Older, larger geese are tougher, and are more commonly braised or used in casseroles.

Baked Chicken
with Vegetables

Gebackenes Hähnchen mit Gemüse

The tomatoes, onions and peppers make this a colorful and healthy dish. *Makes 4 servings.*

1 teaspoon salt

1/4 teaspoon ground sweet paprika

1 (2 1/2- to 3-lb.) chicken, cut up

3 tablespoons butter or margarine

2 medium onions, thinly sliced

2 medium, green bell peppers, halved lengthwise and sliced

1 teaspoon vegetable oil

1/2 cup Chicken Broth (page 57) or chicken bouillon

3 medium tomatoes, cut in 6 wedges each

1/2 cup (2 oz.) shredded sharp Cheddar or Swiss cheese

Combine salt and paprika in a small bowl. Rub chicken with salt mixture. Let stand 15 minutes. Melt 2 tablespoons of the butter or margarine in a large skillet over medium heat. Add onions; sauté until tender, about 10 minutes. Stir bell peppers into onions; sauté 3 minutes. Place sautéed onions and peppers in a medium bowl; set aside. Heat remaining 1 tablespoon butter or margarine and the oil in same skillet. Add chicken; sauté over medium heat 8 to 9 minutes on each side or until browned.

Preheat oven to 350F (175C). Arrange chicken in a shallow baking dish. Stir broth or bouillon into cooking juices in skillet and add to chicken. Spoon cooked onions and peppers over chicken. Arrange tomato wedges over onions and peppers. Top with shredded cheese. Cover with a tight-fitting lid. Bake 35 minutes. Remove lid. Bake 10 more minutes or until cheese lightly browns. Serve hot.

Chicken in White Wine Sauce

Hähnchen in Weissweinsosse

Substitute three small cut-up chickens, if desired. The rest of the recipe will stay the same. *Makes 5 or 6 servings.*

10 chicken-breast halves	1 1/2 cups white wine
Salt	1/2 cup chopped fresh tarragon
Freshly ground black pepper	1/4 cup chopped fresh thyme
3 tablespoons butter or margarine	3/4 cup whipping cream
2 medium onions, chopped	2 tablespoons chopped fresh parsley
2 tablespoons all-purpose flour	

Sprinkle chicken pieces with salt and pepper. Melt butter or margarine in a large skillet over medium heat. Add chicken; sauté 10 minutes, turning chicken until all sides are browned. Transfer chicken to a greased baking dish; leave drippings in skillet.

Preheat oven to 350F (175C). Add onions to same skillet. Sauté onions over medium heat until tender, about 10 minutes. Sprinkle flour over onions; cook 2 minutes, stirring gently. Add wine to onion mixture. Stir, then pour mixture evenly over chicken. Bake, uncovered, 1 hour. Sprinkle chicken with tarragon and thyme and spoon cream over chicken. Bake, uncovered, 30 minutes or until tender. Place chicken in a warm serving dish. Spoon hot cooking juices over chicken. Garnish with parsley.

Baked Chicken Breasts with Mushrooms

....

Gebackene Hähnchenbrust mit Champignons

German cooks are likely to use wild mushrooms when they're in season, which is twice per year, springtime and fall. The rest of the time they rely on cultivated varieties similar to white mushrooms. *Makes 6 servings.*

1/4 cup all-purpose flour

1 teaspoon salt

1/4 teaspoon freshly ground black pepper

6 chicken-breast halves, skinned and boned

3 tablespoons butter or margarine

1 cup white wine

1/2 cup Chicken Broth (page 57) or chicken bouillon

1 lb. fresh mushrooms, sliced

Cooked rice or mashed potatoes (optional)

1/2 cup sour cream

1 tablespoon dried bread crumbs

1 tablespoon all-purpose flour

Preheat oven to 350F (175C). Mix flour, salt and pepper in a shallow medium bowl. Evenly coat chicken by rolling chicken in flour mixture. Set flour-covered chicken aside on a wire rack. Melt 2 tablespoons of the butter or margarine in a medium skillet over medium-high heat. Add chicken; sauté about 10 minutes, turning chicken until all sides are browned. Place chicken in a 9-inch-square baking dish. Pour wine and broth over chicken. Cover with a tight-fitting lid. Bake 30 minutes.

Meanwhile, melt remaining 1 tablespoon of the butter or margarine in a medium skillet over medium-high heat. Add mushrooms; sauté 6 to 8 minutes or until tender. Add mushrooms to chicken. Cover and bake another 30 minutes. While baking chicken, prepare rice or mashed potatoes, if desired.

Remove chicken from juices and keep warm in oven. In a small bowl, mix sour cream, bread crumbs and 1 tablespoon flour. Stir sour-cream mixture into cooking juices; return mixture to oven. Cook until the resulting sauce begins to boil. Serve chicken with side dish of rice or mashed potatoes, if desired. Top with hot sauce and mushrooms.

Chicken Roll with Vegetables

Hähnchenrolle mit Gemüse

Here you'll end up with an extra-special dish that can be served hot or cold, as an entree or sliced as a sandwich filling. *Makes 4 to 6 servings.*

10 chicken-breast halves, boned and
   skinned
2 tablespoons butter or margarine
3 medium carrots, chopped
2 medium onions, chopped
1 medium parsley root or parsnip,
   chopped

1 1/4 cups Chicken Broth (page
   57) or chicken bouillon
2 eggs, beaten
1/4 cup frozen or fresh green peas
Salt to taste
Freshly ground black pepper to taste

Place chicken between plastic wrap and pound about 5 times with a heavy cleaver or meat mallet or until chicken is about 1/4 inch thick. Trim each chicken piece into a rectangular shape, cutting away about one-fourth of the meat. Mince meat trimmings.

Grease a large baking dish. Melt butter or margarine in a large skillet over medium heat. Add carrots, onions, parsley root or parsnip, and 1/4 cup broth or bouillon. Cook 15 minutes or until liquid is reduced to about 2 tablespoons. Reduce heat to low. Stir eggs and peas into cooking vegetables. Simmer until eggs are set, stirring constantly. Add minced chicken, salt and pepper. Cook, stirring frequently, 3 to 4 minutes. Remove from heat. Let cool.

Preheat oven to 325F (165C). Evenly spread minced chicken mixture on flattened chicken. Roll chicken pieces from short end, jelly-roll style. Secure with wooden picks. Place chicken rolls in greased dish. Pour remaining 1 cup broth or bouillon over chicken. Bake 1 hour or until fork tender. Serve hot or cold, sliced for sandwiches.

Sautéed Chicken

Geröstetes Hähnchen

This quick and easy dish can be made ahead and heated up later. *Makes 6 to 8 servings.*

1 teaspoon salt	1/2 cup all-purpose flour
1/2 teaspoon garlic salt	1 cup dried bread crumbs
1 teaspoon sweet ground paprika	2 tablespoons butter or margarine
1/2 teaspoon freshly ground black pepper	1 cup Chicken Broth (page 57) or chicken bouillon
2 (2 1/2- to 3-lb.) chickens, cut up	1 lemon, sliced into wedges
2 eggs	Parsley sprigs for garnish

In a small bowl, combine salt, garlic salt, paprika and pepper. Rub chicken all over with salt mixture. Place on a baking sheet and let stand at room temperature 15 minutes.

Beat eggs in a medium bowl. Place flour in a second medium bowl, and bread crumbs in a third medium bowl. Roll a chicken piece in the flour. Shake off excess. Dip chicken in beaten egg, then roll in bread crumbs, pressing crumbs evenly into chicken. Place coated chicken on a wire rack. Repeat process with remaining chicken pieces. Let stand 15 minutes at room temperature to firm coating. Or, refrigerate until ready to cook.

Melt butter or margarine in a large skillet over medium heat. Place coated chicken, skin side down, in skillet; sauté 8 minutes. Turn chicken and sauté 8 more minutes. Drizzle broth or bouillon over chicken. Cover with a tight-fitting lid. Reduce heat to low; simmer 8 minutes. Turn chicken, cover and simmer 8 more minutes. Uncover; sauté over medium-high heat 5 to 6 minutes on each side or until crisp. Arrange cooked chicken on a platter. Garnish with lemon wedges and parsley sprigs.

Simmered Chicken

Sieden Hähnchen

The combination of sweet onions and tangy sour cream makes a special chicken dinner treat. *Makes 4 to 6 servings.*

1 (3- to 3 1/2-lb.) chicken, cut up
1 teaspoon salt
1/4 cup all-purpose flour
1 teaspoon ground sweet paprika
4 tablespoons butter or margarine
2 medium sweet onions, chopped

2 cups Chicken Broth (page 57)
 or chicken bouillon
1/2 lb. fresh mushrooms, sliced
1 cup sour cream
2 tablespoons chopped fresh parsley

Preheat oven to 325F (165C). Grease a large baking dish. Place chicken pieces in a large bowl; rub with salt and let stand 15 minutes. Combine flour and paprika in a pie pan. Roll chicken pieces in flour mixture until evenly coated. Melt 3 tablespoons of the butter or margarine in a large skillet over medium heat. Add floured chicken; sauté, turning until chicken browns on all sides, about 15 minutes.

Arrange chicken in greased baking dish. Add onions to skillet with drippings. Sauté over medium heat until tender, about 10 minutes. Spoon sautéed onions over chicken. Add broth or bouillon. Cover with a tight-fitting lid and bake 45 minutes.

Melt remaining 1 tablespoon butter or margarine in a medium skillet over medium heat. Add mushrooms; sauté until softened. Spoon cooked mushrooms over chicken. In a small bowl, stir sour cream with a spoon until softened. Spoon over chicken. Garnish with parsley. Cover and bake another 15 to 20 minutes or until chicken is tender. Serve hot.

Fried Chicken

Brathähnchen

One of the most popular ways to prepare and serve chicken in Germany. The extra time it takes to refrigerate the battered chicken parts helps the batter adhere to the chicken so it won't fall off easily. *Makes 4 to 6 servings.*

1 (3-lb.) fryer chicken, cut up

3 teaspoons salt

1/2 teaspoon freshly ground black
   pepper

1 cup all-purpose flour

2 eggs

1/2 cup beer

2 tablespoons melted butter or
   margarine

2 tablespoons minced fresh parsley

Vegetable oil for deep-frying

Rub chicken with 2 teaspoons of the salt and 1/4 teaspoon of the pepper. Cover loosely with plastic wrap and refrigerate 1 hour.

Sift flour and remaining salt and pepper into a medium bowl. Beat in the eggs and beer until smooth. Add butter or margarine and parsley; stir to combine. Dip chicken, 1 piece at a time, in batter, turning chicken to coat heavily and evenly with batter. Let excess batter drip off. Place battered chicken on a baking sheet so they don't touch one another. Refrigerate, uncovered, 1 hour.

Preheat oven to 350F (175C). In a large saucepan or deep-fryer, heat vegetable oil to 360F (180C). Fry chicken until it turns a light golden color, about 10 minutes. Remove chicken; drain on paper towels. Arrange fried chicken in a shallow baking dish. Bake, uncovered, 20 to 30 minutes or until crispy and browned.

Chicken Livers

Gëflügelleber

Although this recipe suggests you serve the savory livers over rice, you can also spoon them over dumplings, noodles, and even toast. *Makes 4 to 6 servings.*

3 tablespoons butter or margarine
1 medium onion, chopped
1 3/4 to 2 lbs. chicken livers, each
   liver cut in half
2 tablespoons all-purpose flour
1 1/2 cups Beef Broth (page 58)
   or chicken bouillon
1 tablespoon tomato paste
1/3 cup sherry

1/2 teaspoon salt
1/4 teaspoon freshly ground black
   pepper
1 teaspoon brown sugar
About 4 to 5 oz. canned sliced
   mushrooms, drained
2 tablespoons chopped fresh parsley
4 to 6 cups cooked rice (optional)

Melt butter or margarine in a large skillet over medium heat. Add onion; sauté until onions are almost tender, about 5 minutes. Add livers; cook over medium heat about 1 minute on each side. Remove livers from skillet; set aside. Stir flour into sautéed onions; cook, stirring, over medium heat until bubbly. Stir in broth, tomato paste and sherry, stirring to combine. Cook until mixture boils and thickens. Add salt, pepper and brown sugar. Gently stir sautéed livers, mushrooms and parsley into cooking juices. Heat livers thoroughly. Serve over hot cooked rice, if desired.

Chilled Chicken & Cheese

Gekühlt Küken und Käse

C hicken-breast meat is usually favored for this recipe. It goes well with practically any cheese. *Makes 6 servings.*

Mixed lettuce leaves

1 1/2 lbs. Gouda, Steppenkase, or natural smoked cheese, cut into 1/4-inch-thick slices, then cut into 1/2-inch-wide strips

1 lb. boneless, cooked chicken, diced

1 medium cucumber, unpeeled, thinly sliced

8 red radishes, sliced

1 1/2 cups plain nonfat yogurt

3 tablespoons lemon juice

1 tablespoon chopped chives

1 teaspoon chopped fresh parsley

1 teaspoon chopped fresh dill

1/2 teaspoon sugar

1/4 teaspoon salt

1/4 teaspoon freshly ground black pepper

Line a medium-sized shallow serving bowl with lettuce leaves. Arrange cheese strips, chicken, cucumber and radishes over lettuce. In a small bowl, combine yogurt, lemon juice, chives, parsley, dill, sugar, salt and pepper. Spoon resulting yogurt mixture over cheese, chicken, cucumber and radishes. Cover and refrigerate until chilled. Serve chilled.

Baked Cornish Hens

Gebacken Cornish Hähner

For a different but delicious dish, use two cut-up chickens instead of Cornish hens. *Makes 4 servings.*

3 tablespoons butter or margarine

4 Cornish hens, thawed, if frozen, and cut in half

4 garlic cloves, crushed

1 tablespoon salt

1/4 teaspoon freshly ground black pepper

1/4 teaspoon ground sage

1/8 teaspoon ground thyme

1 1/2 cups dry white wine

4 medium tomatoes, peeled, sliced and seeded

1 small zucchini or yellow squash, thinly sliced

1 tablespoon potato starch or cornstarch mixed with 1 tablespoon water

Preheat oven to 350F (175C). Melt butter or margarine in a large skillet over medium-low heat. Add hens; sauté 10 minutes on each side or until both sides are golden brown. Arrange hen pieces in a shallow baking dish. Add cooking juices from skillet. Sprinkle hens with garlic, salt, pepper, sage and thyme. Cover and bake 20 to 25 minutes.

Add wine to cooking juices in baking dish. Arrange tomatoes and squash over hens. Cover; bake 15 minutes or until tender. Place hens on a warm platter. Pour 1/4 cup cooking juices into a small saucepan. Stir in potato starch or cornstarch mixture until well blended. Pour in remaining cooking juices. Bring to a boil over medium heat, stirring constantly, and boil until thickened. Reduce heat to low; simmer 5 minutes. To serve, spoon sauce over hens. Serve hot.

Roast Turkey Breast

Truthahnbrustbraten

Select slices of bacon that are sturdy throughout their lengths, so the bacon strips won't pull apart while you're wrapping them around the turkey breasts. *Makes 10 to 12 servings.*

4 (about 1 1/2-lb.) turkey-breast halves	1 large onion, chopped
Salt	1 1/2 lbs. sauerkraut
Freshly ground black pepper	1 bay leaf
8 bacon slices	1/4 cup white wine
2 tablespoons vegetable oil	1/4 lb. seedless green or red grapes

Preheat oven to 375F (190C). Rinse turkey and pat dry with paper towels. Rub turkey with salt and pepper. Stretch 2 pieces bacon around each breast half and secure with wooden picks. Heat oil in a large skillet over medium heat. Add onion; sauté until tender, about 10 minutes. Add turkey and cook over medium heat, browning on all sides. Remove skillet from heat.

In a baking dish large enough to hold turkey, spread an even layer of sauerkraut. Add bay leaf and wine. Arrange turkey-breast halves on sauerkraut, pushing breast-halves partially into sauerkraut. Spoon cooked onion and juices over turkey and sauerkraut. Top with seedless grapes. Cover with foil or a tight-fitting lid; bake 1 1/2 to 2 hours or until turkey is tender and juices run clear when pierced with a knife. Remove foil or cover for last 10 minutes, if desired. Slice turkey and arrange over sauerkraut in same baking dish. Serve hot.

Roast Turkey with Stuffing

Gefüllter Truthahnbraten

This recipe will also work well with wild turkeys, which tend to be considerably smaller. Just proportionately scale back the ingredients. Or, if you still want the extra stuffing, cook it in an ovenproof container toward the latter part of the roasting time. *Makes 14 to 16 servings.*

1 (12- to 14-lb.) turkey, thawed,
   if frozen
1 1/2 tablespoons plus 1 teaspoon
   salt
2/3 cup water
1/4 cup butter or margarine
1 large onion, finely chopped
1 cup finely chopped celery
10 slices white bread
1 cup milk
3 eggs, separated

1 tablespoon finely chopped fresh
   parsley
1/2 teaspoon freshly ground black
   pepper
1/4 teaspoon ground cloves
1/4 teaspoon ground nutmeg
1/4 cup golden raisins
2 tablespoons sherry
1/4 cup butter or margarine, melted
1/4 cup red wine

Preheat oven to 350F (175C). Remove giblets from neck and turkey cavity; reserve for stock or soup. Rinse turkey under cold running water; pat dry with paper towels. Rub turkey, inside and out, with 1 1/2 tablespoons salt. Place turkey on a rack, breast side down, in a shallow roasting pan. Pour water into roasting pan.

Melt butter or margarine in a medium skillet over medium heat. Add onion and celery; sauté until onion is tender, about 10 minutes. Let cool. In a large bowl, combine bread with milk. Mix with your hands until bread absorbs milk; squeeze excess milk out of bread. To squeezed bread, add egg yolks, remaining 1 teaspoon salt, parsley, pepper, cloves, nutmeg, raisins and sherry. In a medium bowl, beat egg whites until stiff but not dry. Mix egg whites into stuffing mixture. Spoon stuffing mixture into turkey cavity; roast 1 hour.

Combine melted butter or margarine and red wine in a cup. Roast turkey, basting with butter mixture every 20 minutes, for a total of 4 to 5 hours or until juices run clear when a knife is inserted between breast and thigh. Place turkey on a large platter. Cover with foil and let stand 20 to 30 minutes before carving. Pour pan juices into a small saucepan, if desired. Place over medium heat; cook, stirring constantly, 3 to 4 minutes. Spoon cooked juices over turkey slices and stuffing.

Braised Goose

Gans Gedunstet

Friends and relatives will flock to your table to try this hearty dish. *Makes 8 to 10 servings.*

1 (8- to 10-lb.) goose, cut up
1 tablespoon salt
1 teaspoon freshly ground black
   pepper
1 teaspoon ground sweet paprika
3 tablespoons vegetable oil

5 garlic cloves, slivered
About 2 1/2 cups Chicken Broth
   (page 57) or chicken bouillon
1 (6-oz.) can tomato paste
1 cup uncooked long-grain white rice

Lay goose pieces out on a flat surface. Using a meat mallet or the flat surface of a cleaver, pound goose 3 or 4 times on each side. Combine salt, pepper and paprika in a small dish. Rub goose all over with salt mixture. Place in a large bowl. Cover and refrigerate 1 hour.

Heat oil in a large heavy skillet over medium heat. Add goose and garlic; sauté 7 to 8 minutes on each side, turning until browned on both sides. Add 1 cup of the broth. Cover with a tight-fitting lid. Reduce heat to low; simmer 1 1/2 hours or until almost tender, turning once.

Combine tomato paste and remaining 1 1/2 cups broth in a small bowl. Spoon rice into juices in skillet. Pour broth mixture over rice and goose. Simmer, covered, 30 minutes or until goose is tender and rice is cooked. If rice is not moist enough, add a little more broth or bouillon or water. To serve, spoon hot rice over braised goose parts.

Roast Goose with Chestnut Stuffing

Gefüllter Gänsebraten mit Esskastanie

Chestnuts are traditionally served around Christmas time. If desired, leave a handful of chestnuts out of the filling mixture to help garnish the serving platter. *Makes 6 to 8 servings.*

1 (8- to 9-lb.) goose
1/4 cup butter or margarine, softened
1 teaspoon dried crumbled sage
1 teaspoon dried chopped rosemary
Salt
Freshly ground black pepper
1 lb. chestnuts, roasted, peeled and chopped
3/4 lb. dried, pitted prunes, soaked overnight in water to cover, drained and chopped

2 large apples, peeled, cored and sliced
Goose giblets, finely chopped
3/4 lb. bulk pork sausage
1/2 cup dry white wine
About 1 lb. (3/4- to 1-inch diameter) boiled potatoes, warm to hot at serving time
Fresh parsley sprigs

Rinse goose and pat dry with paper towels. Rub 1 tablespoon of the butter or margarine, sage and rosemary all over inside of goose. Rub outside of goose with salt and pepper. Melt remaining 3 tablespoons butter or margarine in a large skillet over medium heat. Add chopped chestnuts and prunes, apples, goose giblets and sausage; sauté chestnut mixture 12 to 15 minutes or until apples are cooked but not falling apart. Let chestnut mixture cool.

Preheat oven to 475F (245C). Spoon chestnut mixture loosely into goose cavity and neck. Fasten neck skin of goose to back with skewers. Prick skin all over with a fork. Place goose, breast side up, on a rack in a shallow roasting pan. Roast, uncovered, about 30 minutes or until goose is browned, pricking goose occasionally with a fork to let the fat escape and basting with wine. When goose is browned, reduce heat to 375F (190C) and cook about 2 more hours or until goose is tender. At any time during cooking, if the goose appears to be getting too brown, loosely cover with foil for the remaining cooking time. Remove goose from pan and let stand 10 minutes; transfer to a warm serving platter. Arrange small warm or hot boiled potatoes around goose; garnish with sprigs of parsley and whole cooked chestnuts, if desired.

Pork & Lamb

Schwein und Lamm

Pork

The pig has always been held in the highest regard throughout Germany and all of Central and Eastern Europe. Pork, hands down, is the most frequently eaten meat in Germany. In fact, conservative estimates indicate that for every ten pounds of meat consumed by Germans, six are pork. The rest consist of veal and beef, then wild game, lamb and mutton.

From times when Stone Age tribes hunted and ate wild boar, through the days of the Roman colonization of Germanic lands over 2,000 years ago, wild boar was practically as common as domestic pork is today. Near the city of Cologne, which was founded as a Roman outpost, archeologists discovered an ancient villa with a mosaic floor depicting a feast that focused on a well-attended wild-boar roast. In those times, that was the norm: whole wild boar, roasted on a spit over an open fire.

During the Middle Ages, a number of methods were being used to help preserve both wild boar and the more domesticated varieties of pig. Before the days of refrigeration, pigs were generally slaughtered during late fall, when cold temperatures helped prevent spoilage and when it was convenient to put up the pork in wooden casks alternately layered with meat and salt. Such salted pork or "salt pork" was prepared mainly for household use and later for consumption by mariners at sea and armies traveling large distances from home. Smoking was another option that helped preserve select cuts of meat such as bacon and ham so they'd last for months at a time. Pork preserved in brine, from a process that came to be known as "corning," helped round out the day's selection. Of course, don't forget that available pork, and infrequently other meats, were also ground, seasoned and prepared into sausages. Back then, pork, in one form or another, was practically the only kind of meat that peasants could get their hands on.

Why is pork so popular? Beyond custom and tradition, there are other, more practical reasons. First of all, pigs are a lot more prolific than cattle or sheep. Second, pigs are a lot easier to care for than cattle and other meat-producing animals. Most farms, even the smallest ones, raise one or more pigs, fattened on table scraps and leftovers from the garden. Beef cattle and sheep need lots of space and grain or plant food to survive. Pigs, on the other hand, can forage for themselves much more efficiently, can thrive on a greater variety of foods and are happily kept in much smaller pens. Plus, a properly fed pig gains about twice the weight per pound of feed as does any other large animal raised for food. One point further in favor of pork is that literally every bit of the pig, from the feet to the ears to the tail, is used in some fashion. Fresh, pickled and smoked pork parts provide ingredients for hundreds of recipes and specialties.

One cured or cured and smoked pork product is ham, which the Germans love. The word *ham* is said to have come from the Old English term *hamm,* referring to the thigh or the hind leg of a pig. The most famous German ham is the world-renowned dry-cured and smoked Westphalian variety, which is somewhat similar in texture to prosciutto. "Dry-cured" means that the ham was not injected with brine in the manner by which most hams are cured, but rather rubbed with a dry-salting mixture in the old-fashioned, traditional way. Westphalian ham is naturally smokier than prosciutto as well as denser and chewier. It has certainly stood the test of time, having been prepared over 2,000 years ago for Romans and German peasants alike from one end of the German territories to the other. The production of Westphalian ham eventually became a cottage industry for many a German family who relied upon plundering herds of pigs that roamed free through the thick forests of Westphalia.

Westphalia's fine ham is best suited for an uncooked appetizer, served with pretzels and cheese, fruit or a light sauce. Slice the ham thinly—a little will go a long way. In recipes calling for large amounts of ham, other hams will do, but when top-ranked quality and taste is desired, the Westphalian ham is second to none. It's expensive, but the lengthy smoking it receives makes it the ham to use for special occasions. Although Westphalian ham is not available in every Western supermarket or corner grocery, it's often stocked in larger meat markets and can be ordered from practically any international mail-order gourmet catalog worth its salt.

The pork recipes in this chapter just skim the surface of German pork cookery. Pork roasts are featured in special dinners, including the version here (page 168), prepared with a flavorful filling of chopped prunes, bread crumbs and crumbled bits of bacon. Marinated pork spareribs (page 169) are often served at picnics and outdoor beer gardens, to be enjoyed with plenty of dark bread and mugs of frothy pilsner. Pork cutlets or schnitzels rival those made of veal and have on numerous occasions impersonated veal cutlets in home kitchens and restaurants.

Favorite pork accompaniments include sauerkraut, fresh cabbage and apples, which are frequently cooked slowly with chops or roasts so the meat gradually acquires their never-too-tart or tangy flavors.

Baked ham, here (page 174) stuffed with a filling of sausage, onion, bread crumbs and herbs, is an entree from which leftovers are always appreciated. Baked Ham Slices and Hot Ham Rolls with Asparagus and Ham Noodle Casserole are other popular dishes eaten at various meals from morning to night.

Lamb

Lamb has always been a rather small part of the traditional German diet, but its influence continues to expand due to the influx of immigrants from Turkey and the Middle East, who have introduced numerous lamb recipes through restaurants and take-out kiosks in the larger cities.

Lamb is a tender meat with a distinctive flavor unlike other meats. The meat itself is covered by a thin membrane that feels like paper and is called the "fell." The fell is generally removed before cooking.

Stuffed Pork Roast

Gefüllter Schweinebraten

Before stuffing the pork-roast pocket, stretch the inside of the pocket open a little with a sturdy serving spoon, or with your hand. Stuffing should not be packed solid; it should be firmly arranged, though, evenly placed from the bottom of the roast's pocket to just below the top. *Makes 8 to 10 servings.*

- 1 (4 1/2- to 5-lb.) bone-in pork-loin roast
- 1 cup chopped pitted prunes
- 2 tablespoons brandy
- 1 1/2 cups dried bread crumbs
- 3 bacon slices, crisp-cooked and crumbled
- 2 cups Chicken Broth (page 57) or chicken bouillon
- 3 tablespoons lemon juice
- 1 teaspoon grated lemon peel
- 1/2 teaspoon ground marjoram
- 1 1/4 teaspoons salt
- 1 teaspoon freshly ground black pepper
- 1/2 teaspoon ground thyme
- 3 tablespoons vegetable oil

Using a sharp knife, cut a vertical pocket in pork roast along ribs. In a medium bowl, soak prunes in brandy; let stand 30 minutes at room temperature. Add bread crumbs, bacon, about 1 cup of the broth or bouillon (enough to make a moist filling), lemon juice, lemon peel and marjoram; gently mix. Combine salt, pepper and thyme in a small bowl. Pat roast dry with paper towels. Rub roast with salt mixture. Let stand 15 minutes.

Preheat oven to 325F (165C). Heat oil in a large skillet over medium-high heat. Add roast; cook until browned on all sides. Let roast cool enough to handle safely. Stuff pork roast pocket with bread-crumb mixture. Close top of pocket with wooden skewers. Place stuffed roast in a shallow roasting pan. Add remaining 1 cup broth or bouillon to pan. Roast, uncovered, 2 to 2 1/2 hours or until tender. Baste every 20 minutes, adding enough water to make sure at least 1 cup cooking juices remains in roasting pan throughout cooking time. When done, remove meat and strain cooking juices. Slice roast and serve hot with side dish of strained juices.

Marinated Pork Spareribs

Marinierte Schweinerippchen

Sweet more than sour is the rule for these ribs. Take care when stirring the fruit into the sauce that the fruit remains intact. Same goes for mixing the ribs with the fruit and sauce. Mix only as much as necessary. *Makes 6 to 8 servings.*

3 1/2 to 4 lbs. pork spareribs
1 3/4 cups dry red wine
1/2 cup apricot preserves
1 tablespoon Dijon mustard
2 teaspoons salt
1 teaspoon freshly ground black
    pepper
4 juniper berries
2 tablespoons vegetable oil
1 cup Meat Broth (page 62) or
    beef bouillon

1/2 cup half and half
1/3 cup all-purpose flour
6 canned pear halves, drained and
    chopped
4 canned pineapple rings, drained
    and chopped
6 canned peach halves, drained and
    chopped
1/4 cup slivered almonds
2 tablespoons chopped parsley

Trim ribs; cut into 8 to 10 sections. Arrange ribs in the smallest shallow nonreactive roasting pan the ribs will fit in. In a small bowl, combine wine, apricot preserves, mustard, salt, pepper and juniper berries. Pour wine mixture over ribs. Cover and refrigerate overnight, turning ribs occasionally and evenly basting with marinade. Remove ribs, reserving marinade.

Heat oil in a large skillet over medium-high heat. Add ribs; sauté about 10 minutes or until ribs are browned on both sides. Add reserved marinade and broth or bouillon to ribs. Bring liquids to a boil, then reduce heat to medium-low. Cover with a tight-fitting lid; simmer 1 hour. Remove ribs from skillet and keep ribs warm. In a small bowl, combine half and half with flour. Stir mixture into cooking juices; cook over medium-low heat, stirring, until sauce thickens. Gently stir pears, pineapples and peaches into sauce; cook 5 more minutes. Add cooked ribs to sauce. Spoon sauce over ribs. Cover and simmer 10 minutes over low heat. Serve ribs hot, with hot sauce and fruits spooned over ribs. Garnish with almonds and parsley.

Spicy Sauerkraut & Pork

Würziges Sauerkraut und Schwein

The peppercorns, juniper berries and allspice berries are what gives this casserole dish its snap. Leftovers will be well-received when reheated in a microwave oven. *Makes 10 to 12 servings.*

1 tablespoon vegetable oil	8 juniper berries
2 medium onions, chopped	4 allspice berries
4 lbs. sauerkraut, rinsed and drained	2 teaspoons sugar
2 medium carrots, shredded	3 (1-lb.) pieces smoked pork loin,
3 bay leaves	ham or Canadian bacon
12 black peppercorns	1 qt. Chicken Broth (page 57),
1/2 teaspoon caraway seeds	chicken bouillon or water

Preheat oven 350F (165C). Heat oil in a large skillet over medium heat. Add onions; sauté until tender, about 10 minutes. Arrange one-third of the sauerkraut over the bottom of a large, deep baking dish. Sprinkle one-third of the carrots and onions over sauerkraut. Add another third of the sauerkraut and onions in a second layer. Sprinkle another third of the carrots and remaining onions over second layer of sauerkraut. Arrange remaining sauerkraut in a third layer. Top with remaining carrots.

Distribute bay leaves, peppercorns, caraway seeds and juniper and allspice berries over sauerkraut. Sprinkle sugar evenly over sauerkraut and spices. Place pork loin, ham or Canadian bacon pieces on sauerkraut, slightly pressing meat into sauerkraut mixture. Pour broth, bouillon, or water over meat and sauerkraut. Bake, covered, 3 hours or until meat is done. Slice meat and rearrange over sauerkraut. Discard bay leaves. Serve hot.

Pork & Cheese Cutlets

Schweinefleisch und Käseschintzel

Make sure pork cutlets are thoroughly cooked before topping them with cheese. If the pork has the least bit of pink color, it's not yet cooked enough. *Makes 8 servings.*

8 (3/4- to 1 1/4-inch-thick) pork loin
   rib chops
1 cup all-purpose flour
1 1/4 teaspoons salt
3/4 teaspoon freshly ground black
   pepper
3/4 teaspoon ground sweet paprika

3 eggs, lightly beaten
1 1/2 cups dry bread crumbs
1/3 cup vegetable oil
8 thin slices Emmentaler cheese
Horseradish Sauce (page 172) or
   Dried Mushroom Sauce (page
   129) (optional)

Bone pork chops. Trim excess fat from meat. Score 1-inch cuts at three places on each pork chop edge to prevent curling while cooking. Place pork pieces between 2 sheets of plastic wrap. Using a meat mallet, pound 6 times on each side or until pork pieces are about 1/2 inch thick.

Combine flour, salt, pepper and paprika in a shallow dish. Place eggs and bread crumbs in separate shallow dishes. Dip pounded pork pieces in flour mixture, then dip in egg and bread crumbs, pressing bread crumbs evenly onto pork. Place breaded pork pieces on a rack. Let stand 10 minutes. Heat oil in a large skillet over medium-low heat. Add pork cutlets; cook, turning occasionally, 20 minutes or until cooked through. Remove cutlets from skillet and arrange on baking sheet.

Preheat broiler. Place 1 cheese slice on each cutlet. Broil cheese-covered cutlets several minutes or until cheese melts and slightly browns. Serve hot, with Horseradish Sauce or Dried Mushroom Sauce, if desired.

Horseradish Sauce

Meerreitich

Prepared horseradish loses its pungency after opening. Use a fresh bottle for the most flavor. Horseradish Sauce may be used with pork cutlets, fish, egg or casserole dishes. *Makes about 2 1/2 cups.*

2 tablespoons butter or margarine	1 1/4 cups Meat Broth (page 62)
1 1/2 tablespoons all-purpose flour	1/2 teaspoon lemon juice
1 cup sour cream	1 3/4 teaspoons sugar
3 tablespoons prepared horseradish	Salt

Melt butter or margarine in a small skillet over medium heat. Stir in flour; cook until golden brown. Let cool. In a small bowl, stir cooled flour mixture into sour cream. Blend in horseradish. Heat broth in a small saucepan. Stir in sour cream mixture, lemon juice and sugar. Season with salt to taste. Remove from heat. Cool slightly. Serve warm.

Pork Chops with Apples

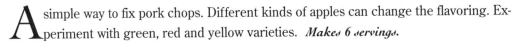

Schweinekoteletts mit Äpfeln

A simple way to fix pork chops. Different kinds of apples can change the flavoring. Experiment with green, red and yellow varieties. *Makes 6 servings.*

2 tablespoons butter or margarine	2 firm apples, peeled, cored and sliced
6 thick pork loin rib chops	Salt to taste
1/4 cup chicken broth	1 1/2 tablespoons chopped fresh
2 medium onions, sliced	parsley

Melt butter or margarine in a large skillet over medium-high heat. Add pork chops; sauté until browned on both sides. Add chicken broth. Cover with a tight-fitting lid and cook over medium-low heat 1 hour, turning occasionally. Add onions and apples; cook, covered, 10 minutes. Uncover; cook 10 more minutes or until apples are tender and a golden color. Season with salt to taste. Garnish with parsley. Serve hot.

Pork Loaf

Schweinehackbraten

The weight, used to press the pork loaf as the loaf cools, is used both to firm up the loaf and to give the loaf a more symmetrical shape that lends itself well to sandwich fillings. *Makes 6 to 8 servings.*

1 lb. fresh pork, cut into pieces	*1 1/2 teaspoons ground sage*
1 lb. ham, cut into pieces	*1 egg white*
1 garlic clove, peeled	*1/2 cup half and half or milk*
1 small onion, quartered	*4 bacon slices*
2 teaspoons salt	*1/4 cup vinegar*
1 teaspoon freshly ground black pepper	*Mustard Sauce (page 216) or prepared horseradish (optional)*
2 teaspoons curry powder	

Using a meat grinder or food processor fitted with the metal blade, grind fresh pork, ham, garlic clove and onion. Do not puree or process too fine. Add 1 teaspoon of the salt, pepper, curry powder and sage; grind again. Stir egg white and half and half or milk into meat mixture. Shape meat mixture into an oval loaf about 8 × 4 inches. Arrange bacon slices along the center of a piece of cheesecloth about 14 × 10 inches. Fold cheesecloth tightly around the loaf and secure with butcher's string.

Bring about 4 quarts water to a boil in a large stockpot. Add vinegar and remaining 1 teaspoon salt. Gently add meat loaf to water. Return to a boil. Cover and simmer 2 1/2 hours over medium-low heat. Remove meat loaf. Cool, pressing meat beneath a weight to flatten surface of loaf. Refrigerate overnight. Serve chilled, sliced, with Mustard Sauce or horseradish, or serve reheated as a main dish.

Stuffed Baked Ham

Gefüllter Schincken

This distinctive way to prepare baked ham will prove to be a hit at any party or social gathering you host. And it's simple to do. *Makes 6 to 8 servings.*

3 lbs. lean boneless ham
1/2 lb. bulk breakfast or pork
    sausage
1 small onion, finely chopped
1 egg
1/2 cup soft bread crumbs
2 tablespoons finely chopped fresh
    parsley

1 teaspoon finely chopped fresh leaf
    marjoram
1 teaspoon finely chopped fresh thyme
1/2 teaspoon salt
1/4 teaspoon freshly ground black
    pepper
1 tablespoon olive oil
1 teaspoon sweet ground paprika

With a sharp knife, cut two pockets in ham, from top of ham down, perpendicular to one another, without cutting through bottom or sides of ham. Cut about 3/4 inch of ham from each pocket. Using a meat grinder or food processor fitted with the metal blade, process ham that was removed from pockets with sausage. Do not puree or process too fine.

Preheat oven to 350F (175C). In a large bowl, combine ham and sausage, onion, egg, bread crumbs, parsley, marjoram, thyme, salt and pepper. Stuff ham pockets with ham and sausage mixture. Rub ham with oil and sprinkle with paprika. Place stuffed ham in a baking dish. Cover ham with foil and bake 1 hour. Remove foil; bake 20 more minutes or until top of ham browns and stuffing is cooked. Serve sliced, hot or cold.

Baked Sliced Ham

Geschnittener Bratschinken

Before cooking the ham slices, score edges of each ham slice by cutting 2 inches toward center in three places on each slice so ham will not curl up while cooking.
Makes 8 servings.

2 (2-inch-thick) center-cut ham slices	2 cups Chicken Broth (page 57)
6 medium onions	or chicken bouillon
2 red bell peppers	6 whole cloves
3 tablespoons butter or margarine	1 tablespoon ground sweet paprika
1/4 cup packed brown sugar	

Preheat oven to 350F (175C). Arrange ham slices in a shallow roasting pan so both slices are flat. Remove skins from onions and slice onions crosswise into thirds, keeping their rings intact. Remove stems and seeds from bell peppers and cut peppers into large chunks. Arrange onions and peppers around ham slices with flat sides of onions face down in roasting pan. Equally dab butter or margarine on top of onions, then spoon brown sugar evenly on top of onions, next to butter or margarine. Carefully pour broth or bouillon into roasting pan. Add cloves. Sprinkle paprika over ham slices. Cover with a tight-fitting lid and bake 1 hour or until onions are tender. Uncover; bake 10 more minutes. Serve hot, with cooked vegetables and juices.

Variation
Serve ham slices with Cumberland Sauce (page 176).

Cumberland Sauce

Cumberlandsosse

Serve with ham slices or over roast pheasant, turkey or duck. *Makes about 1 1/2 cups.*

1 large orange	1/4 cup apple juice or cider
6 tablespoons red wine	2 teaspoons prepared mustard
1/4 cup currant jelly	1/8 teaspoon ground cinnamon

Grate orange peel into a medium saucepan. Squeeze juice from orange; set aside. Add wine to peel; cook over medium heat 3 minutes. Add jelly, orange juice, apple juice or cider, mustard and ground cinnamon. Beat with a wire whisk until frothy. Pour into a small serving bowl.

Hot Ham Rolls with Asparagus

Heisse Schinkenrolle mit Spargel

If possible, select at least some slender asparagus stalks. Then arrange one slender stalk with two larger ones for each ham roll. *Makes 8 servings.*

Béchamel Sauce (page 108)	1 teaspoon ground white pepper
24 asparagus spears	3 tablespoons chopped fresh parsley
4 center-cut ham slices	

Prepare Béchamel Sauce; set aside. Preheat oven to 350F (175C). Lightly grease a baking dish. Rinse asparagus under cold running water; pat dry. Snap off and discard tough bottoms of asparagus. Cut center-cut ham slices in half. Place 3 asparagus spears on each half of ham slice. Sprinkle white pepper over asparagus and ham. Roll ham slices, jelly-roll style, so asparagus spears are in center, with tips of asparagus protruding from rolled ham slice. Secure individual rolled ham slices with wooden picks. Arrange ham and asparagus rolls in greased baking dish. Pour sauce over rolls. Bake, covered, 40 minutes or until asparagus is tender. Garnish with parsley and serve immediately.

Ham & Noodle Casserole

Schinken-Nudelpfanne

Thrifty cooks will save bits and pieces from other baked ham dishes and use them in this casserole. Bits of baked ham that have absorbed cooking juices will have additional flavor. *Makes 6 servings.*

1 tablespoon vegetable oil
2 1/2 cups diced ham
2 tablespoons butter or margarine
2 tablespoons all-purpose flour
1 cup half and half
1 cup (4 oz.) shredded Cheddar
  cheese

1 1/2 tablespoons prepared
  horseradish
3 cups cooked Homemade Noodles
  (page 93)
1/2 cup cooked frozen green peas
1/2 cup dry bread crumbs
1 teaspoon sweet ground paprika

Preheat oven to 350F (175C). Grease a baking dish. Heat oil in a medium skillet over medium heat. Add ham; sauté until browned. Set aside. Melt butter or margarine in a medium saucepan over medium-low heat. Add flour, stirring to form a smooth paste. Stir in half and half; cook, stirring constantly, until a smooth, thick sauce forms. Slowly mix cheese into flour mixture, stirring until cheese melts. Stir horseradish into cheese sauce.

In a medium bowl, toss together noodles, ham and peas. Arrange 1/2 cup noodle mixture in greased dish, then pour or spoon half of the cheese sauce over noodle mixture. Top with remaining noodle mixture. Pour or spoon remaining sauce evenly over noodles, ham and peas. Sprinkle bread crumbs and paprika over sauce. Bake, uncovered, 40 minutes or until thoroughly heated and browned on top. Serve hot.

Pig's Feet

Schweinsfusse

If desired, pig's knuckles can also be used for this recipe, which is hugely popular when served with sauerkraut, grilled sausages and German rye bread. *Makes about 18 servings.*

5 lbs. pig's feet, split lengthwise	15 black peppercorns
1 lb. pork shanks	3 bay leaves
1 lb. veal with bone	1 tablespoon salt
3 1/2 qts. water	Fancy lettuce leaves
4 medium carrots	Lemon juice or vinegar to taste

Place pig's feet, pork shanks and veal in a stockpot. Add water; bring to a boil over medium-high heat. Boil, uncovered, 10 minutes. Skim off surface foam with a slotted spoon. Reduce heat to low. Add carrots, peppercorns, bay leaves and salt. Simmer, uncovered, 4 1/2 to 5 hours or until meat can be easily removed from bones. Strain cooking liquid into a large saucepan. Let meat and bones cool. Remove meat from bones; discard bones. Cut meat into cubes or pieces about 1/2 inch long. Thinly slice cooked carrots. Arrange equal amounts of meat and carrots in about 18 individual serving cups or dishes. Pour cooking liquid to cover in each cup or dish. Refrigerate until liquid sets.

To serve, remove thin layer of congealed fat from chilled dishes. Line small serving plates with lettuce leaves. Turn out each individual portion onto lettuce-lined serving dishes, briefly dipping cup or dish outer surface in warm water if necessary. Sprinkle with a little lemon juice or vinegar to taste.

Roast Leg of Lamb

Gebratene Lammkeule

The mustard coating on this roast provides a distinctive touch—for both flavor and appearance. *Makes 10 to 12 servings.*

1 (6- to 7-lb.) leg of lamb	1/2 teaspoon ground cloves
2 garlic cloves, cut into 6 pieces each	1 (5- to 6-oz.) jar Dijon mustard
1/4 cup salt	1/2 cup sherry
1 tablespoon freshly ground black pepper	1/2 cup Chicken Broth (page 57) or chicken bouillon
1 teaspoon sugar	1/2 cup water

Preheat oven to 350F (175C). Carefully trim as much fat as possible from lamb. Using a sharp knife, cut about 12 (1-inch-deep × 1-inch-wide) slits on top and sides of lamb. Insert pieces of garlic into slits. In a small bowl, combine salt, pepper, sugar and cloves. Spread salt mixture all over roast, evenly rubbing it on with your hands. Using a flexible spatula or wide-blade knife, carefully spread mustard in a thin, smooth coat on sides and top of lamb, spreading like a thin layer of frosting.

Place lamb on a rack in a roasting pan. Add sherry, broth or bouillon and water. Cover with a tight-fitting lid; bake 2 hours, basting every 15 minutes with cooking juices. Remove cover. Bake 30 minutes to 1 hour more, continuing to baste every 15 minutes, until lamb is tender or degree of doneness reached. If needed, add enough water to keep at least 1 cup cooking juices in roasting pan throughout the cooking time.

To serve, remove roast and arrange on a platter. Slice individual portions as needed. Strain cooking juices and serve alongside lamb in a gravy bowl.

Lamb Kebabs

Lamm Kebab

Start this recipe very early in the day, or better yet, the day before, so the lamb has plenty of time in the marinade. *Makes 4 to 6 servings.*

1/3 cup red wine vinegar	3 lbs. lean lamb, cut into 1- to
3 tablespoons olive oil	1 1/2-inch pieces
2 garlic cloves, crushed	1 lb. fresh mushrooms, whole if small,
1 teaspoon crumbled dried marjoram	or cut into bite-size pieces if large
1 teaspoon salt	2 green bell peppers, cut into chunks
1/2 teaspoon freshly ground black	1 red bell pepper, cut into chunks
pepper	2 sweet red onions, cut into chunks

Combine vinegar, oil, garlic, marjoram, salt and pepper in a large, shallow glass bowl. Add lamb pieces; mix well. Cover and refrigerate overnight, mixing occasionally.

Preheat an outdoor barbecue or a broiler. Drain lamb, reserving marinade in a small bowl. Thread lamb alternately with mushrooms and chunks of green pepper, red pepper and onion on 4 to 6 metal skewers. Brush uncooked kebabs with marinade. Place kebabs 4 to 5 inches from heat source. Cook 10 to 12 minutes per side or to desired level of doneness, brushing with marinade every few minutes. Serve hot.

Lamb Stew

Lammeintopf

This may sound like a lot of work, but it's really not. There are just a lot of small steps in making a great stew. *Makes 8 to 10 servings.*

3 lbs. lamb	1 garlic clove, crushed
1/4 cup all-purpose flour	1 tablespoon chopped fresh parsley
1 teaspoon salt	1 teaspoon rosemary
1/3 teaspoon freshly ground black pepper	1 bay leaf
1/4 teaspoon onion powder	1 cup thickly sliced carrots
3 tablespoons vegetable oil	2 tablespoons butter or margarine
1/2 cup dry white wine	12 small white onions
2 cups drained canned tomatoes	1 tablespoon sugar
1 1/2 cups Chicken Broth (page 57) or chicken bouillon	10 small new potatoes
1/2 cup chopped celery	1/2 cup (1/2-inch pieces) green beans
	1/2 cup frozen green peas
	Rice or noodles to serve

Preheat oven to 350F (175C). Cut lamb into bite-size pieces. Combine flour, salt, pepper and onion powder in a shallow bowl. Place lamb pieces in flour mixture; mix until lamb pieces are evenly coated. Heat oil in a large skillet over medium heat. Add flour-coated lamb; sauté until browned on all sides, about 10 minutes. Remove browned lamb and arrange in a large casserole dish. Add wine to cooking juices in skillet; cook over low heat 2 minutes, stirring. Pour wine and cooking juices over lamb. Arrange tomatoes, broth or bouillon, celery, garlic, parsley, rosemary and bay leaf in casserole dish with lamb. Cover with a tight-fitting lid; bake 1 1/2 hours.

Remove lamb from oven. Uncover and let cool to warm. Skim off surface fat from pan juices. Bring 3 inches salted water to a boil in a small saucepan. Add carrots. Return to a boil; cook 5 minutes, then drain.

Melt butter or margarine in a small skillet over medium heat. Add onions; sauté until almost tender, about 10 minutes. Sprinkle onions with 1/2 tablespoon of the sugar; cook 2 more minutes or until golden brown. Remove cooked onions from skillet and set aside. Place carrots in same skillet; sprinkle with remaining 1/2 tablespoon sugar. Sauté carrots until lightly browned. Add onions and carrots to lamb. Gently stir potatoes into casserole. Cover and bake 40 more minutes.

In a small saucepan, cook beans in boiling water 5 minutes. Drain cooked beans and add beans and peas to casserole. Bake 30 more minutes or until beans are tender. Remove bay leaf. Serve hot with rice or noodles.

Lamb in Sour Cream Sauce

Lamm in Cremesosse

Except when browning lamb at the beginning of this recipe, remember to keep cooking temperatures low so the meat won't cook too quickly. Slow cooking will result in a meat that's as tender and flavorful as possible. *Makes 6 to 8 servings.*

2 tablespoons butter or margarine
1 (4- to 4 1/2-lb.) lamb shoulder
2 medium onions, thinly sliced
1 cup Chicken Broth (page 57)
   or chicken bouillon
1/4 cup dry red wine

2 tablespoons ground sweet paprika
1 teaspoon salt
1/2 teaspoon freshly ground black
   pepper
1 1/2 cups sour cream
3 tablespoons chopped fresh parsley

Preheat oven to 350F (175C). Melt butter or margarine in a Dutch oven over medium-high heat. Add lamb. Cook, uncovered, 10 minutes, browning all sides. Remove lamb; set aside. Add onions, broth or bouillon, wine, paprika, salt and pepper to cooking juices. Cover with a tight-fitting lid and simmer over low heat 10 minutes, stirring occasionally. Add lamb. Cover and bake 1 hour or until lamb is tender.

Remove lamb from Dutch oven; keep warm. Let cooking juices cool slightly. Mix sour cream in a small saucepan. Strain about 2 tablespoons cooking juices from Dutch oven into saucepan with sour cream; stir to combine. Strain remaining cooking juices into sour-cream mixture; stir to combine. Simmer over low heat, stirring, until hot; do not boil. Slice lamb and arrange on a warm platter. Spoon hot sauce over sliced lamb. Sprinkle parsley over lamb and sauce. Serve hot.

Curried Lamb

Lamm mit Curry

This savory dish is traditionally served on a bed of hot cooked rice. Good accompaniments include chopped hard-cooked eggs, sweet pickles, crispy bacon bits and even slivered almonds. *Makes 4 to 6 servings.*

1/4 cup all-purpose flour
1 lb. lean lamb, cut into bite-size
    pieces
2 tablespoons vegetable oil
1/2 cup thinly sliced carrots
1 medium onion, chopped
1/2 cup chopped celery root or celery
1 garlic clove, minced
1 cup Beef Broth (page 58), Veal
    Broth (page 60) or beef bouillon

2 tablespoons curry powder
1 teaspoon salt
1/2 teaspoon freshly ground black
    pepper
1/2 teaspoon ground thyme
1 bay leaf
6 to 8 cups cooked rice
2 medium tomatoes, peeled and
    chopped

Place flour in a shallow dish. Add lamb pieces, mixing until evenly coated with flour. Heat oil in a large skillet over medium-high heat. Add flour-coated lamb; sauté 7 to 8 minutes or until all sides are browned. Reduce heat to medium. Add carrots, onion, celery root or celery and garlic; sauté 5 minutes, stirring. Add broth or bouillon, curry powder, salt, pepper, thyme and bay leaf. Cover with a tight-fitting lid; simmer 1 hour or until all vegetables are tender.

While lamb is cooking, prepare rice. Gently stir tomatoes into lamb mixture. Cover and simmer 10 minutes. Remove bay leaf. To serve, spoon hot lamb, vegetables and juices over rice.

Veal

❦

Kalb

*A*fter poultry and pork, veal is the next most popular meat in Germany, just ahead of beef. The Germans like veal's light, delicate flavor and the way it marries with whatever herbs or seasonings are used to flavor it. But they also recognize that veal is a lean meat, with little marbling or fat in the young white to light-pink meat, that if not carefully watched, can easily be overcooked and dried out.

Many German families living on small or large farms, or even in homes on the outskirts of larger towns and cities, own at least one milk cow. The milk cows bear calves, which helps increase the cows' milk-producing abilities and also provides a steady source of fresh veal.

There are distinct differences between the ways that Germans and other Europeans cut veal and how Americans do it. European butchers tend to separate the meat into the various muscles that the meat parts naturally consist of. Separating individual muscles at their seams results in smaller cuts of solid meat—smaller roasts and membrane-free slices for cutlets. Although the purchase price for European-style veal cuts may be higher, it's because the cuts are pure meat, waste-free.

American-style cutting, on the other hand, is not as precise. It doesn't take into account the natural contours and component muscles of the meat. Instead of finding veal pared down into small roasts or cutlets, veal steaks or larger roasts are produced with band saws. Whole slices are cut from the leg, for instance. The slices, including portions of the sirloin tip, the top round, the bottom round and the eye of the round, are all stretch-wrapped as one large piece. To successfully process meat this way—especially veal—the meat has to be fully chilled.

Beyond the way it is cut, veal in Germany is prepared in a manner similar to that of many pork dishes. First of all, boneless slices and thin cuts of veal leg or loin are pounded with a meat mallet or the flat side of a cleaver into the famous cutlets. The story of *Wiener Schnitzel,* tender veal breaded with a crust of crispy egg and bread crumbs, is by itself unique. Back in the fifteenth century, in the homes of northern Italian aristocrats, it was customary to eat dishes covered by an incredibly thin layer of gold foil. Why gold foil? Because physicians of the day strongly believed that gold—since it never tarnished—possessed healing properties which could strengthen the heart and other vital organs. The practice became so popular that it threatened to completely deplete the country's gold supply, so eventually the leaders in Venice banned the use of gold foil in cooking. However, chefs of the time were not to be denied; instead they produced an imitation gold foil with a mixture of eggs and white bread crumbs that was applied to the veal cutlets and sautéed until golden. Years later, in Vienna, cooks found that by dipping the veal lightly in flour first, the coating adhered to the veal much more strongly. Thus evolved the "perfect" *Wiener Schnitzel.*

Other veal dishes, just as delicious if not as famous, include stews and roasts. Veal Paprika (opposite) is a zesty dish of bite-size veal pieces sautéed with garlic and onion, then cooked with paprika and the mild flavors from white wine, chicken broth or bouillon and sour cream. Veal Goulash (page 186) is flavored with sweet tomato paste, fresh tomatoes, red bell peppers and onions. Stuffed Breast of Veal (page 188) features a bread and mushroom filling seasoned with parsley, nutmeg and marjoram. Stuffed Veal Chops are a unique alternative to the standard stuffed pork-chop dinner and yet another stuffed roast, Stuffed Veal Roast (page 192), with the filling stuffed into the indentations left by removing the ribs from a veal rib roast.

Veal Paprika

Kalbspaprika

Although paprika is the national spice of Hungary, the Germans have it, too. Paprika is the dried powder of a sweet, mostly mild red pepper. Hotter varieties are available, but in any case, the best paprikas come from Hungary. Unfortunately, sometimes household cooks buy large quantities that they don't use fast enough. Paprika, even when refrigerated in airtight containers, eventually turns bitter as it ages. Taste yours before you season this recipe. If it's a dingy brown color and doesn't taste sweet, it's time to replenish your supply. *Makes 6 servings.*

2 1/2 lbs. veal shoulder	2 tablespoons chopped parsley
3 tablespoons vegetable oil	1 cup dry white wine
2 garlic cloves, crushed	1 cup Chicken Broth (page 57) or
2 large onions, sliced	chicken bouillon
1 tablespoon ground sweet paprika	2 tablespoons cornstarch
1 teaspoon salt	2 tablespoons cold water
1/2 teaspoon freshly ground black	1 cup sour cream
pepper	

Cut veal into bite-size pieces. Heat oil in a large skillet over medium-high heat. Add garlic; sauté until browned, stirring constantly, about 2 minutes. Remove garlic from skillet; discard. Reduce heat to medium. Add veal; sauté veal until evenly browned, about 10 minutes. Add onions; cook, stirring occasionally, until onions are tender, about 5 minutes. Stir paprika, salt, pepper and parsley into veal and onion mixture. Reduce heat to low. Add wine; cover with a tight-fitting lid. Simmer 45 minutes or until veal is tender. Add a little of the broth or bouillon if more juices are needed.

In a small bowl, blend cornstarch with the cold water. Stir remaining broth or bouillon into cornstarch mixture. Add to veal and onions; cook until thickened, stirring frequently. Stir sour cream into veal and onions, gently mixing to combine. Heat until hot, but do not allow the cooking juices to boil. Serve veal hot, with onions and cooking juices.

Veal Goulash

Kalbsgulasch

Make sure when sautéing the veal that you keep it from burning. Veal is on the lean side. Because it's so tender and there's so little fat throughout the muscles, it's very sensitive to heat and won't stand up well to higher temperatures. *Makes 8 to 10 servings.*

2 lbs. lean veal, from shoulder, leg, or breast

2 tablespoons vegetable oil

1 large onion, chopped

2 cups Veal Broth (page 60), Chicken Broth (page 57) or chicken bouillon

3/4 teaspoon ground sweet paprika

1/2 teaspoon freshly ground black pepper

1/4 teaspoon ground sage

2 medium red bell peppers, sliced into 1/2-inch strips

2 medium tomatoes, cut into wedges

1 tablespoon tomato paste

1 1/4 cups red wine

1/4 cup water

1 tablespoon cornstarch

1/2 teaspoon salt

Noodles, potatoes, Potato Pancakes (page 130) or rice to serve

Cut veal into 1/2-inch cubes. Heat oil in a large skillet over medium-high heat. Add veal and onions; sauté until veal browns on all sides, about 10 minutes. Place browned veal and onions in a large saucepan. Add broth or bouillon, paprika, pepper and sage. Cover and cook over medium heat 1 hour.

Add bell peppers, tomatoes and tomato paste; stir gently. Cover and cook 10 minutes. Add wine. Cover and simmer over low heat 10 minutes. In a small cup, blend water and cornstarch until smooth. Stir into meat mixture. Season with salt. Bring to a boil and cook, stirring, until slightly thickened, about 5 minutes. Serve hot over noodles, potatoes, potato pancakes or rice.

Veal Fricassee

Kalbsfrikassee

After you try this dish with veal, substitute chicken the next time, just for variety's sake. Keep everything else in the recipe the same. *Makes 6 to 8 servings.*

2 tablespoons vegetable oil

2 1/2 to 3 lbs. boneless veal shoulder
  or leg, cut into bite-size pieces

1 medium onion, chopped

About 3 cups Chicken Broth (page
  57) or chicken bouillon

1 teaspoon salt

1/2 teaspoon freshly ground black
  pepper

1/4 teaspoon ground cloves

2 carrots, sliced

2 celery stalks, sliced

1 cup sliced fresh mushrooms

1 tablespoon chopped fresh parsley

2 tablespoons butter or margarine

2 tablespoons all-purpose flour

Juice of 1/2 lemon

Rice, boiled potatoes or noodles to
  serve

Heat oil in a large skillet over medium-high heat. Add veal; sauté 6 to 8 minutes or until browned on all sides. Remove veal; set aside. Add onion to skillet; sauté over medium heat until tender, about 10 minutes. Add broth or bouillon, salt, pepper, cloves, carrots, celery and browned veal. Cover with a tight-fitting lid; simmer over medium-low heat, 30 minutes. Add mushrooms and parsley. Cover and simmer 10 more minutes.

Melt butter or margarine in a small saucepan over low heat. Slowly stir in flour; cook, stirring constantly, until flour mixture turns a golden color. Remove veal and vegetables from heat. Carefully drain cooking juices into a medium bowl. If needed, add enough additional broth or bouillon to drained cooking juices to make 2 cups. Slowly add cooking juices to flour mixture, stirring over medium-low heat until thickened. Stir sauce and lemon juice into cooled veal and vegetables; cook, covered, over medium-low heat 10 minutes. Serve hot, over rice, boiled potatoes, or noodles.

Stuffed Breast of Veal

Gefüllte Kalbsbrust

When shopping for veal, consider that the best cuts are tender, moist and a white to pale pink color. Veal that's red or turning red is likely to come from an older, tougher animal. Older veal can be improved somewhat by soaking it in milk in the refrigerator overnight. *Makes 6 to 8 servings.*

10 slices day-old bread

1 cup milk

2 tablespoons butter or margarine

1 small onion, minced

1 cup chopped fresh mushrooms

2 eggs, lightly beaten

1 tablespoon chopped fresh parsley

1 teaspoon ground nutmeg

1 teaspoon salt

1/2 teaspoon dried leaf marjoram

1/2 teaspoon freshly ground black
    pepper

3 tablespoons vegetable oil

1 (5-lb.) breast of veal with deep
    pocket cut next to bone for stuffing

1 cup Beef Broth (page 58) or beef
    bouillon

3/4 cup dry white wine

1 bay leaf

Soak bread in milk in a large shallow bowl. Squeeze out excess milk. Melt butter or margarine in a small skillet over medium heat. Add onion and mushrooms; sauté until onion is tender, about 5 minutes. Let onions and mushrooms cool.

In a large bowl, combine bread, onion, mushrooms, eggs, parsley, nutmeg, salt, marjoram and pepper. Mix well. Fill veal pocket with stuffing mixture. Close opening with wooden or metal skewers. Lightly rub outside of veal with salt and pepper.

Preheat oven to 350F (175C). Heat oil in a Dutch oven over medium-high heat. Add veal; brown veal on all sides, about 10 minutes. Gently add broth or bouillon, wine and bay leaf. Cover and bake 2 1/2 to 3 hours or until veal is tender. Discard bay leaf. To serve, slice into individual portions and place on warmed platter. Spoon cooking juices, onions and mushrooms over stuffed-veal slices. Serve hot.

Stuffed Veal Chops

Gefüllte Kalbskoteletts

If possible, ask your butcher to cut the pockets into the veal chops for you. Explain that you'll be stuffing the chops and you want them thick enough to stuff, at least 1 inch thick. *Makes 6 servings.*

3 slices white bread

3 tablespoons butter or margarine

3/4 cup chopped spinach

3 tablespoons chopped chives

3 (1/2-inch-thick) veal liver slices, finely chopped

1 medium boneless veal chop, chopped

3 tablespoons white wine

3 tablespoons half and half

1 teaspoon salt

1/2 teaspoon freshly ground black pepper

1/4 teaspoon ground nutmeg

1/3 cup all-purpose flour

6 thick veal chops, each with a pocket sliced horizontally into chop from edge

2 tablespoons vegetable oil

2 tablespoons chopped fresh parsley

Slice bread into 1/2-inch cubes. Melt 2 tablespoons of the butter or margarine in a medium skillet over medium heat. Add bread cubes; sauté until all sides are lightly browned, about 10 minutes. Remove bread cubes and reserve in a medium bowl. Add spinach and chives to same cooking skillet; sauté 3 to 4 minutes, stirring, until chives are almost tender. Add spinach and chives to sautéed bread cubes. Melt remaining 1 tablespoon butter or margarine in juices in skillet. Add chopped liver and chopped veal; sauté over medium heat until browned.

In a medium bowl, combine browned liver and veal, wine, half and half, salt, pepper and nutmeg. Add chopped liver mixture to bread mixture; toss together. Set stuffing mixture aside.

Spread flour in a shallow dish; lightly press a veal chop into flour so an even coat of flour adheres to chop; repeat with other side of veal chop. Repeat process with remaining veal chops. Heat oil in a large skillet over medium-high heat. Add veal chops; brown on both sides, about 5 minutes per side. Let cool slightly.

Preheat oven to 350F (175C). Stuff chops with spinach mixture; secure pocket openings with wooden picks. Arrange stuffed chops in a shallow baking dish and bake, uncovered, 1 to 1 1/2 hours or until tender. Garnish with chopped parsley. Serve hot.

Viennese Breaded Cutlets

Wiener Schnitzel

This is one of those Germanic dishes that's been intimately tied to German cuisine. Indeed, Americans are more familiar with the German name of the recipe, *Wiener Schnitzel*, than with its English name. *Makes 6 to 8 servings.*

2 lbs. veal cutlets	*2 cups dry bread crumbs*
Salt	*About 1/2 cup peanut or vegetable oil,*
Freshly ground black pepper	*or butter or margarine, or*
3 eggs, lightly beaten	*combination thereof*

Place cutlets between 2 sheets of plastic wrap. Using a meat mallet, pound cutlets to 1/8-inch thickness, with a sliding action instead of a straight up-and-down motion, turning cutlets once. Sprinkle tenderized cutlets lightly with salt and pepper. Spread flour in a shallow dish. Place beaten eggs in a shallow bowl and bread crumbs in another shallow bowl. Dip both sides of a cutlet in flour, so sides are evenly coated. Dip floured cutlet in beaten egg. Let excess egg drip from cutlet, then dip both sides of cutlet in bread crumbs, pressing bread crumbs evenly onto cutlet. Repeat breading process with remaining cutlets. Place breaded cutlets on a wire rack; let stand at room temperature 20 to 30 minutes.

Preheat oven to 250F (120C). Heat 2 tablespoons oil, butter or margarine, or a combination thereof in a large skillet over medium heat. Add several breaded cutlets; do not crowd pan. Cook 4 to 5 minutes on each side, or until both sides are golden brown. Place cooked cutlets on an ovenproof platter or pan; keep hot in oven while cooking remaining cutlets. Repeat process with remaining breaded cutlets, adding oil, butter or margarine to skillet as needed. Do not cover the cooked cutlets in the oven, or their crispy coatings will soften. Serve hot.

Variations

Schnitzel á la Holstein Place a fried egg on top of each cutlet and lay 2 anchovy fillets in the shape of a cross over each egg. Add 5 or 6 well-drained capers near each pair of anchovies. Serve hot.

Cheese Schnitzel Bread cutlets with a mixture of 1 cup bread crumbs and 1 cup grated Parmesan cheese instead of 2 cups bread crumbs. While cutlets are cooking on second side in skillet, place 1 thin slice of Emmentaler cheese over top of each cutlet, then sprinkle a little chopped fresh parsley or ground sweet paprika over cheese. Serve hot, when cheese melts.

Note

The best veal cutlets come from the round muscle of the leg, sliced at a slight angle across the grain, with connective tissues removed and any membranes removed or at least scored to prevent the cutlet from curling while cooking. Other cuts of veal can supply this recipe, too, as long as they can be trimmed in similar fashion and they can take the pounding needed to flatten them out and tenderize them.

Viennese Breaded Cutlets

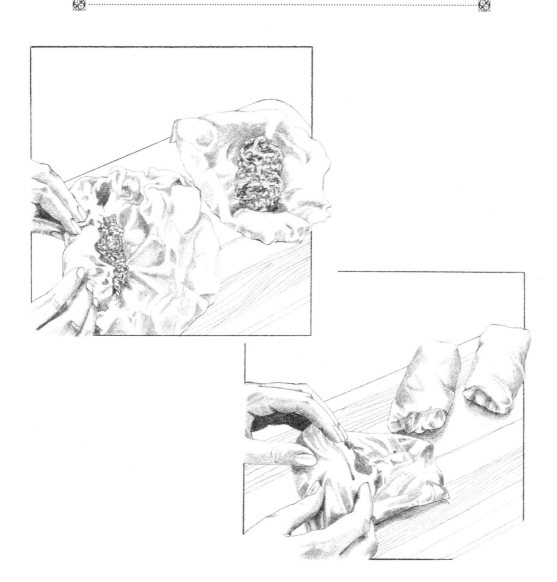

Stuffed Veal Roast

Gefüllte Kalbfleisch Braten

The flavorful stuffing is kept moist in pockets covered with slices of bacon. *Makes 6 to 8 servings.*

1 (4 1/2- to 5-lb.) veal rib roast, with
  bones
2 large day-old rolls
1/2 cup milk
1 tablespoon butter or margarine
10 oz. veal liver, chopped
1/2 cup chopped fresh mushrooms
1/2 lb. bacon slices
2 large onions, finely chopped
2 eggs, lightly beaten

1 teaspoon salt
1/2 teaspoon freshly ground black
  pepper
1/2 teaspoon ground nutmeg
Dried leaf marjoram
1 cup Chicken Broth (page 57) or
  chicken bouillon
Red Wine Sauce (opposite)
  (optional) to serve

Using a sharp, thin-bladed knife, carefully bone roast. Arrange bones in the center of a roasting pan. Break rolls into pieces. Soak rolls in milk in a medium bowl. Lightly squeeze excess milk from roll pieces. Finely chop squeezed rolls.

Melt butter or margarine in a medium skillet over medium heat. Add liver and mushrooms; sauté, stirring, until liver is tender, about 5 minutes; do not overcook. Finely chop half of bacon slices. Place chopped bacon in a large skillet over medium heat; sauté until crisp. Drain excess bacon fat. Add onions to sautéed bacon in skillet. Reduce heat to medium-low. Sauté until onions are tender, stirring frequently, about 5 minutes. Reduce heat to low. Add eggs, salt, pepper, nutmeg, mushroom mixture and chopped rolls to skillet; stir to combine.

Preheat oven to 350F (175C). Gently press equal amounts of the stuffing mixture into indentations in roast where bones were removed. Place roast, stuffing side up, on top of bones in roasting pan. Arrange remaining bacon slices on roast so they cover most of the stuffing mixture. Sprinkle with salt, pepper and marjoram. Add broth or bouillon to bottom of roasting pan. Cover with a tight-fitting lid; roast 2 to 2 1/2 hours or until tender. Remove lid. Roast 10 minutes.

Remove roast from oven and let stand 10 minutes. Strain cooking juices into a small serving dish; spoon off grease. Slice roast and place on a warm serving platter. Serve hot with accompanying cooking juices or with Red Wine Sauce, if desired.

Red Wine Sauce

Rotweinsosse

Serve this sauce over sliced veal roast or beef roast. *Makes about 2 cups.*

3 tablespoons butter or margarine

1 1/2 tablespoons all-purpose flour

1 1/4 cups Meat Broth (page 62)

1 1/2 tablespoons Maggi seasoning

2/3 cup red wine

3/4 teaspoon sugar

Salt

Freshly ground black pepper

Melt butter or margarine in a small skillet over medium heat. Stir in flour. Cook, stirring, until golden brown. Blend in broth and Maggi seasoning. Simmer over low heat 20 to 25 minutes, stirring frequently. Add wine and sugar. Simmer over low heat 5 minutes, stirring constantly; do not boil. Season with salt and pepper to taste.

Veal & Frankfurters

Kalbfleish und Frankfurter

Another version of this simple-to-make entree calls for a slice of beef instead of veal. *Makes 4 servings.*

1 (1 1/2-lb.) veal round steak, boned	1/8 teaspoon freshly ground black
4 frankfurters	pepper
1/4 cup butter or margarine	1 tablespoon chopped fresh parsley
1/2 cup dry white wine	1/2 cup Chicken Broth (page 57)
1/2 teaspoon salt	or chicken bouillon

Place veal slice on a work surface; pound with a meat mallet or side of a heavy cleaver into a rectangular shape about 12 × 8 inches. Place frankfurters on pounded veal, lining 2 frankfurters up lengthwise on each long half of veal slice. Carefully roll up long side of veal slice, jelly-roll style, so frankfurters are at center of veal roll. Tie rolled veal with butcher's string.

Melt butter or margarine in a large skillet over medium heat. Add veal roll. Lightly brown on all sides, about 15 minutes. Add wine; cook until wine is almost gone. Sprinkle veal with salt, pepper and parsley. Add broth or bouillon. Cover with a tight-fitting lid. Reduce heat to low. Simmer 1 1/2 hours or until tender. If too much juice remains, remove cover and cook over medium-high heat until juices are reduced. Remove veal; let cool 6 to 8 minutes. Slice veal; arrange slices on a warm serving platter. Spoon cooking juices over veal slices. Serve hot.

Beef

Rind

Where's the beef? Yes, it is in Germany. But unlike in the United States, beef is not the top meat. It follows the current German leaders, pork and chicken, and lines up closely behind veal.

Beef fits nicely with the new healthy eating revolution that's ongoing throughout Germany. Germans have always associated beef with strength—the power and musculature of beef on the hoof. The massive strength of the bull or, in this case, the steer. If there is one thing that Germans believe in, it's the importance of healthy, fit and strong bodies. Lean beef is indeed a recognized source of protein, iron, vitamins and other nutrients. Beef, as the beef marketers are fond of saying, is high in quality and quantity of protein. It also provides numerous B vitamins that help strengthen and improve vision, appetite, healthy skin and the nervous system.

Throughout Germany, beef is most likely to make a dining-room appearance as thick slices of round or flank steak that have been slowly marinated and cooked in vinegar or red wine and spices and other seasonings such as black peppercorns, bay leaves and cloves, in a recipe known as *Sauerbraten*. As you travel from region to region within Germany, the ingredients in *Sauerbraten* will often change. Rhinelanders, for instance, traditionally have given their beef a sweet-and-sour flavor by adding seedless golden raisins during the cooking process. Bavarians to the south add sour cream or tomato sauce for a tangy result.

Ground beef is prepared in beef patties and various fillings for dumplings and other dishes. When combined with pork or veal, it helps create a huge variety of sausages and a smaller number of loaf-style entrees.

German cooks believe that there's something special about foods prepared with stuffings or fillings: a particular combination can make for a more aromatic, more delectable and more striking dish than can any of the individual components on their own. Or to say it another way, the completed dish can be far more appealing than the mere sum of its ingredients. All told, a stuffed or filled entree is a convenient, compact dish, one that can be served up without a lot of accompaniments and fanfare. Thus, slices of lean beef are often tenderized with a meat mallet, then rolled jelly-roll style along with tasty fillings made of vegetables or other ingredients. The rolls are simmered in flavorful broths, then served hot with a Mushroom Sauce (page 131) or other accompaniment or chilled and sliced as sandwich fillings or appetizers.

Stuffed beef rolls lend themselves to advance preparation for convenient dining or reheating at a later date. Due to the very nature of the dish, the stuffing or filling is encased by a more durable material—in this case, beef—so what is surrounded stays moist and succulent. This technique, in turn, also helps prevent the beef from losing natural flavors and juices.

Beef is also cooked slowly with mushrooms, onions and other vegetables, in numerous one-pot dishes. In bite-size pieces, beef is used alone or is combined with similar chunks of pork to make Bavarian or Hungarian goulashes, which are served hot over noodles, dumplings, rice or potato pancakes.

Even beef bones and meat scraps are important to German cooking. They form the basis of many rich beef broths, which are often used in the preparation of soups, sauces and gravies.

Also popular in Germany is liver, the most preferred type of which is young, tender calf liver.

Tips for Preparing Beef

- For average servings, allow 3/4 to 1 pound beef with bone, 1/3 to 1/2 pound boneless beef or 1/4 to 1/2 pound ground beef.

- Use tongs to turn beef instead of forks, to conserve flavorful juices.

- Boneless cuts of beef, such as rib eye, tenderloin or round roasts are best sliced directly against the grain.

- Brisket of beef, a popular cut in Germany, can be sliced from two or three angles. Slices should be thin and they should be cut at a slight diagonal.

Rhineland Marinated Beef

Rheinischer Sauerbraten

To do sauerbraten "right" is to start preparing it three or four days ahead of time. It's not that big a deal though, because the marinade is what does the work—not you. For old-time sauerbraten, the watchword is *slow*: slow marinating and slow cooking does best. *Makes 8 to 10 servings.*

4 lbs. lean beef chuck, rump or round

1 teaspoon salt

1/2 teaspoon freshly ground black
   pepper

1 large onion, sliced

2 1/2 cups red wine vinegar

2 1/2 cups water

3 bay leaves

12 peppercorns

2 tablespoons granulated sugar

2 tablespoons vegetable oil

3 small carrots, peeled and thinly
   sliced

1/4 cup packed brown sugar

2 tablespoons butter or margarine

2 tablespoons all-purpose flour

1/2 cup seedless golden raisins

Potato Dumplings (page 95) or
   Potato Pancakes (page 130) to
   serve

Rub beef with salt and pepper; place in a deep glass bowl. Arrange onion slices beneath and around beef. In a medium bowl, combine vinegar, water, bay leaves, peppercorns and granulated sugar. Pour over beef and onions. Cover and place in refrigerator. Marinate 3 to 4 days, turning beef occasionally.

Remove meat and pat dry. Strain the marinade into a medium bowl; reserve marinade and onions. Heat 2 tablespoons oil in a large skillet over medium-high heat. Add beef; cook until all sides are browned, about 15 minutes. Remove beef. Add onions and carrots to skillet; reduce heat to medium. Sauté until onions and carrots are almost tender, about 10 minutes. Pour strained marinade into onions and carrots. Add brown sugar; simmer, stirring occasionally, over low heat 10 minutes.

Preheat oven to 350F (175C). Place beef in a baking dish. Pour simmered onion and carrot mixture over beef; cover and bake 3 1/2 to 4 hours or until tender. Remove beef and carefully slice for serving; keep hot. Strain the cooking juices. Melt butter or margarine in a small saucepan over medium heat. Stir flour into melted butter or margarine with a wire whisk. Cook, stirring, until flour turns golden. Add strained marinade and raisins; simmer slowly until marinade thickens. Arrange sliced beef on a serving platter; pour hot marinade over beef. Serve hot with Potato Dumplings or Potato Pancakes, if desired.

Quick Marinated Beef

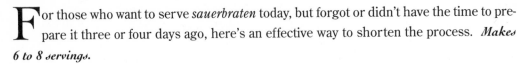

Schneller Sauerbraten

For those who want to serve *sauerbraten* today, but forgot or didn't have the time to prepare it three or four days ago, here's an effective way to shorten the process. *Makes 6 to 8 servings.*

3 1/2 to 4 lbs. beef sirloin steak
1/2 cup dry red wine
1/4 cup lemon juice
1 teaspoon salt

1/4 teaspoon freshly ground black pepper
2 tablespoons butter or margarine
1/2 cup chopped onion

Trim fat and cut steak into 6 pieces. In a large glass or ceramic casserole baking dish, combine wine, lemon juice, salt and pepper. Place beef in wine marinade. Marinate at room temperature 30 minutes, turning four times. Remove beef from marinade, reserving marinade.

Melt butter or margarine in a large skillet over medium heat. Add onion; sauté until tender, about 5 minutes. Add beef; sauté until browned on all sides, about 15 minutes. Pour marinade over beef and onions. Cover with a tight-fitting lid and cook 30 minutes or until beef reaches the desired degree of doneness. Serve immediately, accompanied by hot cooking juices.

Bavarian Goulash

Bayrischer Gulasch

This recipe is never eaten by itself. It's always served over or alongside potatoes, noodles, dumplings or even rice. Leftovers can be refrigerated up to 3 days. *Makes 6 to 8 servings.*

Potato Dumplings (page 95),
    noodles or 1 1/2 to 2 lbs. boiled
    potatoes
1/4 cup vegetable oil or butter or
    margarine
2 lbs. lean beef round, cut into 1- to
    1 1/2-inch pieces
2 large onions, chopped
2 tomatoes, peeled and chopped

1 1/2 teaspoons salt
1/4 teaspoon freshly ground black
    pepper
1 garlic clove, minced
1/8 teaspoon sweet ground paprika
1 bay leaf
2 cups Meat Broth (page 62)
2 tablespoons all-purpose flour
1/4 cup red wine

Prepare dumplings, noodles or boiled potatoes. Heat oil, butter or margarine in a large skillet over medium heat. Add beef; sauté until browned on all sides, about 15 minutes. Add onions; sauté until onions are almost tender, about 5 minutes. Add tomatoes, salt, pepper, garlic, paprika and bay leaf. Stir broth into beef mixture. Cover with a tight-fitting lid and simmer over low heat 1 to 1 1/2 hours or until beef is tender.

In a small bowl, combine 1/4 cup beef cooking juices with flour; stir until smooth. Stir flour mixture into goulash. Cook, uncovered, over low heat 20 minutes. Stir wine into goulash; cook 10 more minutes or until sauce thickens, stirring occasionally. Serve hot over potato dumplings, noodles or boiled potatoes.

Filet Mignon in Wine

Filet in Wein

A little salt, a little pepper and a little sweetness from the onions combines with the aromatic, clean flavor of red wine in sizzling steak juices. It's easy to prepare and simply superb to eat. *Makes 6 servings.*

2 tablespoons butter or margarine	*1 1/2 cups red wine*
6 (2-inch-thick) beef filet mignon	*1 1/2 teaspoons salt*
steaks (about 3 lbs. total)	*3/4 teaspoon freshly ground black*
6 small onions, peeled and halved	*pepper*

Melt butter or margarine in a large skillet over medium heat. Add steaks; sauté about 10 minutes, turning once or until browned on both sides. Reduce heat to medium-low. Add onion halves and wine. Season with salt and pepper. Cover with a tight-fitting lid; simmer steaks 30 minutes or until desired degree of doneness. Serve hot with cooked onions and some of the cooking juices, if desired.

Beef Roll

Rinderroulade

This beef roll makes a wonderful sandwich filling. Just remove from broth or bouillon and let cool. When cool, cover and refrigerate overnight. Unwrap cheesecloth and slice beef roll 3/8 to 1/2 inch thick. *Makes 6 to 8 servings.*

2 (1- to 1 1/2-lb.) beef top- or
    bottom-round steaks
1 teaspoon salt
1 teaspoon freshly ground black
    pepper
1/2 cup milk
1 1/4 cups soft bread crumbs
3 eggs
2 hard-cooked eggs, chopped
1/2 lean ground beef
1/2 lean ground pork
1/4 cup chopped fresh parsley

1/2 teaspoon dried leaf marjoram
1/4 teaspoon garlic powder
6 cups Beef Broth (page 58) or
    Meat Broth (page 62) or beef
    bouillon
2 tablespoons butter or margarine
Mushroom Sauce (page 131)
    (optional) to serve
Prepared horseradish or Beet &
    Horseradish Relish (page 44)
    (optional) to serve

Trim fat from steaks; place each steak between 2 sheets of plastic wrap. Using a meat mallet, pound each to a rectangle about 12 × 8 inches and 1/4 to 3/8 inch thick. When pounding meat, do not use a straight up-and-down movement; use a sliding action to stretch meat more than flatten. Sprinkle 1/4 teaspoon salt and 1/4 teaspoon pepper on the inner side of each steak. Roll each steak tightly.

In a medium bowl, combine milk, bread crumbs, 2 of the eggs, the hard-cooked eggs, ground beef, ground pork, parsley, marjoram, garlic powder and remaining salt and pepper. Unroll steak rectangles. In a small bowl, beat remaining egg with a fork. Brush egg over the inner side of each steak. Pat one-half of filling on each steak, making an even layer to within 1 inch from edges. Roll steaks tightly, lengthwise. Secure with wooden picks.

In a large pot, bring broth or bouillon to a boil. Place each beef roll on a 20 × 16-inch piece of cheesecloth. Tightly roll each beef roll in cheesecloth. Tie ends closed with butcher's string. Wrap string several times along lengths of beef rolls. Place beef rolls in broth or bouillon; cook, covered, over medium-high heat 1 hour. If broth or bouillon does not cover beef rolls, turn rolls every 10 minutes. Remove from broth or bouillon. Carefully unwrap cheesecloth. In a large skillet, melt butter or margarine over medium-high heat. Add beef rolls and cook until browned, about 5 minutes. Slice and serve with Mushroom Sauce, if desired. Or, if served cold, serve as an appetizer with horseradish or relish.

Beef Roll

Tender Steak

Zartes Steak

The word *savory* can be used to describe the steak in this satisfying dish. A favorite steak, soy or even pepper sauce can be substituted for the teaspoon of Maggi seasoning, if desired. *Makes 6 to 8 servings.*

8 pieces (1/2-inch-thick) lean beef round steak (about 2 lbs.)

1/4 cup vegetable oil

3 medium onions, sliced

2 cups fresh whole button mushrooms or 1 cup rehydrated dried mushrooms

1/2 cup dry red wine

2 cups Vegetable Broth (page 63) or Meat Broth (page 62) or beef bouillon

6 medium russet potatoes, peeled and halved lengthwise and sliced crosswise

1 teaspoon Maggi seasoning

Pinch of salt

1/4 cup cold water

1 tablespoon cornstarch

Place steaks between 2 sheets of plastic wrap and pound with a meat mallet about five times on each side. Heat oil in a large skillet over medium-high heat. Add steak; sauté about 10 minutes or until both sides are browned. Transfer beef to another large skillet. Add onions to skillet containing beef drippings; sauté over medium heat until tender, about 10 minutes. Add onions to steak. Place fresh mushrooms in same skillet; sauté over medium heat, about 5 minutes or until tender. If using rehydrated mushrooms, add to steak without sautéing.

Pour wine and broth or bouillon over steak, onions and mushrooms. Cover with a tight-fitting lid and simmer over low heat 30 minutes. Add potatoes, Maggi seasoning and salt. Cover and cook 30 minutes over heat low enough so that liquid does not boil. In a small bowl, blend 1/4 cup cold water and cornstarch until smooth. Gently stir into steak mixture. Cover and simmer 10 minutes over low heat. Serve steak hot with cooked onions, mushrooms, potatoes and juices.

Berlin Beef Rolls

Berliner Rinderroulade

These "personal-size" beef rolls rely on combined flavors of Dijon mustard, dill pickles, bacon and onions for a unique sit-up-and-take-notice taste. *Makes 4 to 6 servings.*

*6 slices boneless beef bottom or top
    round (about 6 × 4 × 1/3-inch
    thick)*
Salt
Freshly ground black pepper
3 tablespoons Dijon mustard

6 thin slices lean smoked bacon
3 small onions, quartered
3 dill pickles, halved lengthwise
3 tablespoons vegetable oil
*2 cups Beef Broth (page 58) or
    beef bouillon*

Trim fat from beef slices; place each slice between 2 sheets of plastic wrap. Using a meat mallet, pound each beef slice five times on each side. Remove plastic wrap; evenly sprinkle salt and pepper over inner sides of beef slices. Spread mustard over beef slices. Arrange strip of bacon on each beef slice, then put 2 onion quarters and 1 dill pickle half over center of each bacon strip. Roll up the beef slices tightly, jelly-roll style. Secure beef rolls with wooden picks.

    Heat oil in a large skillet over medium-high heat. Add beef rolls; sauté until evenly browned on all sides, about 10 minutes. Pour broth or bouillon into skillet. Reduce heat to low. Cover with a tight-fitting lid; simmer 1 1/2 hours or until tender. Serve hot.

Steak Salad

Steak Salat

Top- and bottom-round steak or any other lean cut of beef can be used instead of sirloin. Take care not to broil beef too long. Medium doneness, just a bit pink in the center, is usually what works best. Beef that's well done will not absorb as much marinade as it should. *Makes 6 to 8 servings.*

2 lbs. beef sirloin steak, 1 to
   1 1/2 inches thick
6 oz. canned sliced mushrooms,
   drained
2 medium green bell peppers, sliced
   into thin rings
1/2 cup red wine vinegar
1/4 cup olive oil

1 1/2 teaspoons salt
1/2 teaspoon garlic salt
1/2 teaspoon Maggi seasoning
1/4 teaspoon freshly ground black
   pepper
1/4 teaspoon dried tarragon leaves
Leaf lettuce
12 cherry tomatoes

Preheat broiler. Place meat on broiler rack and cook 3 to 4 inches from heat about 12 minutes per side or until beef reaches medium doneness; cool. Cut meat against the grain into 1/4-inch-thick slices. Arrange meat slices in a shallow glass or ceramic baking dish. Arrange mushrooms on meat. Place bell pepper rings on top of steak and mushrooms.

In a small bowl, combine vinegar, olive oil, salt, garlic salt, Maggi seasoning, pepper and tarragon. Pour over meat and vegetables. Cover and refrigerate 2 hours to overnight, occasionally spooning marinade over vegetables.

When ready to serve, line salad plates with leaf lettuce. Arrange slices of meat on lettuce. With a slotted spoon, remove vegetables and place beside meat slices. Garnish with tomatoes. Serve slightly chilled.

Calf Liver

Kalbsleber

Prepare liver for slicing and cooking by removing the thin outer skin and veining. Calf liver is preferred because it's much more tender than beef liver. *Makes 6 to 8 servings.*

1 cup milk	1 teaspoon ground sage
2 lbs. calf liver, sliced 3/4 inch thick	1/3 cup all-purpose flour
3 tablespoons olive oil	1 1/2 teaspoons salt
2 medium onions, thinly sliced	1/2 teaspoon freshly ground black
1 cup dry white wine	pepper
1 tablespoon lemon juice	2 tablespoons chopped fresh parsley

Place milk in a shallow glass bowl; add liver. Cover and refrigerate 1 hour, turning liver every 15 minutes. Remove liver from milk; discard milk. Heat 1 tablespoon of the olive oil in a medium skillet over medium heat; add onions and sauté until tender, about 5 minutes. Add wine, lemon juice and sage to onions; simmer, covered, 5 minutes. Remove cooked onions and juices from heat; reserve.

Combine flour, salt and pepper in a shallow dish. Dip liver in flour mixture until evenly coated. Heat remaining 2 tablespoons olive oil in a large skillet over medium heat. Add floured liver slices to skillet; sauté over medium heat 3 to 4 minutes on each side or until evenly browned. Add cooked onions and juices. Cover with a tight-fitting lid. Cook over medium-low heat, 5 to 7 minutes or until liver is tender. Do not overcook or liver may become tough. Place cooked liver, onions and juices in a heated serving dish; top with parsley. Serve hot.

Calf Liver in Beer

Kalbsleber in Bier

In German homes, liver is cooked to only one degree of doneness—tender. Anything else will not do. High temperatures or longer-than-recommended cooking times can result in a dish resembling shoe leather, so it takes all of the chef's concentration to cook it right. *Makes 6 servings.*

2 tablespoons vegetable oil

1 large onion, sliced

1 1/2 lbs. calf liver, cut into 3/4-inch pieces

2 tablespoons all-purpose flour

1 cup beer

1/2 cup Beef Broth (page 58) or beef bouillon

1 teaspoon salt

1/4 teaspoon freshly ground black pepper

1/4 teaspoon thyme

1 cup sour cream

2 tablespoons chopped fresh parsley

Dumplings or noodles (optional) to serve

Heat oil in large skillet over medium heat. Add onion; sauté until tender, about 10 minutes. Remove onion from skillet and reserve. Add liver. Cook about 3 to 4 minutes per side, turning until both sides are lightly browned and liver is cooked through. Remove liver and set aside with onion. Add flour to skillet with drippings; cook, stirring, until golden brown. Add beer and broth. Increase heat to high; cook mixture, stirring, 3 to 4 minutes or until a full boil is reached and juices are thickened. Reduce heat to medium. Stir salt, pepper, thyme and sour cream into cooking juices. Add liver and onions. Cook until liver and onions are heated through. Transfer to a warm deep serving dish. Sprinkle with parsley. Serve with dumplings or noodles, if desired.

Sausages & Combination Dishes

Wurst und Kombinationsgerichte

I s any single ingredient or food more "linked" to German cuisine than sausage? Others may approach its popularity, but none surpass it. You might be surprised to learn that sausages, or *Wurst,* did not originate in Germany. Instead, look to the Italians, whose food-preserving skills helped support the Roman occupation of Germanic lands thousands of years ago. Back then there were no refrigerated trailers or rail cars to deliver fresh meat and other provisions to conquering armies. So Roman cooks devised clever methods of preserving rations that included smoking and aging meats and filling gut casings with ground pork, venison and other game meats. Due to the great concentration and lengthy stay of Roman soldiers, especially throughout Bavaria, the locals eventually acquired the sausage-making skills of their colonizers. And when the Romans left, sausages stayed.

Then, little by little, the Germans, in their own methodical way, went about perfecting whole families of *Wurst,* adding variation after variation, establishing regional specialties and starting all sorts of sausage traditions, many of which persist today. It's believed that about 1,700 different kinds of sausage are currently being prepared by German master butchers and sausage makers. Indeed, white, pink, red, tan, brown and black sausage links, rolls and rings in myriad shapes, sizes, flavors and consistencies are offered daily within shiny, glass-covered counters in butcher shops throughout the country, north to south. Within natural pork and sheep casings, with flavors from smoke, spices, herbs and meats in various proportions, sausages appeal to the tastes of young and old, of natives and visitors, of importers and delicatessens and specialty food brokers throughout the world.

The quality of German sausage is recognized everywhere, even by the most hard-to-please critics. While Italian and French chefs sometimes make light of German cuisine as lacking subtlety, they grant a noteworthy exception to German sausages.

The extent of German sausage variety cannot be denied. What's more, the "same" sausage can vary in flavor, texture, appearance and even ingredients from sausage maker to sausage maker, from region to region and even from town to town. Indeed, sausage names often refer to the town or city in which they were first invented, or at least where they are most frequently eaten. Sausages such as *Regensberger, Berliner, Gottinger* or *Frankfurter* are all named for places in Germany. Other sausages carry names that reflect their main ingredient, such as *Lebenwurst* (liver sausage) and *Blutwurst* (blood sausage).

Testaments to just how serious the Germans take their sausages are strict regulations and laws that require sausages to be made of only 100 percent meat, with no "mysterious" fillers or additives of any kind and no artificial colorings, either. So too is the depth of the German sausage lexicon. In the United States, unless you're steeped in national cuisines, such as those of Poland or Hungary, your sausage fluency probably goes no further than hot dogs, ring bologna, small tins of Vienna sausages or various luncheon meats such as thuringer, braunschweiger, hard salami and breakfast sausages. But ask a typical German to itemize sausage varieties he or she is familiar with and the list could go on for a dozen pages. To foreign palates, differences between many sausage varieties may hardly be noticeable. Not so to Germans. Just as an Eskimo can distinguish fine differences in types of snowfall or weather, so too can the Germans distinguish subtle differences in sausages.

To make sense out of sausages, it's best to start with the three basic classes:

- *Kockwurst* or boiled sausages such as *Mettwursts, Sulzwursts,* about sixty kinds of liverwursts and various "blood" or tongue and similar variety-meat sausages. There are over 350 different members of the *Kockwurst* family.

- *Bruhwurst* or perishable sausages such as *Weisswurst, Bockwurst, Bratwurst, Knackwurst* and *Frankfurters* that usually need to be heated or cooked by parboiling, blanching or scalding. This is the largest sausage class, with almost 800 kinds.

- *Hartwurst* or *Rohwurst* or cured, smoked or air-dried long-lasting wursts such as salamis, cervelats and other "hard" sausages that are carried in hikers' and campers' backpacks and eaten as snacks during hot or cold weather. Estimated total varieties of *Hartwursts* or *Rohwursts* mark over 500. These numbers, however, aren't etched in stone. If German sausage names were plotted on a map of Germany, the result would be a wild patchwork of different varieties. And remember, recipes for any one kind of sausage can vary from region to region.

Sausage making, even for the orderly German mind, is as much art as it is science. But it's an art and science that must be learned. Many butcher shops have been passed down for literally hundreds of years within the same family. Like German bakers, sausage makers and butchers must complete rigorous training that includes years of college-level courses in meat cutting as well as a five-year apprenticeship under the tutelage of a certified butcher shop that is not run by individuals related to the student.

Certainly, German sausage making is steeped in tradition. The medieval city of Regensburg, for example, features Bavaria's oldest sausage-making shop, where the *Historische Wurstkuche* sits on the banks of the Danube River, as it has since the twelfth century. And somewhere along the line, German proverbs have feasted upon sausage. Common sayings are spiced with sausage terms. What of *Es geht um die Wurst!* (meaning "The wurst is at stake!"), exclaimed when Germans are faced with a tricky decision. Fat or butter fingers are *Wurstfinger*. And if it's "One or the other," the German citizen might say *Alles wurscht!* (meaning "Oh, well, everything is sausage").

Nowadays many German sausages can be purchased in larger supermarkets or in small butcher shops owned and operated by individuals of German ancestry. A large number of wurst varieties are also available through mail-order catalogs.

Another type of entree Germans love is the stuffed entree, including stuffed tomatoes, stuffed green (or red) bell peppers and the old standby, popular throughout all of Germany and Eastern Europe, stuffed cabbage leaves. Casseroles, too, help extend meat portions and by their inclusion of vegetables, potatoes, noodles, rice and other meatless ingredients, make for healthier eating.

German Sausages

Weisswurst, or white sausage, is a delicately flavored small sausage mostly made of finely ground veal, sometimes with a bit of pork and occasionally brains, lightly seasoned with salt and pepper and often with tiny bits of fresh parsley. *Weisswurst* is slightly cured in a mild brine and is usually steamed and eaten hot from its casing, which is left on the plate. Popular with both visitors and locals alike, it is a specialty of Munich, where it is served late at night through the wee hours of the morning. It's usually the main feature and is most often eaten with rye rolls, big white radishes and pretzels. The only "approved" accompaniment to *Weisswurst* is sweet mustards, in which the slices are dipped.

Bockwurst, somewhat like Vienna sausages, are small, fine-grained, tasty sausages made of veal or beef or pork and, in Berlin, smoked until their whitish color turns pink. Also like Vienna sausages, *Bockwurst* is often sold in cans. It's usually served hot, quickly heated in simmering water. *Bockwurst* got its name from the popular and seasonal dark *Bockbier,* with which the sausage was eaten. Years ago *Bockwurst* was made only during spring, when the popular dark beer was specially brewed. Demand changed that tradition, though, and now *Bockwurst* is available year-round.

Bratwurst, also known as frying sausage, is a sausage whose spicy links are filled with meat combinations of pork and veal or pork and beef. The filling is coarsely ground and flavored with nutmeg, caraway, marjoram, pepper, salt and sometimes mace. But there is no set formula; the combination and degree of seasonings vary according to the taste of the sausage maker. *Bratwurst* is a specialty of Nurnberg, where small, thin versions, called *Schweinwurstel,* are commonly grilled over open wood fires. All told, *Bratwurst* is probably the most popular sausage in Germany.

Bauernwurst resembles a large, fat frankfurter. It is usually made of pork, coarsely and unevenly ground. It's a sausage that is very popular throughout the German country-side. Although this "farmer's" sausage is generally smoked, tradition says it should be steamed for a few minutes and then quickly grilled. Most versions are—as German sausages go—highly seasoned, often containing mustard seeds.

Bierwurst is beer sausage. No, it doesn't actually contain beer, but it goes awfully well with beer. It's a large pinkish sausage, about the diameter of bologna, made of finely ground meat containing bits of smoked pork and fat.

Knackwurst, Knockwurst or "crunchy" sausage is a short, stubby, fat sausage about 4 inches long that can also be called a *Regensburger*—for the Bavarian town of Regensburg, where a spicy version of it is made. *Knackwurst* tends to have crispy skin that makes a crunchy sound when bitten. It's made of beef and pork or of beef alone and is well seasoned with pepper and garlic. Several varieties are even called garlic knockwurst or knackwurst. It's popular with sauerkraut combination dishes and also makes an excellent picnic lunch when heated in a little water, then grilled and eaten with hard rolls and spicy mustard.

Lebenwursts are a family of sausages of widely varying composition, all of which are smoked and cooked and are most often eaten cold with no accompaniments, or sliced in sandwiches and various appetizers. *Braunschweiger* is a liver sausage made of pork, stuffed into a natural pork casing. *Zweibelwurst* is liverwurst with bits of browned onions in it. *Truffelwurst* is, naturally, flavored with truffles. *Sardellenwurst* contains anchovies in its pork-meat mixture. Other versions contain calf liver or pork liver.

Mettwurst, or tea sausage, is a short, stubby and very soft pork sausage, bright paprika-red in color. The most prevalent variety is completely cooked and spread on bread, never sliced. Unless, of course, it's *Hamburger Mettwurst,* a variety that can be cooked until it's solid enough to slice. *Rugenwalder Mettwurst* is a small yet harder salami-like version of this *Mettwurst.*

Lyoner, or the more general-sounding *Fleischwurstring,* is literally a meat sausage ring or circular sausage that's similar to bologna in flavor and texture. The same sausage in a straight, long roll is called just *Fleischwurst.* It's no surprise that both versions are made either of pork, beef or a combination of the two. These sausages are enjoyed both hot and cold, as entrees or snacks.

Thuringer can be purchased in fresh, smoked and partially dried varieties. It's popular in American supermarkets, where it can usually be purchased alongside hard salami and German bologna. The milder, fresh *Thuringer* is made from finely ground pork or pork and veal, dry milk and spices. The cooked, smoked version is made of a coarser ground pork and beef combination, seasoned with mustard, salt and pieces of pepper. The semidry version, a smoked *Cervelat* that will keep for months at a time, has even more bite to it. *Thuringer*'s name hails from the state of Thuringia in the eastern part of Germany.

Blutwurst, or blood sausage, is a favorite German wurst made with fresh pig's blood and a ground-pork base that's combined with larger pieces of pork, tongue or bits of fat, veal or other meats. It's cooked and smoked, almost black in color and sold in links, about two per foot. Larger varieties are sliced and served cold. The name "blood sausage" does not really do this tasty wurst justice. It tastes a lot better than it sounds.

Frankfurters are the sausages the Germans are known for, worldwide. True *Frankfurters* hail from the Frankfurt am Main area. They're 100 percent finely ground pork without fat, tendons or any additives. True *Frankfurters* are stuffed into natural sheep casings and smoked and sold in pairs attached at one end. This is one sausage whose manufacture is tightly regulated. According to German butchers, some people mistakenly call *Frankfurters* "wieners." A visit to practically any supermarket deli in the United States will confirm the use of the term *wieners*. In German, *Wieners* doesn't refer to a sausage; it means "residents of Vienna," which in German is *Wien*. But neither do residents of Vienna walk into a butcher store and order "wieners." They ask for frankfurters instead. Wieners have for some reason been equated to that all-American sausage called the hot dog. Americans tend to use the three terms, *frankfurters, wieners* and *hot dogs* interchangeably.

Sausage with Sweet-Hot Mustard

Wurst mit Scharfsüssem Senf

I f your taste preference leans toward hot, then start out with a spicy prepared mustard of your choice. On the other hand, the brown sugar and honey will mediate nicely between the mustard, horseradish and hot pepper sauce for people who favor milder fare. *Makes 6 to 8 servings.*

1 cup prepared coarse-grained mustard
1/4 cup packed dark brown sugar
1/4 cup honey
3 tablespoons red wine vinegar
2 tablespoons dry mustard
2 tablespoons prepared horseradish
1 teaspoon minced garlic

1/4 teaspoon hot pepper sauce
1/8 teaspoon freshly ground black pepper
2 lbs. cooked bratwurst, knockwurst, kielbasa or other sausage
2 tablespoons butter or margarine
2 medium carrots, cut in strips

In a medium bowl, combine prepared mustard, brown sugar, honey, vinegar, dry mustard, horseradish, garlic, hot pepper sauce and pepper. Cover and refrigerate 2 hours to overnight.

Cut sausage into 1/2-inch-thick slices. Heat butter or margarine in a large skillet over medium heat. Add sausage; sauté until browned on both sides. Drain sausage slices on paper towels. Insert 1 decorative wooden pick into each sausage round; arrange sausage rounds on a warm, ovenproof platter. Keep heated until ready to serve. Place mustard sauce on side, garnished with several carrot sticks.

Pork Sausage & Sauerkraut

Schweinwurst und Sauerkraut

A simple combination of sausage and sauerkraut, flavored with apples and apple juice. A more tart version uses an equivalent amount of sliced small red crabapples, the kind that are used for making jelly. *Makes 6 to 8 servings.*

1 1/2 tablespoons vegetable oil	1 1/2 teaspoons caraway seeds
2 1/2 lbs. pork sausage links	2 apples, peeled, cored and thinly
2 onions, finely chopped	sliced
5 cups sauerkraut	1 cup apple juice

Heat oil in a large skillet over medium heat. Add sausage; sauté 10 to 12 minutes or until browned on all sides. Remove sausage and reserve. Add onions to sausage drippings; sauté until tender, about 10 minutes.

Preheat oven to 350F (175C). In a 3-quart casserole dish, arrange half of the sauerkraut. Place half of the sautéed onions over sauerkraut, then add half of the caraway seeds and apples, evenly arranging them on top of sauerkraut. Add another layer with the remaining sauerkraut, onions, caraway seeds and apples. Top with sausage. Carefully pour apple juice over sausage. Cover with a tight-fitting lid and bake 1 hour. Uncover and bake 30 more minutes. Serve hot.

Variation

Frankfurters may be substituted for sausage. Arrange them on top of sauerkraut for last half hour of baking.

Sausage & Potato Vinaigrette

Wurst und Kartoffelvinaigrette

Take extra care to watch the potatoes closely. It's best to use potatoes that are all about the same size, so some won't cook faster than others. If potatoes are overcooked, they'll fall apart in the recipe. *Makes 6 to 8 servings.*

3 to 3 1/2 lbs. baking potatoes	2 garlic cloves, minced
2 egg yolks (see Note)	1 teaspoon salt
1/2 cup white wine vinegar	1/2 teaspoon sugar
1 teaspoon Dijon mustard	1/4 teaspoon freshly ground black
3/4 cup vegetable oil	pepper
1/4 cup chopped green onions	1 1/2 lbs. garlic knockwurst
2 tablespoons chopped parsley	

Scrub potatoes; place in a large saucepan. Cover with cold water; bring to a boil over medium-high heat. Cook, uncovered, until potatoes are tender, 40 to 50 minutes. Drain; keep potatoes warm.

In a medium-size bowl, combine egg yolks, vinegar and mustard. Vigorously beat with a wire whisk until blended. Slowly add oil, whisking until dressing thickens. Stir in onions, parsley and garlic. Season with salt, sugar and pepper; cover and refrigerate.

Preheat oven to 350F (175C). In a large skillet bring about 1 inch of water to a boil over medium-high heat. Add knockwurst; reduce heat to medium-low. Partially cover; simmer 10 minutes. Drain. Cut knockwurst into 1/4-inch-thick slices. Keep warm. Carefully cut warm potatoes crosswise into 1/3-inch-thick slices. Arrange potatoes on a large ovenproof serving platter. Pour dressing over potatoes. Top with hot sausage. Bake 10 to 12 minutes or until potatoes and sausages are thoroughly heated. Serve hot.

Note

If the eggs in your area sometimes contain salmonella bacteria, omit the egg yolks. The vinaigrette will be thinner and will need to be beaten again before using.

Fresh Bratwurst

Frische Bratwurst

Lean beef can be substituted for the veal, if desired. Remember not to taste the un-cooked sausage mixture. If you want, cook a little bit of the seasoned meat mixture first, then taste and adjust the seasonings, if necessary. *Makes 6 to 8 servings.*

1 lb. coarsely ground lean pork
1 lb. coarsely ground veal
1 egg
2 tablespoons powdered milk
1 tablespoon dried parsley
2 teaspoons ground celery seeds
1 1/2 teaspoons salt
1 teaspoon onion powder
1/2 teaspoon freshly ground black
   pepper

1/2 teaspoon ground ginger
1/2 teaspoon ground coriander
1/2 teaspoon grated lemon peel
1/4 teaspoon dry mustard
About 3 tablespoons water
1 1/2 tablespoons butter or
   margarine
Mustard Sauce (page 216) or
   Horseradish Sauce (page 172)
   to serve

In a large bowl, combine pork, veal, egg, powdered milk, parsley, ground celery seed, salt, onion powder, pepper, ginger, coriander, lemon peel, mustard and water. Using your hands, mix ingredients. Depending on how dry the mixture is—it should be moist—add a little more water if needed. Cover and refrigerate 1 hour. Mix again; refrigerate another 15 minutes.

Melt butter or margarine in a large skillet over medium heat. Form 8 to 10 small oval sausage patties about 1-inch thick. Add patties to skillet; cook until well done, 4 to 5 minutes per side or until browned on both sides and cooked all the way through. Serve hot, plain or with Mustard Sauce or Horseradish Sauce.

Mustard Sauce

Senfsosse

Prepare this sauce just before using. *Makes about 1 cup sauce.*

4 egg yolks
1 stick (8 tablespoons) butter or
  margarine
2 teaspoons lemon juice
Salt

Ground white pepper
1 1/2 tablespoons Dijon or other
  prepared mustard
1/8 teaspoon Worcestershire sauce

Place egg yolks and 4 tablespoons of the butter or margarine in top section of a double boiler over hot (not boiling) water. Cook, stirring vigorously with a small wire whisk, until butter or margarine is melted. Gradually add remaining 4 tablespoons butter or margarine, beating with whisk until well combined with egg-yolk mixture. Remove pan from hot water. Continue beating 2 more minutes, adding lemon juice, salt, white pepper, mustard and Worcestershire sauce. Return pan to bottom part of double boiler, over hot water. Heat and stir 2 more minutes. Serve over hot Bratwurst.

Potato & Sausage Bake

Gebackene Kartoffel und Wurst

Many kinds of sausages can make this dish special. Research your local butcher shops and the meat departments in area supermarkets to see what's available.
Makes 6 servings.

2 lbs. boiled potatoes, in skins, cooled

1 1/2 lbs. sausages

2 eggs, lightly beaten

1 1/2 cups milk

3/4 cup (3 oz.) Gouda, Edam or Cheddar cheese

1/4 cup finely chopped fresh parsley

1 tablespoon ground sweet paprika

Peel and cut potatoes into 1/8-inch-thick slices. Slice sausages in half horizontally. Heat a large skillet over medium heat. Add sausages. Cook sausages, turning, until cooked through and browned, about 15 minutes. Drain on paper towels.

Preheat oven to 375F (190C). Combine eggs, milk, cheese and parsley in a medium bowl. Lightly grease a medium casserole dish. Arrange half of cooked potato slices in a layer on bottom of greased dish. Arrange half of the cooked sausage on top of potato layer. Pour half of the cheese mixture over sausage and potatoes. Repeat layers with remaining potatoes, sausages and cheese mixture. Sprinkle with paprika. Bake, uncovered, 30 minutes or until top of casserole is lightly browned. Serve hot.

Variations

Use pieces of cooked ham or other meat leftovers instead of sausage.

Use 1/2 cup dried mushrooms, soaked overnight and cooked in 1 tablespoon butter until tender, then sliced. Add with sausages. Or use 1/2 lb. fresh mushrooms, sliced and cooked in butter.

Add 2 chopped hard-cooked eggs, with sausages.

Add 1 cup chopped onion, sautéed in 1 tablespoon butter until tender, with potatoes.

Frankfurter-Garlic Salad

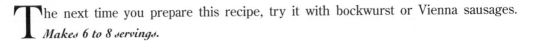

Frankfurter-Knoblauchsalat

The next time you prepare this recipe, try it with bockwurst or Vienna sausages. *Makes 6 to 8 servings.*

2 tablespoons olive oil

1 tablespoon white wine vinegar

1 tablespoon sweet pickle relish, drained

2 green onions, chopped

1 teaspoon Dijon mustard

1/2 teaspoon salt

1/4 teaspoon freshly ground black pepper

1 lb. cooked garlic frankfurters

3 oz. Emmentaler cheese

2 cups shredded red cabbage

Crisp green leaf lettuce

Tomato wedges

In a large bowl, combine oil, vinegar, relish, onions, mustard, salt and pepper. Cut frankfurters crosswise into 1/4-inch-thick slices. Cut cheese into thin strips. Add cabbage, frankfurters and cheese to dressing; gently toss. Cover and let stand at room temperature 30 minutes. Line a serving bowl with leaf lettuce. Spoon salad into bowl; garnish with tomato wedges. Serve at room temperature or slightly chilled.

Stuffed Tomatoes

Gefüllte Tomaten

Fresh, firm, homegrown tomatoes at the peak of their ripeness are best for this dish. *Makes 6 servings.*

3 tablespoons butter or margarine
1 medium onion, chopped
8 oz. ground beef or pork, cooked
1 cup canned tomatoes
1 cup cooked rice
3 tablespoons grated Parmesan
  cheese

1 1/2 teaspoons sugar
1 1/2 teaspoons salt
1/4 teaspoon freshly ground black
  pepper
3 tablespoons fresh chopped parsley
6 medium-large ripe tomatoes
Buttered bread crumbs for topping

Preheat oven to 350F (175C). Lightly grease a large shallow baking dish. Melt butter or margarine in a large skillet over medium heat. Add onion; sauté until tender, about 5 minutes, stirring occasionally. Add beef or pork, canned tomatoes, rice, grated cheese, sugar, salt, pepper and parsley. Cook 8 minutes, stirring occasionally; let cool slightly.

Slice stem ends off fresh tomatoes; discard tomato slices or use in salads. With a spoon, scoop out pulp, leaving a 3/4-inch shell. Stuff tomato shells with meat mixture. Sprinkle bread crumbs on top of stuffing. Arrange stuffed tomatoes in greased baking dish. Pour water around tomatoes to a depth of 1/4 inch. Bake, uncovered, 15 minutes or until top of meat mixture browns. Serve immediately.

Stuffed Red-Cabbage Rolls

Rotkohlroulade

Although this recipe is similar to one of the most popular Polish dishes throughout the world—*golombkies*—it doesn't take a back seat in Germany, either. Naturally, it can be made with green cabbage leaves, too. *Makes 12 to 14 servings.*

1 (3-lb.) head red cabbage	1/4 teaspoon garlic salt
4 tablespoons butter or margarine	1/2 teaspoon freshly ground black
1 small onion, chopped	pepper
1 1/4 lbs. lean ground beef	3 3/4 cups Beef Broth (page 58)
1 1/2 lbs. lean ground pork	1 (6-oz.) can tomato paste
1 3/4 cups cooked white rice	2 tablespoons all-purpose flour
1 teaspoon salt	

With a sharp knife, remove core from cabbage. Carefully remove wilted or decayed outer cabbage leaves; discard. In a large saucepan, bring enough salted water to a boil to cover cabbage. Immerse cabbage in boiling water. Cook over medium-high heat 5 to 7 minutes. With fork or tongs, gently remove leaves as they become tender. Drain well; let cool.

Preheat oven to 325F (165C). Melt 1 tablespoon of the butter or margarine in a small skillet over medium heat. Add onion; sauté until golden brown, about 15 minutes. In a large bowl, combine sautéed onion, beef, pork, rice, salt, garlic salt and pepper.

Trim large stems from cabbage leaves. Spread a cabbage leaf flat, inner side up. Depending on leaf size, place 2 to 3 tablespoons filling on cabbage leaf near base. Fold bottom of leaf over filling, then fold sides toward center. Roll tightly. Repeat with remaining filling and cabbage leaves.

Heat 1 tablespoon of the butter or margarine in a large skillet over medium heat. Place filled cabbage leaves, seam side down, in skillet; cook until browned, 8 to 10 minutes, turning once with a spatula. Arrange cabbage rolls, seam side down, in a medium baking pan. Add 3 1/4 cups broth. In a small bowl, combine 1/2 cup broth and tomato paste. Pour over stuffed cabbage. Cover and bake 45 minutes or until tender.

Melt remaining 2 tablespoons butter or margarine in a small skillet over medium heat. Stir flour into butter or margarine; cook, stirring, until golden brown. Ladle 1 cup broth from stuffed cabbage into flour mixture; blend. Pour mixture over stuffed cabbage; cook, uncovered, until liquid bubbles and thickens slightly. Place stuffed cabbage on a large platter. Pour pan juices into a serving bowl. Serve hot with pan juices.

 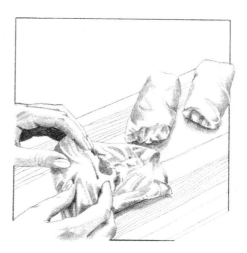

German Casserole

Deutsche Pfanne

If there were a German substitute for spaghetti with tomato sauce, this would almost be it—except for the sauerkraut. *Makes 4 to 6 servings.*

2 cups uncooked noodles

1 lb. sauerkraut, drained

1 lb. ground beef

1 egg, slightly beaten

1/2 cup soft rye bread crumbs

1/4 cup milk

1 teaspoon salt

1/2 teaspoon sugar

1/4 teaspoon freshly ground pepper

1 tablespoon vegetable oil

1 (1 lb.) can canned tomatoes

Cook noodles according to package directions and drain. In a large bowl, gently mix sauerkraut and noodles. In another large bowl, mix ground beef, egg, bread crumbs, milk, salt, sugar and pepper. Using your hands, form meat mixture into about 20 meatballs.

Heat oil in a large skillet over medium heat. Add meatballs; cook until browned on all sides. Carefully stir tomatoes into meatballs. Cook 5 minutes, gently stirring.

Preheat oven to 350F. Place half of noodle and sauerkraut mixture in a large casserole dish. Arrange half of meatballs and tomatoes evenly on noodle-sauerkraut bed. Arrange remaining noodles and sauerkraut over first layer of meatballs. Evenly top with remaining meatballs and tomatoes. Cover and bake 1 hour. Serve steaming hot.

Stuffed Green Peppers

Gefüllte Paprikaschoten

Peppers are ideal, low-fat, nutritious vehicles for extending meat. Green bell peppers aren't your only option here. Try red, yellow or orange peppers or a mixture of several for a colorful and tasty entree. *Makes 6 servings.*

6 large green bell peppers
1 1/2 tablespoons butter or
   margarine
1 large onion, chopped
3/4 lb. ground beef or pork
3 tablespoons cooked white rice
1 egg, lightly beaten
1 teaspoon salt

1/2 teaspoon dried oregano
1/4 teaspoon freshly ground black
   pepper
1/2 cup dry bread crumbs
1 1/2 cups Beef Broth (page 58) or
   Veal Broth (page 60)
Tomato Sauce (page 114)

Preheat oven to 350F (175C). Lightly grease a shallow baking dish. Slice stem ends off bell peppers; dice edible parts of cut ends. With a spoon, scoop out seeds and white pith; discard.

Melt butter or margarine in a small skillet over medium heat. Add diced bell pepper and onion; sauté until tender, about 10 minutes. Let cool. Combine beef or pork, rice and sautéed bell pepper and onion in a medium bowl. Add egg, salt, oregano and black pepper; stir to combine. Stuff pepper shells with ground meat mixture; do not press stuffing mixture in too tightly. Spoon bread crumbs evenly over stuffed-pepper tops. Arrange stuffed peppers in greased baking dish. Pour broth in bottom of baking dish. Cover and bake 50 minutes or until peppers are tender and filling is cooked through. Serve hot with Tomato Sauce.

Beef, Veal & Pork Stew

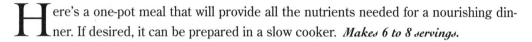

Rind, Kalbs und Schweineintopf

Here's a one-pot meal that will provide all the nutrients needed for a nourishing dinner. If desired, it can be prepared in a slow cooker. *Makes 6 to 8 servings.*

2 tablespoons butter or margarine

2 medium onions, chopped

1/2 lb. lean beef, cubed

1/2 lb. veal, cubed

1/2 lb. pork, cubed

4 carrots, sliced crosswise

1 celery root, peeled and chopped

1 small cabbage, cut into
   2-inch pieces

1 lb. potatoes, peeled and cubed

3 1/2 cups Beef Broth (page 58)

Salt

Freshly ground black pepper

Noodles or Potato-Bread Dumplings
   (page 96) (optional)

Melt butter or margarine in a large skillet over medium heat. Add onions; sauté until almost tender, about 5 minutes. Add beef, veal and pork; sauté 8 minutes or until browned on all sides. Add carrots, celery root, cabbage, potatoes and broth. Cover with a tight-fitting lid. Reduce heat to medium-low; cook 1 1/2 hours or until meats are fork tender. Season with salt and pepper. Serve hot, with noodles or Potato-Bread Dumplings, if desired.

Beef Bavarian

Bayrisches Rind

These flavorful patties can be prepared ahead and reheated later. They're ideal for parties and buffets. *Makes 6 servings.*

2 lbs. lean ground beef
2 eggs, beaten slightly
1 tablespoon grated lemon peel
1 teaspoon salt
1/2 teaspoon onion salt
1/2 cup skim milk
1/2 cup dried bread crumbs

1 tablespoon vegetable oil
3 tablespoons all-purpose flour
1 1/2 cups Beef Broth (page 58)
3 tablespoons lemon juice
2 tablespoons brown sugar
1/4 teaspoon ground ginger
4 whole cloves

In a large bowl, combine beef, eggs, lemon peel, salt, onion salt, milk and bread crumbs until well blended. Using your hands, shape beef mixture into 6 equal-size oval patties, about 1 inch thick. Heat oil in a large skillet over medium heat. Sauté beef patties 12 to 15 minutes, or until browned on both sides. Remove patties. Add flour to pan drippings; stir until combined. Stir broth into flour mixture; simmer, uncovered, until broth mixture thickens, stirring. Stir lemon juice, brown sugar, ginger and cloves into broth mixture. Return patties to skillet. Cover with a tight-fitting lid and simmer over low heat 30 minutes. Remove cloves before serving. Serve hot, spooning gravy over patties.

Game

Wild

Wild game meats are very popular in Germany. Rabbit or hare, venison, wild boar, pheasant and other game can be purchased at select butcher shops. This, however, does not imply that German citizens are able to hunt these animals whenever they want. Germany's forests historically have been strictly regulated and still are. It wasn't many generations ago, for instance, that only the nobility or aristocracy were permitted to hunt and take wild game. In fact, for hundreds of years, up until the second half of the nineteenth century in Germany and much of Europe, game was not available to the lower or even middle classes. Peasants who lived at a forest's edge, with deer feeding at their gardens and wild boar ranging through their fields, were not permitted to hunt. Yet the rich and powerful upper classes stormed through planted fields, causing much destruction of grains and other crops as they harvested all sorts of wild game.

Strict game laws came to be looked at as social traditions associated with the ruling gentry. The penalties for violations could be quite harsh. Poaching a wild boar could result in the poacher's eyes being put out, or snaring a wild hare would result in a fine equated to several years' worth of a peasant's income. Feelings ran so high between the nobility, who owned luxurious hunting lodges at which they entertained visiting noblemen and dignitaries, and the lower classes that there were a number of revolts against the rich landowners.

Rabbits and hares are two of the most accessible game meats in Germany today. In addition to being available in the forests and fields and in butcher shops, they're also raised or "farmed" to help supply the considerable demand.

Rabbit is a rather sweet meat that, as the cliché goes, "tastes like chicken." It can be sautéed, braised, boiled, stewed, roasted, or used in practically any recipe that calls for chicken or pheasant. While young rabbits and hares are tender and mild-flavored and can be successfully roasted, older animals lend themselves to being casseroled or "jugged" because their meat is rather dry, without much fat. The best time of the year to obtain rabbit is in the fall or winter months, when the meat quality is generally at its peak.

If you get your rabbits afield or from a hunter friend or relative, have the rabbits skinned and dressed as quickly as possible after the animals are killed. Scent glands located under the front legs where they join the body should be removed to avoid tainting the meat. Wild rabbits tend to be stronger flavored. If desired, soak rabbit in salted water and a few tablespoons of red wine vinegar to reduce any strong wild-game flavor that might be present. Soaking is not necessary if using farmed or "tame" rabbits.

Other game meats available from time to time include elk, reindeer, bear, squab, quail, partridges, woodcock, pigeons and doves. Some of those meats are imported from other countries.

Jugged Hare or Rabbit

Hasenpfeffer

There must be a million ways to make *Hasenpfeffer* and everyone thinks his or hers is right. It's true. There are basics to follow, but oh so many variations. After trying the recipe, experiment with different herbs and spices in the marinade. *Makes 4 to 6 servings.*

1 (4- to 4 1/2-lb.) rabbit, cut up

1 cup white vinegar

1 cup water

1 cup dry red wine

1 medium onion, sliced

12 peppercorns

5 juniper berries

1 teaspoon whole cloves

1 teaspoon ground allspice

1/2 teaspoon garlic salt

1 bay leaf

Salt

Freshly ground black pepper

3 tablespoons all-purpose flour

3 tablespoons butter or margarine

1/3 cup sour cream (optional)

Boiled potatoes sprinkled with
    parsley to serve

Place rabbit pieces in a deep baking dish or bowl. In a medium saucepan, combine vinegar, water, wine, onion, peppercorns, juniper berries, cloves, allspice, garlic salt and bay leaf. Cook over medium heat 10 minutes. Let marinade cool. Pour marinade over rabbit pieces. Cover and refrigerate 2 days, turning rabbit twice per day.

Remove rabbit pieces from marinade and pat dry. Reserve marinade. Rub rabbit pieces with salt and pepper. Place flour in a shallow bowl. Roll rabbit pieces in flour until rabbit is evenly coated with flour. Heat butter or margarine in a large skillet over medium heat. Add floured rabbit pieces; cook until rabbit pieces are browned on all sides. Strain marinade into rabbit in skillet. Cover and simmer 40 to 50 minutes, or until rabbit is tender. Taste cooking juices for seasonings and add salt and pepper if needed. Stir sour cream into cooking juices, if desired. Serve hot, with cooking juices spooned over rabbit. Serve with boiled potatoes sprinkled with parsley.

Variation
Cook sliced carrots, celery, onions, tomatoes and other vegetables or a combination thereof with rabbit as it simmers.

Braised Rabbit with Mushrooms & Onions

Gescmorter Hase mit Champignons und Zwiebeln

Rabbits and the larger hares come in many sizes. Hares can weigh upward of 12 pounds. Adjust the ingredient amounts as necessary for larger or smaller animals. *Makes 4 servings.*

5 tablespoons butter or margarine

1 large onion, halved then cut in
    chunks

1 (4- to 4 1/2-lb.) rabbit

1 tablespoon salt

2 tablespoons all-purpose flour

1 bay leaf

1 teaspoon grated lemon peel

1/4 teaspoon ground thyme

10 black peppercorns

4 whole cloves

1 cup Chicken Broth (page 57) or
    Veal Broth (page 60)

1 tablespoon red currant jelly

3/4 lb. fresh mushrooms, sliced

About 2 cups dry red wine

Melt 3 tablespoons of the butter or margarine in a large skillet over medium heat. Add onion; sauté until onion is tender, about 10 minutes. Remove onion from skillet; reserve in a small bowl. Add rabbit to skillet. Cook over medium heat 8 to 10 minutes on each side or until both sides are browned. Sprinkle salt and flour evenly over rabbit. Tie bay leaf, lemon peel, thyme, peppercorns and whole cloves into a cheesecloth bag; add to rabbit with broth and currant jelly. Cover with a tight-fitting lid. Simmer over medium-low heat 1 hour, turning rabbit several times. Add sautéed onions to rabbit.

Melt remaining 2 tablespoons butter or margarine in a medium skillet over medium heat. Add mushrooms; sauté until tender. Add mushrooms to rabbit. Pour wine over rabbit. Cover and simmer 30 minutes or until rabbit is tender. Place rabbit on a warm serving platter. If juices are too dry, stir in a little more wine. Discard spices. Cut rabbit into serving pieces. Spoon onions, mushrooms and cooking juices over rabbit. Serve hot.

Pheasant in Wine

Fasan in Wein

Since pheasant breast is so lean, strips of bacon are needed to help keep the meat moist. *Makes 4 to 6 servings.*

1 (3 1/2- to 4-lb.) pheasant, thawed, if frozen	1 cup dry red wine
Salt	1/2 cup Chicken Broth (page 57) or chicken bouillon
Freshly ground black pepper	3 lean bacon slices
1/4 cup butter or margarine, softened	1 cup thinly sliced fresh mushrooms
1 tablespoon vegetable oil	1 tablespoon all-purpose flour
1 medium onion, chopped	1/4 cup half and half
1 bay leaf	

Rinse pheasant under cold water; pat dry with paper towels. Rub inside and out with salt and pepper. Rub pheasant cavity with 1 tablespoon of the butter or margarine. Heat 2 tablespoons of the butter or margarine and 1 tablespoon vegetable oil in a heavy Dutch oven over medium heat. Add pheasant; cook until all sides are browned. Remove pheasant from Dutch oven; set aside on a plate. Add onion and bay leaf to Dutch oven; sauté onion until tender, about 10 minutes. Stir wine and broth into sautéed onion; simmer about 5 minutes.

Return pheasant to Dutch oven. Drape bacon slices over pheasant breast. Cover pan with a tight-fitting lid. Reduce heat to very low; simmer 40 to 50 minutes or until juice between thigh and breast runs clear when pierced and meat is tender. Remove pheasant from Dutch oven; loosely cover with foil and set aside in a warm place.

Melt remaining 1 tablespoon butter or margarine in a medium skillet over medium heat. Add mushrooms; sauté until tender. Combine flour with sautéed mushrooms; cook, stirring, several minutes. Add cooked mushrooms and juices to Dutch oven. Stir in half and half. Cook, stirring, over medium-low heat until juices thicken slightly into a sauce. Discard bay leaf. Remove bacon slices from pheasant. Slice pheasant into serving-size pieces; arrange on warm platter. Spoon sauce over meat. Serve hot.

Stuffed Pheasant

....

Gefüllte Fasan

Flaming cognac sears a delicious flavor into this elegant dish. *Makes 4 servings.*

1 (4- to 4 1/2-lb.) pheasant, thawed, if frozen	1/2 lb. veal
1 tablespoon salt	3 chicken livers
1 teaspoon freshly ground black pepper	2 eggs, slightly beaten
1/4 cup milk	8 thin bacon slices
1 large day-old hard roll	1/4 cup cognac
	1 cup dry red wine
	1 tablespoon all-purpose flour

Rinse pheasant under cold water; pat dry with paper towels. Rub pheasant with salt and pepper, inside and out. Cover and refrigerate 1 hour.

Place milk in a small bowl. Break roll into pieces. Soak roll in milk. Squeeze out excess milk. Grind veal, livers and soaked roll through a meat grinder into a medium bowl, or process in a food processor fitted with the metal blade; do not overprocess or puree. Add eggs to veal mixture and combine.

Preheat oven to 350F (175C). Stuff pheasant cavity with veal mixture. Sew cavity closed and truss pheasant. Wrap pheasant with bacon slices by stretching bacon around breast and securing with butcher's string. Place stuffed pheasant in a baking dish. Bake, uncovered, 30 minutes. Remove dish from oven and set in a place away from combustible curtains and other items. Pour cognac over pheasant. Using a long match, carefully ignite cognac. When flames die out, remove bacon from pheasant. Stir wine into cooking juices. Bake 10 more minutes.

Remove stuffed pheasant from pan and place on a cutting board. Carefully quarter pheasant with a heavy butcher knife or cleaver. Place quartered pheasant on a serving platter; keep warm in oven. Pour cooking juices into a small saucepan. Stir flour into juices and bring to a boil over medium heat. Cook, stirring, until slightly thickened. Serve sauce in a small dish with pheasant. Serve hot.

Spiced Duckling

Würzentlein

It takes a good-size wild duck to make a meal. Much of a duck's frame consists of bones that support the wings. Unlike domestic poultry types raised for their large breasts and legs, a duck is built more for speed of flight, so excess meat would slow it down. *Makes 2 to 4 servings.*

1 (4 1/2- to 5-lb.) duck, thawed, if frozen	1/4 teaspoon ground cloves
1 1/2 teaspoons salt	1/2 cup water
1/4 teaspoon freshly ground black pepper	2 large apples, halved
2 garlic cloves, minced	2 large onions, chopped
1 teaspoon ground ginger	2 cups beer
	1 cup Chicken Broth (page 57) or chicken bouillon

Preheat oven to 400F (205C). Remove giblets and neck from duck cavity. Rinse duck under cold running water; pat dry with paper towels. Remove any excess fat from duck; discard fat. Prick duck skin all over to let fat drain during roasting. Rub duck, inside and out, with salt, pepper, garlic, ginger and cloves. Place duck, breast side up, on a rack in a shallow roasting pan. Pour water in bottom of roasting pan. Place halved apples in duck cavity. Roast duck 45 minutes. Carefully remove duck from pan. Remove rack from pan. Pour fat off from bottom of pan. Discard apples. Return duck to bottom of pan; add onions, beer and broth to pan.

Reduce heat to 375F (190C). Roast duck 1 hour or until inside meat is tender and juices run clear when a knife is inserted between breast and thigh. Cool duck slightly.

Preheat broiler. Using a heavy cleaver or knife, cut duck into quarters. Arrange duck quarters, skin side up, in a shallow baking dish. Broil duck 4 to 5 minutes, until outside of duck quarters are crispy. Serve hot, with cooking juices and onions spooned over each serving.

Rolled Duck

Ente Rolle

A bit tricky, but the presentation will be worth it. The best knife to use while boning the duck is a sharp, narrow-blade boning type. If desired, a chicken of equal size can be substituted for the duck. *Makes 6 main-dish servings.*

1/4 lb. dried pitted prunes	2 eggs, lightly beaten
1 (4- to 4 1/2-lb.) duck	1/4 teaspoon freshly ground
1 1/2 teaspoons salt	black pepper
1/2 teaspoon ground marjoram	1/2 teaspoon ground nutmeg
1/3 cup milk	1 qt. Chicken Broth (page 57),
2 day-old dinner rolls	Meat Broth (page 62) or
1/4 lb. pork liver	chicken bouillon

Place prunes in a medium bowl. Add enough water to cover. Let stand 30 minutes. Drain. Chop prunes and set aside. Remove giblets and neck from duck cavity. Rinse duck under cold running water; pat dry with paper towels. Rub duck inside and out with 1 teaspoon of the salt and marjoram. Let stand 15 minutes. Turn duck, breast side up. Using a sharp, flexible knife, cut the duck skin along one side of the breastbone. Carefully skin duck, cutting about 1/2 inch of meat along with skin where possible, including legs. On a flat working surface, stretch skin out, meat side up. Trim skin as near to a rectangular shape as possible, without cutting off too much skin. Bone remaining meat.

Place milk in a small bowl. Break rolls apart and soak pieces in milk. Gently squeeze out excess milk. Grind boned duck meat, soaked rolls and pork liver through a meat grinder into a large bowl. Add chopped prunes, eggs, remaining 1/2 teaspoon salt, pepper and nutmeg; mix to combine.

Lay out duck skin, meat side up, on a work surface. Spoon ground duck mixture over center of upturned skin. Smooth out mixture over skin, leaving 2-inch margins on all edges. Roll skin jelly-roll style, turning short side up first. Sew ends closed with butcher's string. Wrap roll tightly with butcher's string by turning string around roll at 2-inch intervals. Heat broth or bouillon in a large saucepan. Add duck roll. Cook, partially covered, over medium-high heat, 20 minutes.

Preheat oven to 350F (175C). Remove duck roll from broth or bouillon. Place in a baking dish; add 1 cup cooking juices. Bake, uncovered, 35 to 45 minutes or until fork-tender, turning once. Serve hot as a main dish, or let cool to slice for sandwich filling.

Venison Casserole

Rehschmortopf

If venison proves difficult to find, feel free to substitute any lean cuts of beef. *Makes 8 to 10 servings.*

1/4 lb. bacon, chopped

3 lbs. venison, cut into bite-size pieces

2 tablespoons all-purpose flour

1 1/2 cups water

1/2 cup red wine

1/2 cup red wine vinegar

1 teaspoon salt

1/4 teaspoon freshly ground black pepper

1 bay leaf, crushed

1 garlic clove, crushed

2 tablespoons chopped fresh parsley

1/4 teaspoon ground thyme

2 large onions, chopped

1/4 lb. fresh mushrooms, sliced

1 teaspoon cornstarch (optional)

2 tablespoons water (optional)

Sauté bacon in a large skillet over medium heat until crisp. Drain off all but 2 tablespoons bacon drippings. Add venison; sauté over medium heat, turning occasionally, until browned on all sides. Remove venison; set aside in a medium bowl. Stir flour into pan drippings; cook, stirring constantly, over medium heat until flour turns light brown. Stir water, wine and vinegar into flour mixture until well blended. Add salt, pepper, bay leaf, garlic, parsley, thyme, onions and browned venison. Cover and simmer over medium-low heat 1 hour. Add mushrooms; simmer 20 more minutes or until meat is tender.

Strain cooking juices; if too thin, combine cornstarch and water in a small bowl. Blend 2 tablespoons hot cooking juices with cornstarch mixture. Stir blended cornstarch mixture back into cooking juices. Cook over medium heat, stirring, until sauce thickens.

Venison Party Rolls

Rehfleisch-Partyrolle

This meat roll is especially good for parties and celebration buffets. *Makes 6 to 8 servings.*

2 to 2 1/2 lbs. lean venison steak (1/2 inch thick)	1/2 lb. fresh mushrooms, sliced
1 3/4 cups Beef Broth (page 58) or beef bouillon	1/2 cup all-purpose flour
5 black peppercorns	1 teaspoon salt
1 bay leaf	1/4 teaspoon freshly ground black pepper
4 tablespoons butter or margarine	1 tablespoon cornstarch
1 medium onion, sliced and separated into rings	1 teaspoon Maggi seasoning
	Rice, noodles, dumplings or boiled potatoes (optional)

Place steaks between 2 sheets of plastic wrap and pound with a meat mallet to about 1/4-inch-thick 6 × 4-inch ovals. When pounding meat do not use a straight up-and-down movement; use a sliding action so meat is stretched more than flattened.

In a medium saucepan, combine 1 1/2 cups of the broth or bouillon, peppercorns and bay leaf. Bring to a boil over medium-high heat. Reduce heat to low. Simmer, covered, 10 minutes.

Melt 1 tablespoon of the butter or margarine in a medium skillet over medium heat. Add onion; sauté until tender, about 10 minutes. Place venison ovals on a work surface. Arrange equal amounts of sautéed onion on 1 short end of each oval. Roll up venison rolls, jelly-roll style. Secure with wooden picks.

Melt 1 tablespoon of the butter or margarine in skillet over medium heat. Add mushrooms; sauté until tender. Add to simmering broth mixture.

In a small bowl, combine flour, salt and pepper. Turn venison rolls in flour mixture until evenly coated. Melt remaining 2 tablespoons butter or margarine in a large skillet over medium-high heat. Add venison rolls; sauté 4 to 5 minutes or until all sides are browned.

Place browned venison rolls in broth mixture. Cover with a tight-fitting lid and simmer over low heat 1 to 1 1/2 hours or until tender. In a small bowl, blend cornstarch, Maggi seasoning and remaining 1/4 cup broth or bouillon. Add to venison rolls. Bring to a boil, stirring. Simmer, stirring occasionally, 5 minutes or until thickened. Serve immediately, with rice, noodles, dumplings or boiled potatoes, if desired.

Variation
Substitute beef round steak for venison.

Wild Boar Fillets
with Cherries

Wilder Eber mit Kirschen

Wild boar is a very popular meat in Germany, particularly during the hunting season in the fall. *Makes 4 servings.*

4 (8-oz.) boar fillet steaks	3/4 cup red wine
2 tablespoons vegetable oil	1 tablespoon butter or margarine
Salt	2 cups sweet cherries, stones removed
Freshly ground black pepper	1 teaspoon lemon juice

Lay steaks in a shallow dish. Rub steaks all over with oil. Heat a large skillet over medium-high heat. Add oiled steaks to hot skillet; cook 6 to 9 minutes on each side. Reduce heat to medium-low. Season with salt and pepper. Add wine, butter or margarine, cherries and lemon juice; simmer 5 to 7 minutes or until cherries are soft. Serve steaks hot, topped with cherry sauce.

Variations
Substitute venison, beef, or pork fillets for boar.

Fish & Seafood

Fisch und Meeresfruchte

Germany has little access to saltwater ports, except through its northeast coastline—along the Baltic Sea—and its northwest coastline—along the North Sea. Nor is Germany noted for its freshwater lakes and rivers. Yet over the years, certain fish and seafood recipes have become part of traditional German cuisine. While people living in the regions nearest the sea, to the north, eat a great deal of fresh fish, those living to the south eat it far less frequently. Still, frozen fish of all kinds and the ever-present herring in various forms are available in markets throughout the country.

Both cold- and warm-water fish live in Germany's lakes and rivers. Pike, perch, pike-perch (similar to American walleye), catfish, carp, eel, rainbow trout and salmon are among the most popular freshwater varieties. Saltwater fish such as halibut, cod, sole and haddock and seafood such as crayfish, crab, lobster, mussels and shrimp are available from commercial fisheries. "Blue" trout describes the visual phenomenon that occurs when a freshly killed trout is cooked in boiling water after being brushed with vinegar. When done just so, there's a reaction with the trout's skin that gives the skin a bluish tint. In addition, the trout is traditionally bent into a circle so its tail can be tucked into its mouth, then arranged on a heated plate or platter. If that sounds like too much trouble, though, there are other more practical ways to prepare German-style fish and seafood.

Fish is frequently poached, sautéed and baked in or later seasoned with butter, wine, mustard, sour cream or other sauces. Trout, salmon, pike and pike-perch are all appetizingly stuffed, and various fillets are rolled and filled before they're baked. Fried batter-dipped fish or shrimp or pieces of lobster are served with small boiled parsleyed potatoes, potato pancakes or French fries. Shrimp, mussels and other shellfish have grown in popularity in recent years and can now be found on menus in small restaurants as well as in the finest haute establishments.

Literally thousands of tons of eel are consumed every year in Germany. As an entree it's almost always served with a wine or sour cream sauce. Smoked eel is an appetizer appreciated either by itself or as part of a mixed hors d'oeuvre.

Herring have provided mariners with sustenance for over a thousand years, since fishermen who sailed the North and Baltic seas figured out that they could "salt down" herring and store them in wooden casks for indefinite periods of time. Salted herring became a truly important food supply for peoples in the northern part of Germany and developed into an important trade resource for cities such as Hamburg, Bremen and Lubeck. Even today herring is an integral part of German culture and cuisine, and small casks or similar containers of salted herring are a popular German export item to Western supermarkets and gourmet mail-order companies.

A good deal of fish eaten in Germany is served cold. Several chilled-fish snacks appear in the appetizer chapter.

Baked Fillet of Sole

Gebackenes Seezungenfilet

Sole fillets are perfect for rolling. They're rather slender and almost the same thickness from one end of the fillet to the other. Start rolling from the head end, so the inside of the fillet is on the inside of the finished roll. *Makes 6 to 8 servings.*

2 1/2 to 3 lbs. sole fillets	2 oz. pimientos, drained
2 eggs, lightly beaten	10 ripe olives, chopped
1 cup dry bread crumbs	2 tablespoons chopped fresh dill
1 cup milk	1 garlic clove, minced
2 tablespoons butter or margarine	1 teaspoon celery salt
1 lb. fresh mushrooms, sliced	1/4 teaspoon ground thyme
2 tablespoons all-purpose flour	1/4 teaspoon ground tarragon
1 cup half and half	1/8 teaspoon ground white pepper

Preheat oven to 350F (175C). Grease a 13 × 9-inch baking dish. Rinse fish fillets under cold water; pat dry with paper towels. Roll up each fillet. Place beaten eggs in a small bowl and bread crumbs in another small bowl. Dip a rolled fillet in beaten eggs, then in bread crumbs, evenly pressing crumbs into rolled fillet. Place breaded fillet, seam side down, in greased dish. Repeat with remaining fillets. Pour 1/2 cup of the milk in between rolled fillets. Bake 20 to 25 minutes or until fish just begins to flake when tested with a fork.

While fish is baking, melt butter or margarine in a medium saucepan over medium heat. Add mushrooms; sauté until mushrooms are tender. Stir flour into cooked mushrooms. Gradually stir in half and half and remaining 1/2 cup milk. Cook, stirring constantly, until thickened. Add pimientos, olives, dill, garlic, celery salt, thyme, tarragon and white pepper; simmer 10 minutes over low heat. If sauce is too thin, cook longer; if too thick, add a little more milk. Pour hot sauce around and over cooked fillets. Bake 10 more minutes or until fillets are heated through. Serve hot.

Stuffed Trout

Gefüllte Forelle

If you can get a 5- or 6-lb. trout, a single fish will do. Pike, salmon and carp may also be prepared this way. *Makes 6 to 8 servings.*

1 teaspoon salt

1/2 teaspoon freshly ground black
   pepper

1/4 teaspoon ground sweet paprika

2 (2 1/2-lb.) trout, ready to cook

1/2 cup plus 3 tablespoons butter or
   margarine

2 large onions, chopped

1 large celery root, shredded, or
   3 celery stalks, chopped

3 medium apples, peeled, cored and
   chopped

1 1/2 tablespoons chopped fresh
   parsley

1 cup finely chopped fresh
   mushrooms

About 4 cups croutons

1 1/2 teaspoons sugar

1/2 teaspoon ground thyme

Juice of 1/2 lemon

3 eggs

About 2/3 cup white wine

Combine salt, pepper and paprika in a small bowl. Rub salt mixture evenly over fish cavities. Cover; refrigerate 20 minutes. Preheat oven to 350F (175C). Grease a shallow baking dish large enough to hold fish.

Melt butter or margarine in a large skillet over medium heat; reserve 3 tablespoons in a small bowl for basting fish. Add onions and celery root or celery to skillet; sauté until tender, about 10 minutes. Reduce heat to low. Add apples, parsley and mushrooms; simmer, stirring, until mushrooms are tender; remove skillet from heat. Add croutons, sugar, thyme, lemon juice, eggs and wine; stir to combine. If stuffing mixture is too dry, add a little more wine; if too moist, add a few more croutons. Cool.

Loosely fill fish cavities with stuffing, allowing room for expansion during cooking. Place fish in greased dish, 1 fish facing right, the other facing left. Bake 30 to 40 minutes, basting with melted butter or margarine about every 10 minutes, or until fish changes from translucent to opaque throughout and flakes easily with a fork. Serve hot.

Broiled Salmon Steaks

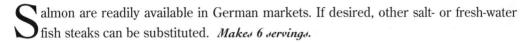

Grillen Lachs Steak

S almon are readily available in German markets. If desired, other salt- or fresh-water fish steaks can be substituted. *Makes 6 servings.*

6 (1-inch-thick) fresh or thawed frozen salmon steaks, about 2 lbs. total	1/2 teaspoon freshly ground black pepper
Juice of 1 lemon	1 garlic clove, minced
1/2 cup butter or margarine, melted	1 tablespoon chopped onion
1/4 teaspoon ground sweet paprika	1 tablespoon fresh chopped parsley
1/2 teaspoon salt	1 cup (4 oz.) shredded Emmentaler cheese

Lightly grease a broiler pan or grill. Preheat broiler or grill. Arrange salmon steaks on broiler pan or grill. Sprinkle lemon juice over salmon. Brush with melted butter or margarine. Sprinkle paprika, salt and pepper over salmon. Broil or grill salmon 5 to 7 minutes on each side, basting frequently with butter or margarine, or until steaks are cooked through and salmon flakes easily with a fork.

In a small saucepan, combine remaining melted butter or margarine, garlic, onion and parsley; cook over low heat 5 minutes. Arrange salmon on a warm serving platter. Sprinkle cheese over salmon. Spoon hot melted butter or margarine mixture over salmon and cheese. Serve hot.

Trout in Sauce

Forelle in Sosse

Rainbow trout are commonly found throughout Germany today, but it wasn't always so. The rainbow is a transplant from North America, introduced to Germany's inland waters in the latter part of the nineteenth century. *Makes 4 to 6 servings.*

1 (2 1/2- to 3-lb) trout, ready to
    cook, cut crosswise into 1 1/2- to
    2-inch pieces
Salt
3 cups Vegetable Broth (page 63)
    or Fish Broth (page 64)
1 celery root, chopped
1 medium onion, chopped
1/2 cup dry red wine
1 tablespoon grated lemon peel
1/8 teaspoon freshly ground black
    pepper

1/4 teaspoon ground ginger
Juice of 1/2 lemon
1 cup dark beer
1 tablespoon sugar
1 teaspoon honey
2 tablespoons raisins
2 tablespoons chopped almonds
2 tablespoons butter or margarine
1 tablespoon all-purpose flour
Salt to taste
Lemon slices

Rinse fish with cold running water; pat dry with paper towels. Rub trout inside and out with a little salt. Cover with plastic wrap and refrigerate 30 minutes. In a medium saucepan, combine broth, celery root, onion, wine, lemon peel, pepper, ginger and lemon juice. Simmer, uncovered, over low heat 30 minutes.

Place fish in a large skillet. Strain broth mixture into skillet with fish. Cover with a tight-fitting lid. Cook over low heat 20 to 30 minutes or until fish changes from translucent to opaque. Gently remove fish from skillet and transfer to a serving platter. Arrange pieces in the shape of the original trout. Keep fish warm in oven.

Strain cooking juices into a medium saucepan. Add beer, sugar, honey, raisins and almonds. Simmer 10 minutes over medium-low heat. Strain into a small saucepan. Melt butter or margarine in a small skillet over medium-low heat. Stir flour into butter or margarine; cook, stirring, until flour turns golden. Stir flour mixture into strained cooking juices; simmer, stirring occasionally, 15 to 20 minutes. Season with salt to taste. To serve, pour hot cooking juices over trout. Garnish with round lemon slices cut halfway and twisted in the shape of an "S."

Poached Fish Fillets with Shrimp Sauce

Pochiertes Fischfilet mit Garnelensosse

Trout, pike, salmon, haddock, cod or practically any other fish fillets will work here. *Makes 6 to 8 servings.*

2 tablespoons butter or margarine
2 tablespoons all-purpose flour
1 1/2 cups half and half
1 teaspoon sweet ground paprika
1 teaspoon salt
1/2 teaspoon white pepper

1 cup thinly sliced fresh mushrooms
1 lb. small cooked shrimp, shelled
3 to 3 1/2 lbs. fish fillets (about 1/2
   inch thick)
1 cup milk
Parsley sprigs

Melt butter or margarine in the top section of a double boiler. Slowly stir flour into melted butter or margarine. Gradually stir in half and half. Cook, stirring, until sauce thickens. Add paprika, 1/2 teaspoon of the salt, 1/4 teaspoon of the white pepper, mushrooms and shrimp. Cook in double boiler 30 minutes, stirring occasionally.

If fish fillets are over 4 inches wide, slice lengthwise in half. Roll each piece of fillet jelly-roll style and fasten each with a wooden pick. Place a lightly oiled large skillet over medium heat. Combine milk, remaining 1/2 teaspoon salt and remaining 1/4 teaspoon white pepper in skillet. Carefully place fillets in milk mixture; cover with a tight-fitting lid. Reduce heat to medium-low; simmer 15 to 20 minutes, or until fish flakes easily with a fork. Using a slotted spatula, remove fish and arrange on a warm platter; remove wooden picks. Pour hot shrimp sauce over fish. Serve immediately, garnished with parsley.

Baked Perch with Herbs

Backbarsch mit Krauter

Perch is a favorite panfish available year-round. *Makes 6 servings.*

6 large (10- to 13-inch) fresh whole
    perch (about 1 lb. each), ready to
    cook
Salt
Freshly ground black pepper
6 bay leaves, crumbled
2 tablespoons chopped fresh sage
    leaves, or 1 tablespoon dried sage

2 tablespoons chopped fresh
    rosemary leaves, or 1 tablespoon
    dried rosemary
3 tablespoons butter or margarine
2 tablespoons lemon juice
2 tablespoons olive oil
2 tablespoons chopped fresh parsley

Preheat oven to 425F (220C). Grease a shallow baking dish large enough to hold fish in one layer. Rinse fish inside and out with cold running water. Pat fish dry with paper towels. Sprinkle fish inside and out with salt and pepper. Spoon equal amount of bay leaves, sage and rosemary inside each fish. Place 1 teaspoon butter or margarine inside each fish. Arrange fish in baking dish; sprinkle with lemon juice, olive oil and parsley. Cover with a tight-fitting lid or foil; bake 20 to 25 minutes or until fish is cooked through and flakes with a fork. Serve hot.

Baked Stuffed Shrimp

Gefüllte Garnelen

Because the shrimp are not really "stuffed" (the stuffing is placed upon, not in the shrimp), you could get away with smaller, less expensive shrimp for this dish. But larger ones are indeed preferred. *Makes 6 servings.*

24 medium-large raw shrimp, shelled
   and deveined, with tails on
1/3 cup Chicken Broth (page 57)
   or chicken bouillon
6 tablespoons butter or margarine
2 garlic cloves, minced
1/2 teaspoon freshly ground black
   pepper

1 cup finely chopped onion
3/4 cup soft bread crumbs
2 tablespoons sour cream
1 teaspoon salt
1/2 teaspoon dried thyme leaves
1/2 teaspoon dried tarragon leaves
Chopped fresh parsley
Lemon wedges

Preheat oven to 350F (175C). Curl each shrimp and secure with wooden picks. In a shallow baking pan, combine broth or bouillon, 4 tablespoons of the butter or margarine, garlic and pepper. Simmer broth mixture 6 minutes.

Melt remaining 2 tablespoons butter or margarine in a small skillet over low heat. Add onion and bread crumbs; cook 5 minutes. Let cool. Add sour cream, salt, thyme and tarragon; stir to combine. Place 1 heaping teaspoon stuffing on the center of each curled shrimp. Carefully arrange stuffed shrimp in a single layer in the hot broth mixture. Baste with some of the broth mixture. Cover and bake 15 to 20 minutes or until shrimp are pink. Remove wooden picks. Sprinkle parsley over shrimp. Serve hot with lemon wedges.

Batter-Fried Fish

In Teiggebackener Fisch

Raw cleaned shrimp or lobster pieces are also excellent choices for this recipe. Create a seafood basket, using the same batter for all. *Makes 6 to 8 servings.*

2 lbs. fish fillets

3 eggs, separated

1 cup beer

1 1/2 cups sifted all-purpose flour

1 teaspoon salt

1/4 teaspoon ground sweet paprika

2 tablespoons chopped fresh parsley

1/2 cup butter or margarine, melted

Vegetable oil for deep-frying

Lemon wedges

Rinse fish; pat dry with paper towels. Cut into 2- to 4-inch pieces. In a medium bowl, beat egg yolks and beer together. Beat flour, salt, paprika, parsley and butter or margarine into beer mixture. Let batter stand 1 hour at room temperature.

In a medium bowl, beat egg whites until stiff peaks start to form. Fold beaten egg whites into batter. If batter is too thick, add a little more beer; if it's too thin, add a little more flour.

Heat vegetable oil for frying to 365F (185C). Dip 1 piece of fish into batter; turn fish to coat with batter. Let excess batter drip off. Gently lower battered fish into hot oil. Fry about 5 minutes, or until both sides are golden brown, turning once. Cook fish in batches so oil does not cool off too much. Drain fish on paper towels. Repeat with remaining pieces of fish. Serve hot, garnished with lemon wedges.

Fish Croquettes

Fischkroketten

Serve plain, with onions sautéed in a little butter, or serve with fresh hot Chicken Broth or Fish Broth, if desired. *Makes about 40 croquettes.*

2 lbs. fresh or thawed frozen fish
    fillets, skinned
2 day-old dinner rolls
1 cup milk
2 large eggs
1 1/4 teaspoons salt
1/4 teaspoon white pepper
1/4 teaspoon ground sweet paprika

1 1/2 tablespoons chopped fresh
    parsley
3 qts. Chicken Broth (page 57) or
    chicken bouillon
1 1/2 qts. hot Chicken Broth or Fish
    Broth (page 64) (optional), to
    serve

Using a meat grinder, grind fish into a medium bowl. In a small bowl, soak rolls in milk until milk is absorbed. With your hands, squeeze excess milk from rolls. Grind squeezed rolls; add to fish along with eggs, salt, white pepper, paprika and parsley. Blend fish mixture. With wet hands, form fish mixture into walnut-size balls. Place each ball on a greased baking sheet.

    In a large saucepan, bring 3 quarts broth or bouillon to a boil over high heat. Gently drop fish balls into boiling liquid; return to a boil. Reduce heat to medium; cook, uncovered, 10 to 12 minutes or until croquettes float. Cover with a tight-fitting lid; cook 5 to 7 minutes or until a total of 20 minutes is reached. Remove croquettes with a slotted spoon; discard cooking liquid. Place croquettes on a platter. Serve plain or with broth, if desired.

Eel in Sauce

Aal in Sosse

Skinning an eel takes practice. If possible, have it done at the fish market. If you've got to do it yourself, make a shallow incision around the body. Wearing a cotton or other glove on one hand, hold the eel firmly by the head with your gloved hand and with your other hand, pull skin from head to tail with one firm downward stroke. *Makes 4 to 6 servings.*

1 cup dry white wine	10 black peppercorns
1 1/2 cups water	1 small onion, sliced
1/2 cup apple juice	1 (2 1/2-lb.) eel, skinned
Juice of 1/2 lemon	and cleaned,
2 tablespoons minced fresh parsley	cut into 1 1/2- to 2-inch lengths
2 tablespoons minced fresh dill	1 tablespoon butter or margarine
2 tablespoons minced fresh chervil	1 tablespoon all-purpose flour
2 bay leaves	2 egg yolks
1/2 teaspoon salt	1/4 cup sour cream

In a large saucepan, combine wine, water, apple juice, lemon juice, 1 tablespoon of the parsley, 1 tablespoon of the dill, 1 tablespoon of the chervil, bay leaves, salt, peppercorns and onion. Bring to a boil over medium-high heat; simmer 10 minutes, uncovered. Add eel. Reduce heat to medium-low. Simmer, uncovered, 20 minutes. With a slotted spoon, remove eel from cooking liquid. Place eel on a serving dish; keep warm in oven.

Melt butter or margarine in a small saucepan over medium heat. Stir flour into melted butter or margarine; cook, stirring, until flour mixture turns a golden color. Strain enough eel cooking liquid into flour mixture to form a smooth sauce.

In a medium bowl, beat egg yolks and sour cream until smooth. Fold sour-cream mixture into sauce until combined. Add remaining parsley, dill and chervil; simmer over low heat, stirring, until heated through. To serve, pour heated sauce over warm eel pieces. Serve immediately.

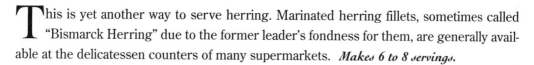

Herring in Cream Sauce

Hering in Cremesosse

This is yet another way to serve herring. Marinated herring fillets, sometimes called "Bismarck Herring" due to the former leader's fondness for them, are generally available at the delicatessen counters of many supermarkets. *Makes 6 to 8 servings.*

1 lb. marinated herring fillets, cut into 1/2-inch pieces
1 onion, thinly sliced
3/4 cup sour cream
3/4 cup plain yogurt

Juice of 1 lemon
1 teaspoon sugar
2 tablespoons chopped fresh dill, or
1 tablespoon dry dill weed

Place herring and onion in a medium bowl. In a small bowl, combine sour cream, yogurt, lemon juice and sugar. Pour sauce over herring; gently combine. Cover and refrigerate overnight. Before serving, sprinkle with dill. Serve chilled.

Herring Salad

Heringsalat

By starting out with pickled herring, you'll enjoy the results of a dish that used to take several days to prepare. Be sure to drain the herring before using it, though, because you'll have your own marinade before this recipe is completed. *Makes 6 to 8 servings.*

1 (1-lb.) pickled herring, drained and cut into 1 1/2- to 2-inch chunks

1/2 cup diced green bell pepper

2 small tart apples, diced

Juice of 1 1/2 lemons

1/4 cup chopped onion

1/4 cup olive oil

1/4 cup white vinegar

1 tablespoon chopped fresh dill

Combine all ingredients in a medium bowl. Cover and refrigerate 1 hour to overnight, turning herring several times. Serve chilled.

Bread & Rolls

Brot

A woman is leaning over her backyard fence, discussing her son's career choice with a neighbor. "Well," she says, "Manfred just couldn't pass his baker's exams, so he's taking up brain surgery."

That may be stretching the truth a bit—but not by much. Not just anyone can operate a bakery in Germany. Anyone can *own* a bakery, but only a properly trained and certified baker can bake the goods. Germany takes its bread very, very seriously. Becoming a master baker is an honored trade for which years of study and apprenticeship are required. A visit to the most out-of-the-way German bakery will confirm this by revealing a wonderful display of round and oval, long and short, and rectangular and square loaves of many colors and textures, with eye-pleasing braided or smooth or rough-scored crusts, some crispy and shiny. There are small rolls with hard crusts and many others of varying sizes. The smells in a German bakery are mouth-watering: sweet yeasts, sugars, salts, fruits and flours. Everything shiny and neat, where the smallest rolls can be individually purchased and where the baker's assistant will gladly slice exactly what you want from a torpedo-size loaf of rye.

Bread making goes on mostly late at night and early in the morning, supplying restaurants and shops and hotels with fresh supplies on a daily basis. Germans, unlike many Americans, will put up with a lot, but they demand that their breads and rolls be baked daily. Prepackaged breads and rolls have yet to make the inroads in German bakery markets that they have elsewhere. In fact, not too many years ago breads in Germany were still delivered door-to-door, hung on door knobs in bags, placed on window sills, or left in boxes on porches, like old-fashioned home-delivered milk. Because German bakers are so good at their trade, and bread and rolls so readily available, the home baking of bread is not as popular as it once was.

Today Germans think nothing of walking home from the market with loaves of crusty bread sticking out from the left arm and other groceries from the right. White bread is a rarity. Ryes, whole wheats and other hearty seed breads such as dill and caraway are available in a variety of combinations, textures and colors from golden to black. Sourdough mixtures are popular. Pumpernickel rye is baked and served almost everywhere, usually with butter and cold meats or cheese. The dark breads are mostly heavy, dense, and sometimes coarse-grained breads that keep well when wrapped in plastic, brown paper, or foil. Mail-order imported food catalogs frequently feature large pumpernickel loaves because the loaves keep so well and taste so good. But all breads are not heavy and dark. There are French breads, too.

Slicing bread is mostly a casual affair: whoever is doing the eating does the cutting. Loaves are rarely sliced evenly, as breads in the United States are. The main reason is a practical one: the loaves hold up better when kept intact. On the other hand, good teeth are needed to negotiate the sturdy crusts.

Crusty and softer white, rye and wheat rolls are found on practically every breakfast table, day in, day out. Unlike typical German breads, German rolls consist mostly of white flour.

Soft pretzels or pretzel-rolls are everywhere in Germany, sold fresh in bakeries, shops, outdoor stands, beer gardens, you name it. They're a fast food with a history, eaten plain or with spicy mustards, eaten with sausages, eaten for breakfast, lunch and dinner.

There are sweet breads, too. One being *Stollen,* a delicious traditional Christmas yeast bread that contains golden raisins, candied fruit, almonds and if desired, a helping of rum or brandy. Sometimes referred to as *Dresden Stollen* because of its origin, it's a sweet bread that stores very well. In fact, many household cooks will bake it at least a week in advance before serving. Different German cooks use *Stollen* recipes that vary considerably, but all are baked to a lovely golden brown, with a shiny yet soft crust that's been liberally brushed with melted butter two or three times as the hot loaf cools when removed from the oven. Some families have special ways to shape the dough—into the form of a cross, for instance. Sometimes *Stollen* is sprinkled with powdered sugar, and it's frequently baked in small loaves or cakes and given to friends and relatives as gifts. Traditionally, a small loaf of *Stollen* is kept until Easter, a practice that links one important celebration with another.

Soft Pretzels

Brezen

Instead of or in addition to coarse salt, try topping these pretzels with sesame, caraway or poppy seeds. Or make a mixed batch. From the same dough recipe you can also make fewer but larger pretzels. Just lengthen the baking time to match the larger size and be careful not to overcook them. When "tieing" the pretzels, it may help you to have a sample pretzel available—even a small store-bought one. *Makes 24 pretzels.*

1 1/4 cups warm water (105 to 115F, 40 to 45C)	*1 1/2 teaspoons salt*
	2 tablespoons vegetable oil
1 (1/4-oz.) package active dry yeast	*1 egg*
2 teaspoons sugar	*1 tablespoon milk*
About 4 cups all-purpose flour	*Coarse salt*

In a small bowl, combine 1/4 cup of the warm water, yeast and sugar. Let stand in a warm place until yeast mixture turns bubbly, 5 to 10 minutes. In a large bowl, combine 3 1/2 cups of the flour and salt. Add remaining 1 cup water, oil and yeast mixture; mix thoroughly. Turn dough out on a lightly floured surface. Knead dough until smooth and elastic, adding flour if needed to prevent sticking. Don't worry if some flour is left over.

Lightly grease several large baking sheets. Roll dough into a rope about 16 inches long. With a knife, divide dough into 24 equal-size pieces. Roll each piece of dough into a strip about 10 inches long. Form standard pretzel shapes by crossing the strip ends in a loop, then pressing the ends back against the body of the pretzel. Place pretzels as they are formed on greased baking sheets, leaving enough room for expansion during baking. Loosely cover pretzels with a clean cloth and let rise in a warm place until they almost double in size, about 20 minutes.

Preheat oven to 425F (220C). Beat egg and milk in a small bowl for a glaze. Lightly brush unbaked pretzels with egg glaze. Sprinkle each pretzel with salt. Bake 15 to 20 minutes, or until light golden. Avoid overbaking.

Dinner Rolls

....

Brotchen

Try substituting rye flour for the whole-wheat flour. Or use other combinations of different flours available. *Makes 24 cloverleaf dinner rolls.*

1 cup warm water (105 to 115F, 40 to 45C)	*2/3 cup butter or margarine, melted*
2 (1/4-oz.) packages active dry yeast	*2 cups whole-wheat flour*
2 tablespoons sugar	*2 cups unbleached all-purpose flour*
3 eggs	*1 teaspoon salt*
1/2 cup honey or sugar	*1 egg white*
	2 teaspoons milk

In a small bowl, combine warm water, yeast and sugar. Let stand in a warm place until yeast mixture turns bubbly, 5 to 10 minutes. Beat eggs with honey or sugar until pale and creamy. Add butter or margarine and yeast mixture. Sift flours and salt together; add to egg mixture. Mix until dough is smooth and elastic. Place dough in a lightly greased bowl; turn dough to coat evenly. Cover dough with plastic wrap; refrigerate overnight.

Grease 2 muffin baking pans (24 muffin cups). Divide dough into 24 pieces. Separate each piece into 3 equal portions; roll each portion into a small ball. Place 3 balls in each prepared muffin space. Cover with a clean cloth; let rise in a warm place until doubled in size, about 30 minutes.

Preheat oven to 375F (190C). In a small bowl, mix egg white and milk for a glaze. Brush rolls with egg white glaze. Bake rolls 12 to 15 minutes or until golden brown.

Variation

Lightly grease 2 baking sheets. Divide dough into 20 equal pieces. Form 10 pieces into oval shapes and 10 remaining pieces into round shapes. With a sharp knife, score 2 (1/4-inch-deep) slashes in the top of each roll. The slashes can be parallel to each other or crisscrossed. Arrange on prepared baking sheets with at least 2 inches between each roll to allow for expansion. Cover with a clean cloth, let rise and brush with egg white glaze as above. Bake 15 minutes or until golden brown. *Makes 20 oval and round dinner rolls.*

Rye Bread

Roggenbrot

Although this recipe calls for half rye and half white flour, you can experiment with different proportions. *Makes 1 loaf, about 10 servings.*

1 cup warm water (105 to 115F, 40 to 45C)

1 (1/4-oz.) package active dry yeast

2 teaspoons sugar

3/4 cup warm milk (105 to 115F, 40 to 45C)

3 tablespoons safflower oil

2 tablespoons molasses

1 1/2 cups rye flour

1 teaspoon salt

1 1/2 cups unbleached all-purpose flour

1 egg white

2 teaspoons water

2 teaspoons caraway seeds

In a small bowl, combine warm water, yeast and sugar. Let stand in a warm place until yeast mixture turns bubbly, 5 to 10 minutes. In the bowl of a large heavy-duty electric mixer, combine milk, safflower oil, molasses and yeast mixture. Beat in 1 cup of the rye flour and salt. Slowly add all-purpose flour and remaining rye flour, beating or stirring until dough is moderately stiff. Beat 10 minutes, adding a little additional warm milk or flour if required to produce a smooth, elastic dough. Lightly grease a large bowl. Add dough, turning to coat entire surface of dough. Cover dough with a clean cloth. Let rise in a warm place until doubled in size, about 2 hours.

Punch down dough. Form 1 round, slightly flattened loaf. Grease a baking sheet. Arrange loaf on prepared baking sheet. Cover and let loaf rise in a warm place until doubled in size, about 1 hour.

Preheat oven to 375F (190C). With a sharp knife, score top of loaf with 2 lengthwise 1/2-inch-deep slashes and 2 slashes of same depth crisscrossed crosswise. In a cup, combine egg white, 2 teaspoons water and caraway seeds for a glaze. Brush loaf with glaze. Bake 45 to 55 minutes or until crust is a dark golden brown and loaf sounds hollow when tapped. Remove from baking sheet and cool on a rack before slicing.

White Bread

Weissbrot

This delightful white bread will fill your kitchen with odors of sweet yeast and fresh flour. At one time, white bread was enjoyed only by the ruling class. *Makes 2 loaves, 10 to 12 servings.*

1 (1/4-oz.) package active dry yeast
1 cup warm water (105 to 115F, 40 to 45C)
2 teaspoons sugar
1 cup milk, scalded and cooled to lukewarm

2 1/2 tablespoons sugar
1 1/2 teaspoons salt
3 cups all-purpose flour
1 egg white, lightly beaten
2 teaspoons water

In a small bowl, combine yeast, 1/4 cup of the warm water and 2 teaspoons sugar. Let stand in a warm place until yeast mixture turns bubbly, 5 to 10 minutes. In the bowl of a large heavy-duty electric mixer, blend scalded milk, the remaining 3/4 cup warm water, 2 1/2 tablespoons sugar and salt. Add yeast mixture; mix to combine. Slowly add flour, mixing flour and yeast mixture into a smooth, elastic dough. If dough is too sticky, add a little more flour; if dough is too dry, add a little more warm water. Beat dough 5 more minutes, then form dough into a ball. Lightly grease a large bowl. Add dough, turning to coat entire surface of dough. Cover dough with a clean cloth. Let dough rise in a warm place until doubled in size, about 2 hours.

Punch down dough. Divide dough into 2 equal portions. Shape each portion into a rectangular loaf. Lightly grease 2 (8 × 4-inch) loaf pans. Arrange loaves in prepared pans. Cover with a clean cloth. Let rise in a warm place until loaves rise above pans, 1 1/2 hours.

Preheat oven to 350F (175C). In a cup, combine beaten egg white and 2 teaspoons water for a glaze. Brush egg white glaze over loaves. Bake 45 to 55 minutes, or until crusts are a light golden and loaves sound hollow when tapped. Remove from pans; let loaves cool on a wire rack before slicing.

Whole-Wheat Country Bread

Bauernbrot

The importance of whole-wheat bread in Germany has been stressed lately, as principles of sound nutrition have taken a firm hold throughout the country. *Makes 2 round loaves, about 12 servings.*

2 cups warm water (105 to 115F,
    40 to 45C)
1 (1/4-oz.) package active dry yeast
2 tablespoons honey
3 cups whole-wheat flour

2 cups unbleached all-purpose flour
1 teaspoon salt
3 tablespoons milk
1 tablespoon melted butter or
    margarine

In a small bowl, combine 1/4 cup of the warm water, yeast and honey. Stir until honey dissolves. Let stand in a warm place until yeast mixture turns bubbly, 5 to 10 minutes. In a large bowl, combine flours and salt. In the bowl of a large heavy-duty electric mixer, combine yeast mixture, the remaining 1 3/4 cups warm water and flour mixture; mix until a smooth, elastic dough results. If dough is too sticky, add a little more flour; if too dry, add more warm water. Lightly grease a large bowl. Add the dough, turning to coat entire surface of dough. Cover dough with a clean cloth. Let rise in a warm place until doubled in size, about 1 1/2 to 2 hours.

Punch down dough; divide dough in half. Form 2 round, slightly flattened loaves. Lightly grease a large baking sheet. Arrange loaves on prepared baking sheet. Cover and let rise 1 hour.

Preheat oven to 350F (175C). Using a sharp knife, score 3 parallel (1/2-inch-deep) slashes in the top of each loaf. In a cup, mix milk and melted butter or margarine for a glaze. Brush loaves with butter glaze. Bake 50 to 60 minutes or until loaves are golden brown and sound hollow when tapped. If loaves appear to be browning too quickly, cover lightly with foil when browned enough. Remove from baking sheet and cool loaves on racks.

Brown Bread

Graubrot

Unlike the other recipes in this chapter, this is a quick bread, leavened by a reaction of the buttermilk and baking soda, not yeast. *Makes 1 loaf, 4 to 6 servings.*

1 1/2 cups unbleached all-purpose
    flour
1 cup rye flour
1 cup whole-wheat flour
1/2 cup packed brown sugar
1/2 cup finely chopped walnuts

1/2 cup raisins
1 teaspoon salt
2 cups buttermilk
    (see Note, page 18)
1/2 cup dark molasses
2 teaspoons baking soda

Preheat oven to 325F (165C). Lightly grease a 9 × 5-inch loaf pan. In a large bowl, combine all-purpose flour, rye flour, whole-wheat flour, brown sugar, walnuts, raisins and salt. In a medium bowl, combine buttermilk or sour milk, molasses and baking soda, stirring with a wooden spoon. The buttermilk or sour milk mixture will begin to bubble. When it does, stir it into the flour mixture; stir until all ingredients are thoroughly combined in a thick batter. Spoon batter into prepared pan.

Bake 55 to 65 minutes or until a wooden pick inserted in center of loaf comes out clean. Using a spatula to loosen the sides, gently turn loaf out of pan; let cool on a wire rack.

Pumpernickel Bread

Schwarzbrot

This coarse, dark bread is universally devoured by Germans and German bread lovers around the world, especially when accompanied by butter, cold cuts, ham, cheese and frothy beer. *Makes 2 loaves, 12 to 14 servings.*

1 1/2 cups warm water (105 to 115F, 40 to 45C)

3 (1/4-oz.) packages active dry yeast

2 teaspoons sugar

1/2 cup molasses

1 1/2 tablespoons salt

2 tablespoons solid vegetable shortening

2 tablespoons caraway seeds

2 3/4 cups rye flour

About 3 cups unbleached all-purpose flour

Cornmeal

In a small bowl, combine 1/2 cup of the warm water, yeast and sugar. Let stand in a warm place until yeast mixture turns bubbly, 5 to 10 minutes. In a large bowl, combine remaining 1 cup warm water, molasses, salt, shortening, caraway seeds and yeast mixture; beat until smooth. Slowly beat rye flour into yeast and molasses mixture. Mix in all-purpose flour; work into a soft, smooth dough. Turn dough out onto a lightly floured surface. If dough is too moist, add a little more flour; if too dry, add a little more warm water. Knead 5 minutes. Lightly grease a large bowl. Add dough, turning to coat entire surface of dough. Cover dough with a clean cloth. Let rise in a warm place until almost doubled in size, about 1 1/2 hours.

Punch down dough. Separate dough into 2 equal portions. Form 2 round, slightly flattened loaves. Score a 3/4-inch-deep "X" in tops of both loaves with a sharp knife. Grease a large baking sheet; sprinkle with cornmeal. Cover loaves with a clean cloth; let rise until doubled, about 1 hour.

Preheat oven to 375F (190C). Bake 30 to 35 minutes or until crusts are dark brown and loaves sound hollow when tapped. Remove from baking sheets and cool on racks before slicing.

Old-Country Rye

Bauernbrot

The cocoa gives this old-fashioned rye a unique flavor. *Makes 1 loaf, about 12 servings.*

2 (1/4-oz.) packages active dry yeast

1 1/2 cups warm water (105 to 115F, 40 to 45C)

2 teaspoons sugar

1/2 cup light molasses

4 tablespoons melted butter or margarine

2 tablespoons caraway seeds

1 tablespoon salt

2 cups rye flour

2 1/2 cups whole-wheat flour

1/4 cup unsweetened cocoa powder

2 tablespoons cornmeal

In a small bowl, combine yeast, 1/2 cup of the warm water and sugar. Let stand in a warm place until yeast mixture turns bubbly, 5 to 10 minutes. In the bowl of a large, heavy-duty electric mixer, combine remaining 1 cup warm water, molasses, 2 tablespoons of the butter or margarine, caraway seeds, salt and yeast mixture; mix well. Add rye flour, 1 cup whole-wheat flour and cocoa; mix until smooth. Add remaining flour, mixing or stirring until dough is moderately stiff. Beat 10 minutes, until dough becomes smooth and elastic, adding a little more warm water or flour if required. Lightly grease a large bowl. Add dough, turning to coat entire surface of dough. Cover dough with a clean cloth. Let rise in a warm place until almost doubled in size, about 2 hours.

Punch down dough. Form 1 oval, slightly flattened loaf. Grease a baking sheet; sprinkle center part of baking sheet with cornmeal. Place loaf on baking sheet, over cornmeal. Let loaf rise in a warm place until doubled in size, about 1 hour.

Preheat oven to 375F (190C). Brush loaf with remaining 2 tablespoons melted butter or margarine. Bake 45 to 55 minutes or until crust is dark brown and loaf sounds hollow when tapped. Remove from baking sheet and cool on a rack.

Fruit Bread

Stollen

Among the earliest known sweeteners in Germany were honey and dried fruits. This Christmas recipe relies heavily on colorful candied or "glacéed" fruits. *Makes 2 loaves, 10 to 12 servings.*

1/3 cup golden raisins
1/4 cup chopped candied citron
1/3 cup chopped candied cherries
1/3 cup chopped candied orange or
    other citrus peel
1/2 cup light or dark rum
3/4 cup warm water (105 to 115F,
    40 to 45C)
1 (1/4-oz.) package active dry yeast
2 teaspoons plus 1/2 cup granulated
    sugar
1/4 teaspoon salt

1/2 teaspoon almond extract
1/2 cup milk
3 eggs
3/4 cup butter or margarine, melted
3 1/2 cups all-purpose flour
1 tablespoon grated lemon peel
1/2 cup blanched slivered almonds
1/3 cup powdered sugar (optional) to
    decorate
Cherries or candied citron leaves
    (optional) to decorate

In a medium bowl, combine raisins, citron, cherries, orange or other citrus peel and rum. Cover with plastic wrap and refrigerate overnight. Drain candied fruit, reserving the rum. Place candied fruit on paper towels to dry further.

In a small bowl, combine 1/4 cup of the warm water, yeast and 2 teaspoons sugar. Let stand in a warm place until yeast mixture turns bubbly, 5 to 10 minutes. In a large bowl, combine remaining 1/2 cup warm water, 1/2 cup sugar, salt, almond extract, milk, eggs, 1/2 cup melted butter or margarine, yeast mixture and reserved rum; beat thoroughly. Stir flour into sugar and yeast mixture until a soft, smooth dough results. Turn out dough on a lightly floured surface. Knead dough 5 minutes. If dough is sticky, add a little more flour. If dough is too dry, add a little more warm water. Gently work the drained candied fruit, lemon peel and almonds into dough. Lightly grease a large bowl. Add dough, turning to coat entire surface of dough. Cover dough with a clean cloth. Let rise in a warm place until almost doubled in size, 1 1/2 to 2 hours.

Punch down dough. Separate dough into 2 equal portions. On a lightly floured work surface, roll out dough into a 10 × 7 × 1/2-inch-thick rectangle. Fold lengthwise, bringing about one-third of width to middle. Fold opposite third to middle, overlapping edge of first fold along centerline of dough by about 1 inch. Press the center seam firmly, so edges lay flat and won't come apart while baking. Pinch the ends by squeezing dough together with your fingertips to seal. Repeat rolling and folding process with second portion of dough. Grease a large baking sheet. Place both stollen on opposite ends of prepared baking sheet. Brush with remaining 1/4 cup melted butter. Let rise in a warm place until doubled in size, 1 hour.

Preheat oven to 375F (190C). Bake 35 to 40 minutes or until golden brown. Remove from baking sheet and cool on wire racks. If desired, sift powdered sugar over stollen and decorate with cherries or candied citron.

Almond Pretzels

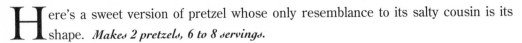

Mandelbretzen

Here's a sweet version of pretzel whose only resemblance to its salty cousin is its shape. *Makes 2 pretzels, 6 to 8 servings.*

1/3 cup warm water (105 to 115F, 40 to 45C)

1 (1/4-oz.) package active dry yeast

2 teaspoons sugar

1/3 cup warm milk

1/2 teaspoon salt

1/4 cup butter, melted

1 egg

2 1/4 cups all-purpose flour

Almond Filling (see below)

1 egg white

1 teaspoon water

2 tablespoons slivered almonds, chopped

ALMOND FILLING

1 cup almond paste

1/3 cup sugar

6 tablespoons butter, room temperature

In a small bowl, combine 1/3 cup warm water, yeast and sugar. Let stand in a warm place until yeast mixture turns bubbly, 5 to 10 minutes. In a large bowl, combine warm milk, salt, melted butter, egg and yeast mixture; beat until smooth. Add flour, stirring to make a soft dough. Turn out dough on a lightly floured surface. Knead dough until soft and elastic, 5 to 10 minutes. Grease a large bowl. Add dough, turning to coat entire surface of dough. Cover dough with a clean cloth. Let rise in a warm place until almost doubled in size, about 1 hour. Prepare Almond Filling: Blend almond paste, sugar and butter in a medium bowl.

Punch down dough. Divide dough into 2 equal portions. On a lightly floured working surface, roll out half of dough into a 25 × 3-inch rectangle. Spread half of filling over rolled dough. Roll, jelly-roll style, and pinch edges closed. Carefully twist the long dough roll into a pretzel shape. Repeat process with other dough portion and remaining filling. Grease a large baking sheet. Arrange pretzels on opposite ends of prepared baking sheet. In a cup, mix egg white with 1 teaspoon water for a glaze. Brush pretzels with glaze. Sprinkle with chopped almonds. Cover and let rise in a warm place until doubled in size, 1 hour.

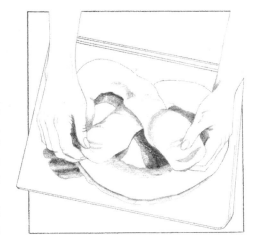

Preheat oven to 350F (175C). Bake 25 to 30 minutes or until golden brown. Serve warm.

Desserts

Nachspeisen

Desserts in Germany mean cakes and tortes and cookies and jam-filled doughnuts and pastries and sweet breads and puddings and creams and prepared fruits and ice creams. But of all these, the German fondness for baking shines through. The famous Black Forest Cherry Cakes with their chocolate and cherry and cherry brandy flavors, the many cookies that are sweetened with honey and peppered with bits of fancy candied fruits and the fancy molded springerle cookies all attest to German baking skills. "May your introduction be short and sweet," goes an old German proverb.

That goes for the opening words of this introduction, too. On to the desserts!

Coffeecake

Kaffeekuchen

This simple coffee cake is all the typical German family needs to fuel a rousing discussion of politics, sports or work topics around the dinner table. *Makes 1 (13 × 9-inch) cake, 12 to 14 servings.*

1/4 cup warm water (105 to 115F, 40 to 45C)

1 (1/4-oz.) package active dry yeast

1/4 cup plus 1 tablespoon sugar

2 cups plus 2 tablespoons all-purpose flour

2 eggs

1/4 cup butter or margarine, melted

1/2 cup milk, warmed

2 cups all-purpose flour

Crunchy Topping (see below)

1 (16-oz.) can thinly sliced peaches in syrup, drained

CRUNCHY TOPPING

1/2 cup all-purpose flour

1/4 cup packed brown sugar

1/4 cup granulated sugar

1/4 cup butter or margarine, chilled

1 teaspoon vanilla extract

Pinch of salt

In a small bowl, combine warm water and yeast. Add 1 tablespoon sugar and 2 tablespoons flour. Let stand in a warm place until yeast mixture turns bubbly, 5 to 10 minutes.

Place eggs and 1/4 cup sugar in a large bowl; beat until pale and fluffy. Add melted butter or margarine and milk to egg mixture. Beat until well blended. While beating, slowly add 2 cups flour to make a soft dough. Using your hands, turn dough out on a floured surface and knead 8 to 10 minutes, until smooth and elastic. Place dough in a greased bowl, turning to coat all sides. Cover with a clean damp cloth; let rise in a warm place, free from drafts, until doubled in bulk.

Place dough on a lightly floured surface. Punch dough down, then form it into a ball. Roll out dough into a 13 × 9-inch rectangle, forming corners with your hands. Grease a 13 × 9-inch baking pan. Fit dough into greased pan. Cover with a cloth and let rise in a warm place 1 hour or until doubled in bulk.

Preheat oven to 375F (190C). Prepare Crunchy Topping; set aside. With a paper towel, pat peach slices dry. Arrange peaches on top of dough, as desired. Sprinkle Crunchy Topping over peaches and dough. Bake 30 minutes or until topping turns a light golden brown. Let cool in pan.

Crunchy Topping

In a blender or food processor, combine all ingredients until crumbly. Or, in a medium bowl, evenly cut all ingredients together with a pastry blender until crumbly.

Old-Fashioned Spice Cake

Gewürzkuchen

If you've got the time, start this traditional dessert two weeks in advance to let the dough age to perfection. *Makes 1 (13 × 9-inch) cake, 12 to 14 servings.*

1 1/3 cups honey	2 teaspoons ground cloves
1 cup granulated sugar	1 teaspoon ground ginger
1/2 cup plus 2 tablespoons unsalted	2 eggs
butter or margarine	1/4 cup milk
About 4 cups all-purpose flour	2 tablespoons Soft Candied Orange
1 1/2 teaspoons baking soda	Peel (page 294)
1/4 teaspoon salt	1/2 cup finely chopped walnuts
2 teaspoons ground cinnamon	Powdered sugar to sprinkle

Combine honey, granulated sugar and butter or margarine in a medium saucepan. Bring to a boil, stirring over medium heat. Remove from heat. Let cool.

Combine flour, baking soda, salt, cinnamon, cloves and ginger in a large bowl. Add honey mixture, eggs, milk, candied orange peel and walnuts. Mix into a rich dough. Turn out dough on a lightly floured surface; knead until smooth, about 15 minutes. Add a little more flour if dough is too moist. Form dough into a ball. Cover with foil and refrigerate 2 weeks.

Preheat oven to 325F (165C). Butter a 13 × 9-inch baking pan. On a lightly floured work surface, roll out dough into a 13 × 9-inch rectangle. Lightly flour rolled dough and roll up on a rolling pin. Unroll dough rectangle into buttered baking pan. Bake 45 to 50 minutes, or until wood pick inserted in center comes out clean. Let cool 2 or 3 minutes. Turn cake out from pan. Let cool on a wire rack. Sprinkle top of cake with powdered sugar.

Variation

When cake cools, slice horizontally into 3 layers. Spread 1 1/4 cups thick plum or cherry jam on top of bottom two layers. Stack cake layers. Sprinkle top of cake with powdered sugar.

Plum Cake

Pflaumenkuchen

Use only fresh ripe plums for this aromatic and attractive dessert. Be aware that if you plan to use Vanilla Sugar for this recipe, you need to prepare the sugar at least two weeks in advance. *Makes 1 (10-inch) round cake.*

Vanilla Sugar (see below)
2 cups all-purpose flour
1 teaspoon baking powder
1/2 cup plus 3 tablespoons unsalted
   butter or margarine, room
   temperature
3 tablespoons sour cream
1/2 cup plus 3 tablespoons powdered
   sugar, sifted separately

1 egg yolk
1 teaspoon vanilla extract
Freshly grated peel of 1 lemon
1 1/2 lbs. fresh ripe plums, halved
   lengthwise, pitted and tossed with
   lemon juice

VANILLA SUGAR
2 cups sugar

2 vanilla beans

Prepare Vanilla Sugar 2 weeks before using.

Place flour and baking powder in a large bowl. Add butter or margarine, sour cream, 1/2 cup powdered sugar, egg yolk, vanilla extract and lemon peel. Work flour mixture with your hands into a medium-soft dough. Press dough into a ball. Cover dough and refrigerate 30 minutes.

Preheat oven to 430F (220C). Butter sides and bottom of a round 10-inch spring-form pan. Slice dough into round pieces about 1/2 inch thick. Reserve 1 end slice, then place remaining dough slices in a flat layer on pan bottom. Press dough slices together and smooth dough together with your fingertips. Roll reserved dough piece into a rope about 1/4 inch thick. Place dough rope inside of pan, against bottom dough layer. Gently press dough rope into bottom dough and pan sides.

Arrange plums, cut sides up, on bottom dough layer. Gently press plums into dough. Bake 20 to 25 minutes or until a wooden pick inserted in center of cake comes out clean. Remove from oven. Combine 3 tablespoons powdered sugar and 1/2 teaspoon Vanilla Sugar in a small bowl. Sprinkle sugar mixture over plums. Let cool.

Vanilla Sugar

Place sugar and vanilla beans in a small jar or container. Cover with an airtight lid. Set aside in a cool, dry place. Shake occasionally. Store 2 weeks before using. *Makes 2 cups.*

Peach Cake

Pfirsichkuchen

For the absolutely best-looking cake possible, choose peaches that are firm but ripe, without a hint of green and without large dark-colored bruises. *Makes 1 (13 × 9-inch) cake, 12 to 14 servings.*

Almond Topping (see below)
1 1/2 cups all-purpose flour
2 teaspoons baking powder
1/4 teaspoon salt
1/2 cup butter or margarine, chilled
2 eggs

ALMOND TOPPING
1 cup slivered almonds, processed
   into a consistency approaching a
   fine powder
1/4 cup butter or margarine,
   room temperature
1/2 cup all-purpose flour
1/2 cup packed brown sugar

1/4 cup milk
1 tablespoon grated lemon peel
10 large ripe peaches, peeled, pitted,
   sliced and tossed with lemon juice
1/2 cup sugar
Apricot Glaze (see below)

APRICOT GLAZE
3/4 cup apricot preserves
2 tablespoons water

Preheat oven to 350F (175C). Lightly grease a 13 × 9-inch cake pan. Prepare Almond Topping; set aside. Sift flour, baking powder and salt into a food processor fitted with the metal blade. Add butter or margarine; process until mixture resembles coarse meal. In a medium bowl, beat eggs with milk. Add flour mixture and lemon peel to egg mixture; stir until combined. Pour batter into greased pan.

    Carefully arrange peaches on top of the batter, peeled sides up. Sprinkle peaches evenly with sugar. Sprinkle Almond Topping evenly over sugared peaches. Bake 40 to 50 minutes or until a wooden pick inserted in cake comes out clean. Let cake cool about 15 minutes. Prepare Apricot Glaze. Brush cake with hot Apricot Glaze. Let cool.

Almond Topping

In a medium bowl, mix together almond powder, butter or margarine, flour and brown sugar.

Apricot Glaze

Press apricot preserves through a sieve into a small saucepan. Blend in water. Cook over low heat 2 or 3 minutes or until preserves melt.

Black Forest Cherry Cake

Schwarzwälder Kirschtorte

Although maraschino cherries make an excellent garnish for this rich dessert, fresh pitted sweet cherries can also be used. You needn't be restricted with your decorations, either. This cake has many times been prepared as ornately as you could imagine.
Makes 1 (9-inch) cake, about 12 servings.

2 (8 oz.) squares dark or semisweet chocolate, room temperature

1 (15- or 16-oz.) can of pitted tart cherries, drained

1/3 cup plus 2 tablespoons cherry brandy

3 (9-inch-round) Chocolate Cake Layers (see below)

2 cups whipping cream

2 tablespoons half and half

1/3 cup powdered sugar

About 18 maraschino cherries, well drained

CHOCOLATE CAKE LAYERS

3 cups cake flour

2 1/3 cups sugar

1 cup unsweetened cocoa powder

2 teaspoons baking soda

1 teaspoon salt

1/3 teaspoon baking powder

1 3/4 cups milk

1 cup vegetable shortening

5 eggs

1 teaspoon vanilla extract

Using a vegetable peeler, shave the chocolate squares into thin curls and pieces. Chill curls and pieces in refrigerator until ready to use.

In a medium bowl, soak tart cherries in 1/3 cup cherry brandy; set aside at room temperature 2 to 3 hours, stirring occasionally.

Prepare 3 (9-inch-round) cake layers. With a dinner fork, perforate the top of each cooled cake layer all over to a depth of about 1/2 inch, so cake layers will freely absorb sprinkled cherry brandy. Drain tart cherries and set aside, reserving drained brandy. Evenly sprinkle drained brandy over the 3 cake layer tops.

In a chilled medium bowl, combine whipping cream, half and half, powdered sugar and 2 tablespoons cherry brandy; beat until stiff peaks form. Place 1 cake layer on a serving plate. Spread cake layer top with one-quarter of whipped cream mixture; top with half of the tart cherries, leaving a 1-inch margin around outside edge of cake without cherries. Repeat process with whipped cream and remaining cherries for second cake layer, placing finished second layer on top of the first. Top with the third cake layer.

Frost sides of entire cake with half of the remaining whipped cream mixture. With a spoon, carefully press smaller chilled chocolate curls and pieces onto whipped cream mixture all around the sides of the cake. Garnish top edge of cake all around with 12 equally spaced dollops of remaining whipped cream mixture. Top each dollop with a drained maraschino cherry. Arrange remaining larger chocolate curls and pieces in center of cake top, leaving a little room in center of chocolate pieces for remaining drained maraschino cherries. Keep cake refrigerated until ready to serve.

Chocolate Cake Layers

Preheat oven to 350F (175C). Grease and flour 3 (9-inch-round) cake pans. In a large bowl, sift together cake flour, sugar, cocoa, baking soda, salt and baking powder. Add milk, shortening, eggs and vanilla. Using an electric mixer set at low speed, beat until well mixed, making sure all ingredients are thoroughly blended by occasionally scraping the sides of the bowl. Beat 5 more minutes on high speed.

Pour one-third of the cake batter into each prepared pan. Bake 30 to 35 minutes or until a wooden pick inserted in cake centers comes out clean. Cool cake layers in pans on wire racks 10 minutes; carefully remove from pans and cool completely on racks.

Black Forest Cake Roll

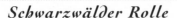

Schwarzwälder Rolle

When attractively decorated with chocolate or real leaves and flowers, this cousin of the Black Forest Cherry Cake makes a picture-perfect dessert for the finest occasion. *Makes 1 (15-inch) cake roll, about 6 servings.*

Chocolate Leaves (see below)	*1/2 teaspoon salt*
4 eggs	*1/2 cup powdered sugar, sifted*
2/3 cup granulated sugar	*1 cup whipping cream*
1 tablespoon water	*16 oz. cherry preserves*
1 teaspoon vanilla extract	*7 to 10 whole pitted sweet cherries*
2/3 cup all-purpose flour	*(or whole or large chunks of*
1/4 cup unsweetened cocoa powder	*cherries removed from cherry*
1/2 teaspoon baking powder	*preserves)*

CHOCOLATE LEAVES

3 oz. semisweet chocolate	*About 20 small fresh rose leaves,*
1 teaspoon vegetable shortening	*rinsed and patted dry*

Prepare Chocolate Leaves. Preheat oven to 350F (175C). Line a 15 × 10-inch jelly-roll pan with waxed paper. Lightly butter the top side of waxed paper and sprinkle with a little flour.

In a large bowl, beat eggs until light. Gradually add granulated sugar while beating. Beat until light and fluffy. Fold water and vanilla into beaten eggs. Sift flour, cocoa, baking powder and salt into a small bowl; fold into egg mixture. Pour batter into prepared pan. Bake 12 to 15 minutes or until top springs back when lightly pressed; do not overbake.

Let cake cool in pan 2 to 3 minutes. Place a clean cloth on a work surface; sprinkle 1/4 cup of the powdered sugar lightly over cloth. Turn cake out onto sugared cloth. Roll up warm cake and towel together; set aside to cool on wire rack, setting cake on its seam so it stays rolled.

While cake is cooling, beat cream in a chilled medium bowl until stiff peaks form. Fold remaining 1/4 cup powdered sugar into beaten cream. Unroll cake and spread cherry preserves over cake, leaving a 1-inch border on all sides. Top cherry preserves with about 1 cup of whipped cream mixture. Reroll cake, helping to do so by lifting up the towel. Place cake roll, seam side down, on a serving platter. Evenly frost top and sides of cake roll with remaining whipped cream mixture. Run a fork lengthwise across top and sides to form a striped pattern. Garnish with sweet pitted whole cherries or chunks of cherries. Arrange chocolate leaves over cake roll, near cherries.

Chocolate Leaves

In a small saucepan, melt chocolate and shortening together over low heat; stir to combine. Spread rose leaves out on waxed paper. Brush 1/8-inch layer of melted chocolate mixture on top sides of leaves with a pastry brush. When chocolate hardens and is dry, carefully peel each rose leaf from chocolate. Refrigerate chocolate leaves or freeze and store until ready to use. Makes about 20 chocolate leaves.

Variation
Edible real flowers can be substituted or used to decorate in addition to chocolate leaves.

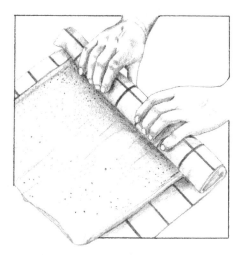 

Poppy Seed Cake

Mohnkuchen

Arrack is a fiery liquor, often flavored with anise, that can be found in the imported foods sections of many large grocery stores. *Makes 1 (10-inch) cake, about 10 servings.*

2 1/2 cups dried poppy seeds
About 1 1/4 qts. water
1/2 cup plus 1 tablespoon unsalted
    butter or margarine, room
    temperature
1 cup sugar

1 cup all-purpose flour
2 teaspoons baking powder
7 egg whites
1/2 teaspoon arrack or other
    flavoring

Place poppy seeds in a large bowl. Bring water to a boil in a medium saucepan. Pour boiling water over poppy seeds. Stir until all poppy seeds are soaked. Cover with plastic wrap and let stand overnight at room temperature. Carefully strain through a fine-mesh strainer; discard liquid. Grind poppy seeds through a grinder into a medium bowl. Grind two more times.

Preheat oven to 350F (175C). Grease a round 10-inch springform pan. In a large bowl, beat butter or margarine and sugar until creamy. Combine flour and baking powder in a small bowl. Beat flour mixture into butter or margarine mixture. In a large bowl, beat egg whites until stiff, adding arrack or other flavoring. Fold egg whites and ground poppy seeds into butter or margarine mixture. Pour batter into greased springform pan. Bake 55 to 60 minutes or until a wooden pick inserted in center comes out clean. Let cool 4 to 5 minutes. Remove pan sides. Let cake cool on a rack.

German Cake

Kuchen

This is but one of dozens of basic German cakes that are commonly made by German household cooks. It can be made with or without the nuts. *Makes 1 (8-inch) round cake.*

1/2 cup butter or margarine, room temperature
1 cup plus 1 tablespoon sugar
4 eggs, room temperature
1 tablespoon lemon juice
1/2 tablespoon grated lemon peel

1 cup all-purpose flour
1 teaspoon baking powder
1/4 cup chopped almonds, pecans or hazelnuts
1/4 teaspoon ground cinnamon

Preheat oven to 350F (175C). Lightly butter an 8-inch-round baking pan. Sprinkle a little flour over the bottom of the buttered pan; tap out excess. In a large bowl, beat butter or margarine and 1 cup sugar 3 to 4 minutes or until light and creamy. Beat in the eggs, one at a time, beating at least 1 minute after each egg is added. Add lemon juice and lemon peel, beating until combined. Sift flour and baking powder into butter or margarine mixture. Beat until mixture becomes a smooth batter. Gently pour batter into prepared pan.

In a small bowl, mix together nuts, remaining 1 tablespoon sugar and cinnamon. Sprinkle evenly on top of batter. Bake 30 to 35 minutes or until wooden pick inserted in center of cake comes out clean. Cool slightly, tip pan enough to carefully remove cake. Cool on a wire rack. Serve warm or at room temperature.

Bee-Sting Cake

······ *Bienenstich* ······

A winning combination: a moist cake with a creamy filling and nutty almond and honey topping. *Makes 1 (10-inch) cake, about 10 servings.*

Cake Filling (see below)
1/4 cup warm water (105 to 115F, 40 to 45C)
1 (1/4-oz.) package active dry yeast
1/3 cup plus 2 tablespoons sugar
3 cups all-purpose flour

Grated peel of 1 lemon
1/2 cup milk, warmed
2 eggs
1/4 cup butter, melted
Cake Topping (see below)

CAKE FILLING
1 (3.4-oz.) package French vanilla-flavored instant pudding
1 cup milk
1/2 cup whipping cream

ALMOND TOPPING
1/2 cup butter
1 cup honey
1 cup ground almonds
2 tablespoons half and half
1/8 teaspoon ground cinnamon

Prepare Cake Filling. In a small bowl, combine warm water, yeast and 2 tablespoons sugar. Let stand in a warm place until bubbly. Combine flour, lemon peel, milk, 1/3 cup sugar, eggs, butter and yeast mixture in a large bowl; mix with your hands until an elastic dough forms. Knead the dough in the bowl 10 to 15 minutes. Cover dough with a clean cloth and set in a warm place until dough doubles, about 2 hours. Prepare Almond Topping.

Preheat oven to 350F (175C). Grease a 10-inch springform pan. Place raised dough in pan and press dough flat with your fingertips, evenly covering the bottom of pan with dough. Spread the almond topping over the dough in an even layer. Bake 50 minutes or until topping is golden brown and cake is cooked. Let cake cool. Remove cake from pan and horizontally slice cake through center of baked dough. Carefully remove upper layer of cake. Spread cake filling over bottom layer of cake. Gently replace top layer of cake. Slice and serve immediately, or keep refrigerated until needed.

Cake Filling

Prepare instant pudding with milk according to package directions. In a chilled medium bowl, whip cream until stiff peaks form. Fold whipped cream into pudding. Cover pudding mixture with plastic wrap; chill.

Almond Topping

Melt butter in the top section of a double boiler. Stir honey, almonds, half and half and cinnamon into melted butter. Cool.

Gingerbread

························

Lebkuchen

Here's a rich, moist, spicy cake that has a wonderful aroma. *Makes 1 (9-inch) square cake, about 9 servings.*

2 (1-oz.) squares unsweetened
    chocolate
4 tablespoons unsalted butter or
    margarine, room temperature
1 cup sugar
3 eggs
1 cup honey
2 cups all-purpose flour
1 tablespoon ground cinnamon

1 tablespoon ground allspice
1 tablespoon ground cloves
1/4 teaspoon ground nutmeg
1 teaspoon baking powder
1/4 teaspoon salt
1 teaspoon vanilla extract
1/2 cup bourbon or brandy
1 cup pecans, finely chopped

POWDERED SUGAR ICING (OPTIONAL)
2 egg whites
1 1/2 cups sifted powdered sugar
2 tablespoons brandy or other liquor

In the top section of a double boiler, melt chocolate over low heat; let cool.

Preheat oven to 350F (175C). Grease a 9-inch-square pan. In a large bowl, beat butter or margarine and sugar until creamy. Add eggs, one at a time, beating well after each is added. Beat in honey, cooled chocolate, flour, cinnamon, allspice, cloves, nutmeg, baking powder, salt, vanilla extract, bourbon or brandy and pecans; beat until combined. Pour batter into greased baking pan. Bake 40 minutes or until top springs back when lightly pressed. Let cool in pan on rack. Prepare Powdered-Sugar Icing, if desired. When cooled, spread with icing, if using.

Powdered Sugar Icing

In a medium bowl, beat egg whites until frothy. Gradually add powdered sugar, beating constantly. Beat 10 minutes or until glossy. Add brandy or other liquor; beat 2 minutes or until icing stands up in soft peaks.

Apple Crisp Cake

Apfelkuchen

German cooks love to use apples in their baking. Here's a recipe that combines easy-to-make apple filling with a delectably sweet powdered sugar icing. *Makes about 20 pieces.*

2 cups all-purpose flour

1 teaspoon baking powder

Pinch of salt

3/4 cup unsalted butter or margarine, chilled

1 cup sugar

2 egg yolks

1 tablespoon sour cream

Apple Filling (see below)

Powdered Sugar Icing (see below)

Candied Orange Peel (page 294), chopped walnuts or shredded coconut (optional)

APPLE FILLING

1 lb. tart apples, peeled, cored and thinly sliced

1/4 cup water

1 tablespoon cornstarch

1/2 cup sugar

1/8 teaspoon ground cinnamon

POWDERED SUGAR ICING

2 egg whites

1 1/2 cups sifted powdered sugar

1/2 teaspoon lemon juice

Sift flour, baking powder and salt into a medium bowl. Cut butter or margarine into flour mixture until it resembles coarse meal. Add sugar, egg yolks and sour cream. Work mixture quickly with your hands into a rough dough. Press dough into a ball. Cover and refrigerate dough 2 to 24 hours.

Prepare Apple Filling and Powdered Sugar Icing. Preheat oven to 350F (175C). On a lightly floured surface, roll out dough into a 13 × 9-inch rectangle. Lightly flour dough and roll up widthwise on a rolling pin. Unroll dough into a 13 × 9-inch baking pan. Crimp dough edges 1/2 inch up pan sides, like pie crust. Bake 20 to 25 minutes or until golden. Let cool.

Evenly smooth out apple filling over baked crust. Frost by gently spooning powdered sugar icing over apple filling. Decorate with orange peel, chopped walnuts or shredded coconut, if desired. Bake 15 minutes. Let cool. Carefully cut cake into serving-size pieces.

Apple Filling

Place apples and water in a medium saucepan; cook, uncovered, over medium-low heat, stirring, 10 minutes or until apples are broken into small pieces. In a small bowl, combine cornstarch, sugar and cinnamon. Stir into cooking apples. Reduce heat to low; simmer, uncovered, 10 minutes or until thickened, stirring. Let cool.

Powdered Sugar Icing

In a medium bowl, beat egg whites until frothy. Gradually add powdered sugar, beating constantly. Beat 10 minutes or until glossy. Add lemon juice; beat 2 minutes or until icing stands up in soft peaks. If desired, add food coloring or flavorings, such as 1 teaspoon sifted unsweetened cocoa powder or vanilla extract. Use a little more sugar if liquids are added.

Makes about 1 1/4 cups icing.

Cheesecake

Käsekucken

The key to this cheesecake's success is the old-fashioned white farmer's cheese. You can find it in the delicatessen or cheese counters of most large supermarkets, in ethnic food shops, or through mail-order gourmet catalogs. *Makes 8 to 10 servings.*

Cheesecake Crust (see below)

5 eggs, separated

2 cups powdered sugar, sifted

1 tablespoon Vanilla Sugar (page 266)

2 lbs. old-fashioned white farmer's cheese

1 cup unsalted butter or margarine, melted and cooled

1/3 cup all-purpose flour

1 egg, beaten

CHEESECAKE CRUST

3/4 cup all-purpose flour

1/4 cup powdered sugar, sifted

2 1/2 tablespoons unsalted butter or margarine, room temperature

1 egg yolk

Prepare Cheesecake Crust. Preheat oven to 350F (175C). In a large bowl, beat egg yolks, powdered sugar and Vanilla Sugar until pale and creamy, about 5 minutes. Grind cheese through a grinder or process in a food processor fitted with the steel blade until finely ground. Add one-fourth of the cheese and one-fourth of the butter or margarine to egg-yolk mixture. Beat until smooth, about 1 minute. Add another one-fourth of the cheese and one-fourth of the butter or margarine. Beat until smooth. Repeat two more times, until all cheese and butter is used.

In a medium bowl, beat egg whites until stiff. Gently fold one-fourth of the egg whites and one-fourth of the flour into cheese mixture. When smooth, fold another one-fourth of the egg whites and one-fourth of the flour into cheese mixture. Repeat two more times, until all egg whites and flour are used. Spoon cheese mixture into springform pan over prepared crust; smooth the surface. Brush with beaten egg. Bake 55 to 60 minutes or until a wooden pick inserted in center comes out clean. Cool on a rack in pan at least 2 hours.

Cheesecake Crust

Sift flour and powdered sugar into a medium bowl. Add butter and egg yolk. With your fingers, work mixture into a smooth dough. Cover with foil or waxed paper. Refrigerate 2 hours. Preheat oven to 350F (175C). Pat dough evenly over the bottom of a round 10-inch springform pan. Bake 10 minutes or until crust sets. Let cool.

Apple Fritters

Apfelschnitten

Although the apples in many desserts do not have to be carefully prepared, in this recipe try to cut the apple slices as evenly as possible, so each fritter is cooked to the same level of doneness. *Makes about 35 to 40 fritters.*

1 cup all-purpose flour	3 firm, tart apples
1/2 teaspoon salt	3 tablespoons lemon juice
2 eggs, separated	1/3 cup granulated sugar
2 tablespoons butter or margarine, room temperature	1 teaspoon ground cinnamon
	Vegetable oil for deep-frying
1 cup fresh apple cider	1 cup powdered sugar

In a blender or food processor fitted with the steel blade, process flour, salt, egg yolks, butter or margarine and cider. Process until smooth. In a medium bowl, beat egg whites. Fold flour mixture into egg whites until combined.

Peel and core apples; cut into 1/4-inch-thick slices. Sprinkle apple slices with lemon juice and toss with granulated sugar.

Heat 4 to 5 inches oil in a large heavy-duty saucepan over medium-high heat until oil is hot enough to sizzle when a tiny bit of batter is dropped in. Dip an apple slice in batter. Apple slice should be evenly coated with batter; allow excess batter to drip off. Repeat with several more apple slices. Carefully drop battered apple slices into hot oil. Cook 8 to 10 minutes or until apple slices are cooked through and batter is puffy and golden. Drain on paper towels. Repeat process until all apple slices are battered and cooked. Let cool. Sprinkle with powdered sugar before serving.

Berlin Jam-Filled Doughnuts

Berliner Pfannkuchen

Back when President Kennedy was trying to say "Ich bin ein Berliner," or that he was a Berliner, he was literally, in the German language, stating that he was, indeed, a jelly doughnut—a *Berliner. Makes 50 to 60 filled doughnuts.*

4 (1/4-oz.) packages active dry yeast

1/3 cup warm water (105 to 115F,
    40 to 45C)

1 cup plus 2 tablespoons granulated
    sugar

6 3/4 cups all-purpose flour

1 1/4 cups milk, warmed

12 egg yolks

1 teaspoon salt

1/2 teaspoon vanilla extract

1/2 cup butter or margarine, melted
    and cooled

2 tablespoons rum

About 3/4 cup thick cherry, apple or
    other jam

Vegetable oil for deep-frying

Powdered sugar, sifted

In a medium bowl, dissolve yeast in water. Stir in 2 tablespoons granulated sugar and 1/4 cup of the flour. Blend in milk until smooth. Let stand until foamy, 5 to 10 minutes.

In a large bowl, beat egg yolks, 1 cup granulated sugar, salt and vanilla until pale and creamy. Add yeast mixture, melted butter or margarine, 3 cups of the flour and rum. Work mixture into a soft dough, adding about another 3 cups flour. Turn out dough on a lightly floured surface. Clean and grease bowl. Knead dough 8 to 10 minutes or until smooth and elastic, working in additional flour as needed. Place dough in greased bowl, turning to coat all sides. Cover and let rise in a warm place, free from drafts, until doubled in bulk, 2 to 2 1/2 hours. Grease 3 baking sheets.

On a floured surface, roll out about 1 cup of the dough until 1/4 inch thick. Keep remaining dough covered to prevent drying. Using a 2 1/2-inch-round cutter, cut out dough. Place 1/2 teaspoon cherry or other jam on 1 dough round. Lightly place another dough round directly on top of the first, covering jam. Using your fingers, crimp dough edges together tightly to prevent halves from separating during frying.

Place filled doughnut on a floured surface. Using a 2 1/4-inch-round cutter, press over doughnut so crimped rough edge gets trimmed smooth and round. Place filled doughnut on a greased baking sheet. Repeat process with remaining dough and jam until all baking sheets are filled, being careful to leave enough room between each doughnut for spreading when dough rises. Cover each baking sheet of doughnuts with a clean cloth. Let rise in a warm place, free from drafts, until doubled in bulk, about 1 hour.

Pour oil into a deep-fryer or large saucepan to a depth of about 5 inches. Heat to

360F (180C) or until a 1-inch bread cube turns golden brown in 60 seconds. Add doughnuts without crowding, top side down, so bottom will round out during cooking. Fry 3 to 4 minutes or until golden brown. Turn and fry other side about 3 minutes or until golden brown on both sides. Remove cooked doughnuts with a slotted spoon and drain on paper towels. Lightly dust doughnuts with powdered sugar.

Apple Pancakes

··

Apfelpfannkucken

This classic German dish is often served for breakfast but in reality is eaten at any time of the day or night, especially during fall and early winter, when apples are readily available. *Makes 8 to 10 pancakes.*

Apple Filling (see below)
9 eggs
1 1/2 cups milk
1 1/2 cups all-purpose flour
2 teaspoons sugar

1/2 teaspoon salt
About 1 cup butter or margarine,
 melted
Sugar mixed with cinnamon to taste

APPLE FILLING
3 lbs. apples
1 tablespoon lemon juice
2 tablespoons butter or margarine
3/4 cup sugar
Nutmeg and cinnamon to taste

Prepare Apple Filling. In a large bowl, beat eggs until light and frothy. Add milk and beat until combined. Sift flour, sugar and salt into beaten egg mixture. Beat into a smooth batter.

For each pancake, add about 1 1/2 tablespoons melted butter or margarine to a 10- or 12-inch skillet over medium heat. Pour enough batter into hot skillet to cover the bottom with a thin layer. As soon as batter is poured, tilt and rotate the pan so the batter will evenly cover the bottom. Cook over medium heat about 2 minutes, carefully testing doneness of pancake by gently lifting edges with a spatula. When pancake underside is golden brown, turn and cook the other side about 1 minute.

While second side of pancake is cooking, spoon several tablespoons of filling over the center of half of pancake, keeping the filling about 1 inch away from pancake edges. Using the spatula, fold pancake in two, flipping the unfilled side of the pancake up and over the apple filling. Brush top of pancake with melted butter. Sprinkle with sugar-cinnamon mixture. Flip filled pancake and cook about 10 to 15 seconds. Flip pancake over; brush other side with butter. Sprinkle with sugar-cinnamon mixture. Flip pancake and cook 10 to 15 more seconds. Remove from heat. Keep hot in an oven set between 250F (120C) and 300F (150C) while remaining pancakes are cooked. Serve hot.

Apple Filling

Peel and slice apples. Sprinkle with lemon juice. Melt butter or margarine in a small saucepan over medium heat. Add sugar; cook 6 to 8 minutes or until fruit is tender but not mushy. Season with nutmeg and cinnamon. Remove from heat; keep filling mixture warm.

Variation

Serve cooked pancakes without apple filling, seasoned with powdered sugar, cinnamon and sugar, lemon juice, jelly, or jam.

Sand Tarts

Sandtörtchen

For a crisper cookie, make them thinner. If desired, color different parts of the dough with a drop or two of food coloring before rolling and baking the cookies. *Makes about 5 dozen cookies.*

1 cup butter, room temperature	1 egg white, slightly beaten
2 cups sugar	1 tablespoon ground cinnamon
1 egg	Slivered almonds or pecan halves
2 cups all-purpose flour	

Beat butter and 1 1/2 cups of the sugar in a large bowl until creamy. Beat egg into sugar mixture. Gradually blend in flour. Work into a stiff, uniform dough. Cover with foil or plastic wrap; refrigerate dough overnight.

Preheat oven to 350F (175C). Lightly grease several cookie sheets. Lightly flour a work surface. Remove one-fourth of the dough from refrigerator; keep remaining dough chilled. Roll out dough to 1/8-inch thickness. Cut out stars, rounds, diamonds or other medium shapes with cookie cutters. Arrange cookies on greased sheets, leaving several inches of space between each cookie. Repeat process with remaining dough. Brush cookies with beaten egg white.

In a small bowl, combine remaining 1/2 cup sugar and cinnamon. Sprinkle cookies with sugar-cinnamon mixture. Press one slivered almond piece or pecan half slightly into center of each cookie. Bake 8 to 10 minutes or until cookie edges are lightly browned. Cool on cookie sheets 1 minute, then remove to wire racks to cool completely.

Linzer Cookies

Linzer Augen

The raspberry jam used in these cookies is what makes this recipe special. Naturally, you can experiment with red raspberry, black raspberry and many other kinds of thick jams. *Makes about 5 dozen cookies.*

1 1/2 cups unsalted butter or margarine, room temperature	Grated peel of 1/2 lemon
1 cup granulated sugar	1 1/4 cups finely grated hazelnuts
2 eggs	2 egg whites, slightly beaten
3 1/2 cups sifted all-purpose flour	About 2 cups raspberry jam
1/3 teaspoon salt	1/4 cup powdered sugar or 4 oz. melted chocolate (optional)

In a large bowl, beat butter or margarine and granulated sugar until light and fluffy. Beat in eggs. Stir in flour, salt, lemon peel and hazelnuts. Combine mixture into a smooth ball. Cover with foil or plastic wrap; refrigerate 2 hours or overnight.

Preheat oven to 375F (190C). Lightly grease several baking sheets. On a lightly floured surface, roll out dough to 1/8 inch thickness. Use a 2-inch-round cookie cutter to cut out as many rounds as possible. On half of dough rounds, cut out 1/2-inch circles, creating circular "windows" in centers of rounds. With a spatula, arrange rounds on greased baking sheets; brush tops with egg whites, using a pastry brush. Bake 10 to 12 minutes or until lightly browned. Remove rounds from baking sheets; cool on wire racks 15 minutes.

Spread each full round with jam. Top each with a "windowed" cookie. Let cool completely. Sprinkle lightly with powdered sugar or drizzle melted chocolate over cookies.

Molded Anise-Seed Cookies

Springerle

These simple square or rectangular cookies were first baked in Swabia, where they were formed in detailed and sometimes very large molds, which were carved out of wood. They're still often served at Christmastime. *Makes 4 to 5 dozen average-size cookies.*

3 eggs	*1 teaspoon vanilla extract*
1 1/2 cups powdered sugar, sifted	*3 cups all-purpose flour*
1 tablespoon finely grated lemon peel	*1/2 cup anise seeds*

In a large bowl, beat eggs and sugar until pale and creamy. Add lemon peel and vanilla. Sift flour into beaten egg mixture; mix until dough is well blended and fairly stiff. Cover with a clean cloth and refrigerate 4 hours.

Grease several large cookie sheets. Evenly sprinkle greased cookie sheets with anise seeds. On a lightly floured surface, roll out dough to 1/2-inch thickness. Press a well-floured springerle board or rolling pin firmly into rolled dough to emboss designs onto the dough. Cut out cookies around their embossed outlines, or into small squares if a regular pattern has been impressed into the dough. Carefully transfer cookies to anise-sprinkled baking sheets. Let cookies stand overnight, so they slowly dry.

Preheat oven to 325F (165C). Bake 12 to 15 minutes or until set; do not let tops of cookies turn brown.

Spice Cookies

Pfeffernussekuchlein

Make these two to three weeks before Christmas, then mellow by storing with a slice of apple. *Makes about 7 dozen cookies.*

4 eggs

1 1/4 cups sugar

3 1/4 cups all-purpose flour

1 teaspoon baking powder

1/2 teaspoon salt

1 teaspoon ground cinnamon

1/4 teaspoon ground cloves

1/2 cup blanched almonds, finely ground

1/2 cup Candied Orange Peel (page 294), finely chopped

In a large bowl, beat eggs and sugar until light and pale. Sift flour, baking powder, salt, cinnamon and ground cloves into egg mixture. Add almonds and orange peel. Using your hands, form a stiff dough.

Preheat oven to 350F (175C). Lightly grease several baking sheets. Flour a work surface; roll dough out to 1/3-inch thickness. Using a 1 1/4-inch-round cookie cutter, cut out dough rounds. For soft cookies bake immediately, about 15 minutes or until lightly browned; for crispy cookies, cover unbaked cookies on cookie sheets with clean towels and let stand overnight before baking. Preheat oven to 350F (175C); bake 15 minutes or until lightly browned.

Almond Crescents

Mandel-Halbmonde

Almond Crescents are about as traditional a German baked good as you can find. To achieve the proper consistency in this cookie recipe, make sure the almonds are finely ground, not chopped. *Makes 45 cookies.*

1 cup butter or margarine, room temperature	2 teaspoons almond extract
1 cup granulated sugar	2 1/3 cups all-purpose flour
1 teaspoon vanilla extract	1 cup ground almonds
	1 cup powdered sugar

Preheat oven to 350F (175C). Grease several large baking sheets. In a medium bowl, beat butter or margarine with sugar until light and fluffy; add vanilla extract and almond extract. Stir in flour and almonds. Work flour mixture into a firm dough.

Working with 1 tablespoon of dough at a time, shape a log in which the middle is thicker than both ends. Bend dough log into a crescent shape. Place on greased cookie sheet. Repeat until all dough is used. Bake 12 to 15 minutes or until light brown. Sift powdered sugar into a small shallow bowl. While still warm, roll crescents in powdered sugar. Cool on racks.

Peach-Apricot Dessert

Pfirsich-Aprikosen Susspeisen

This sweet dessert can be prepared all year long because it doesn't rely on fresh fruit. *Makes 6 to 8 servings.*

2 (16-oz.) cans sliced peaches, drained	Grated peel from 1/2 orange or 2 tablespoons finely chopped Candied Orange Peel (page 294)
8 oz. dried apricots	1/2 cup crumbled gingersnap cookies
1 (about 6-oz.) jar of pitted Bing cherries with juice	1 cup packed brown sugar
Juice of 1 large orange	1 cup sour cream (optional)

Preheat oven to 350F (175C). In a medium baking dish, combine peaches, apricots, cherries and cherry juice, orange juice and orange peel. Gently arrange crumbled gingersnaps on top of fruit, gently pressing into fruit. Sprinkle brown sugar over gingersnaps. Bake, uncovered, 1 hour or until fruit mixture is thickened and somewhat caramelized. Serve hot, topped with sour cream, if desired.

Honey Cookies

Honigplatzchen

Early bakers had no refined sugars to help sweeten their cakes, cookies and pastries, so they relied on honey, Germany's oldest and most readily available sweetener.
Makes about 6 dozen cookies.

1 cup honey

3/4 cup packed brown sugar

1 cup finely chopped nuts

2 tablespoons grated lemon peel

2 teaspoons lemon juice

3 cups all-purpose flour

1 teaspoon baking soda

1/2 teaspoon ground nutmeg

1/2 teaspoon ground allspice

1/4 teaspoon ground cloves

1 egg, slightly beaten

Blanched almond halves

Chocolate chips

Bring honey to a boil in a medium saucepan over medium heat. Remove honey from heat. Stir in brown sugar, chopped nuts, lemon peel and lemon juice. Cool slightly.

In a medium bowl, combine flour, baking soda, nutmeg, allspice and cloves. Add egg and the honey mixture to flour mixture. Using your hands, form a soft, sticky dough. Cover dough with plastic wrap and refrigerate overnight.

Preheat oven to 375F (190C). Lightly grease several baking sheets. Flour a work surface. Roll chilled dough out to 1/4-inch thickness. Cut out 2-inch rounds with a cookie cutter. Press blanched almond halves evenly around the edges of each cookie round, like petals on a flower. Press a chocolate chip into center of each round. Bake 10 to 12 minutes or until edges of cookies are lightly browned. Let stand 1 minute on baking sheets; remove and cool on wire racks.

Variation

Omit chocolate chips and brush cookies with the following mixture instead. Combine 1 cup granulated sugar and 1/2 cup water in a small saucepan. Bring to a full boil over medium-high heat; boil 5 minutes. Remove from heat. Stir 1/2 cup powdered sugar into hot sugar mixture. Let cool to warm. Brush cookies and almonds with warm glaze. Let cool.

Little Horns

Hornchen

These cookies, although very popular in Germany, are probably a variation of French cookies having the same name. *Makes 35 to 40 cookies.*

2 cups all-purpose flour
1 cup butter, room temperature
4 egg yolks
3 tablespoons sour cream

3 egg whites
1 1/2 cups powdered sugar
2 cups walnuts, ground

Sift flour into the bowl of a food processor fitted with the metal blade. Add butter. Process to combine. Add egg yolks, one at a time, processing until combined. Add sour cream. Process into a smooth and pliable dough.

On a lightly floured surface, roll out dough into a 1-inch-thick rope. Cut dough rope into 35 to 40 equal-size pieces. Using your hands, roll each piece of dough into a ball. Place all dough balls on a plate; cover and refrigerate overnight.

In a medium-size bowl, beat egg whites until frothy. Add powdered sugar and beat until stiff peaks form. Add ground walnuts; beat to combine.

Preheat oven to 350F (175C). Grease several baking sheets. On a lightly floured surface, roll chilled dough balls into rounds about 1/8 inch thick. Place a small dollop of walnut filling on one side of dough round. Roll dough round into the shape of a horn. Repeat with remaining dough and filling. Arrange filled horns on sheets so they have room to expand while cooking. Bake 15 to 20 minutes or until golden brown.

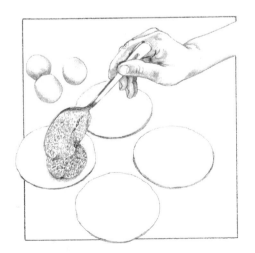
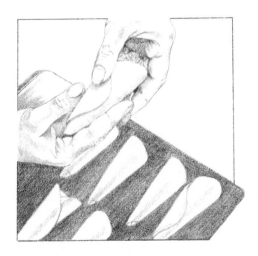

Homemade Ice Cream

Hausgemachtes Eis

Although many small shops and corner vendors sell ice cream in almost every town and city, many a German grandmother still makes her own ice cream for special occasions. *Makes 4 servings.*

2 cups whipping cream
1/3 cup sugar
1/4 cup raisins
1/4 cup chopped walnuts

1/4 cup Candied Orange Peel (page 294)
Walnut halves, maraschino cherries or strawberries (optional)

Place cream in a large bowl. Beat until soft peaks form. Slowly beat in sugar; beat until stiff peaks form. Stir raisins, walnuts and orange peel into cream. Spoon cream mixture into the smallest bowl it will fit in. Smooth top of cream mixture flat. Cover with foil or a tight-fitting lid and freeze overnight.

When ready to serve, dip bottom of bowl in hot water about 5 seconds. Turn out ice cream onto a serving plate. Serve frozen, sliced like cake. If desired, decorate with walnuts, whole cherries or strawberry halves.

Variations
Add 1 teaspoon instant coffee with sugar.
Add 1 tablespoon powdered cocoa with sugar.
Add 1 tablespoon rum to whipping cream.

Strawberry Ice Cream

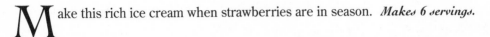

Erbeereis

Make this rich ice cream when strawberries are in season. *Makes 6 servings.*

4 egg yolks
1/4 cup sugar
1 tablespoon Vanilla Sugar (page
    266)

2 cups milk
1 cup fresh strawberries

In a large bowl, beat egg yolks, sugar and Vanilla Sugar until creamy and pale. In a large saucepan, bring milk to a boil over medium heat. Reduce heat to low. Stir egg mixture into heated milk; cook, stirring, 2 minutes. Remove from heat.

In a blender or food processor fitted with the steel blade, process strawberries until pureed; stir into milk mixture. Pour into a medium bowl. Cover and refrigerate until cold. Freeze 2 or more hours, stirring every 20 minutes until frozen.

Variation
For fluffy strawberry ice cream, fold 3 beaten egg whites into mixture before freezing.

Vanilla Pudding

Vanille Pudding

Yes, there is pudding in Germany. It's almost always eaten with plenty of sliced fresh fruit. *Makes 4 to 6 servings.*

3 3/8 cups milk
1/2 cup sugar
1 tablespoon vanilla extract
2 tablespoons potato starch

1 egg white
1/2 lb. fresh peaches, peeled and
    sliced, or strawberries, sliced

Place all but 2 tablespoons of the milk in a medium saucepan; bring to a boil over medium heat. Reduce heat to low. Stir sugar and vanilla into simmering milk; simmer 2 minutes, stirring constantly. Blend potato starch and remaining milk in a small bowl; stir into simmering milk mixture. Increase heat to medium. Bring milk mixture to a boil, stirring constantly. Remove from heat. Let cool 10 minutes.

In a small bowl, beat egg white until stiff. Gently fold beaten egg white into cooked milk mixture. Pour into dessert dishes. Refrigerate 30 minutes or until set. Serve chilled, topped with sliced peaches or strawberries.

Bavarian Cream

Bayrische Creme

Be careful that the mixture, while cooking in the top part of the double boiler, is not allowed to boil. If the mixture gets too hot, the egg yolks won't combine well with the rest of the ingredients. *Makes 6 dessert servings.*

1 package unflavored gelatin	*1 cup milk, scalded*
1/4 cup cold milk	*1 teaspoon vanilla extract*
4 egg yolks	*1 cup whipping cream*
1/2 cup sugar	

In a cup, soften gelatin in 1/4 cup cold milk. In a medium bowl, beat egg yolks until thickened. Gradually beat sugar into egg yolks. Combine egg yolk mixture and scalded milk in the top part of a double boiler. Cook milk mixture over hot water, stirring constantly, until thick enough to coat a spoon. Remove from heat.

Stir vanilla and softened gelatin into milk mixture until gelatin is completely dissolved. Pour into a bowl; refrigerate mixture, stirring occasionally to prevent a crust from forming, until mixture begins to thicken to the consistency of egg white, about 30 minutes.

Whip cream in a chilled medium bowl until stiff peaks form. Fold whipped cream into gelatin mixture. Rinse a 1-quart mold in cold water, then lightly rub it with vegetable oil. Pour cream mixture into lightly oiled mold. Refrigerate cream mixture until firm, about 2 hours. Serve chilled or use as filling in other desserts.

Variations

Almond Bavarian Cream Add 1 teaspoon almond extract with vanilla extract.

Chocolate Bavarian Cream Add 2 (1-oz.) squares unsweetened chocolate or 1 (6-oz.) package semisweet chocolate pieces with scalded milk. Stir until chocolate melts and blends with rest of cream mixture.

Chocolate Mocha Bavarian Cream Add 2 tablespoons instant coffee to above Chocolate Bavarian Cream.

Coffee Bavarian Cream Add 2 tablespoons instant coffee granules with milk.

Apricot Bavarian Cream Fold 1 cup sieved canned apricots and 1 tablespoon lemon juice into chilled mixture with whipped cream.

Strawberry or Raspberry Bavarian Cream Fold 1 cup sliced strawberries or raspberries, sweetened with sugar to taste and drained, into chilled mixture with whipped cream.

Candied Orange Peel

Orangeat

A children's favorite, candied orange peel can be used in numerous cake and cookie recipes—or as a sweet substitute in recipes calling for finely chopped lemon peel. *Makes about 1 1/4 cups candied peel.*

Peel from 6 medium oranges, cut into	*1 cup water*
1/2-inch-wide strips	*1 cup sugar*

Wash orange peel strips under cold running water; pat dry. With a sharp knife, remove white inner part of peels; discard. Coarsely chop peels. Place in a medium heatproof bowl. In a medium saucepan, bring 2 cups water to a boil. Pour boiling water over peel. Let stand 10 minutes; drain. Boil 2 more cups water. Pour over peel. Let stand 10 minutes; drain. Repeat boiling-water process 2 more times.

In a medium saucepan, combine the 1 cup water and sugar; bring to a boil. Reduce heat to low; simmer, uncovered, 5 minutes. Add chopped orange peel; cook, uncovered, over low heat 25 to 30 minutes or until peel mixture becomes translucent and thick. Spoon hot peel mixture into a sterilized jar or other container. Cover with an airtight lid; let cool. Refrigerate.

Variation

Candied Lemon Peel Prepare the peels of 6 large lemons in the same manner. Rinse with boiling water 12 times; let stand 2 minutes each time. When cooking with sugar, add 5 whole allspice berries. Remove allspice berries when peel mixture becomes transparent and thick.

Soft Candied Orange or Lemon Peel Prepare peels in same manner, removing inner white part. Instead of cooking peel with 1 cup water and 1 cup sugar, simply cut orange or lemon peels into 1/4-inch squares. Place 1/4 cup sugar in a small airtight jar or container. Add one-fourth of the peel squares in an even layer over sugar. Top peel with another 1/4 cup sugar. Repeat layering process until all peel and sugar is used. Top fourth layer of peel with another 1/4 cup sugar. Cover with an airtight lid. Store in a cool, dry place 2 weeks before using. For soft candied lemon peel, let stand 4 weeks before using. *Makes about 1 1/2 cups soft candied peel.*

Beverages

································ ❦ ································

Getränke

To the typical German, a beverage can mean many things—anything from milk to fruit juices to cola drinks to schnapps or cherry brandy, or numerous clear fruit spirits to wine to beer. It means all of these drinks and others.

While Germans are noted for their heavy beer drinking, there seems to be a change in the works there. Stricter drinking and driving penalties, along with increasing attention to health, have had a moderating effect on some beer-drinking Germans. On the other hand, wine drinking is up, but not nearly as high as it is in France or Italy.

Beer

Beer is unquestionably the favorite adult drink in Germany. Germans drink upward of 35 gallons of it per year. And that misleading figure includes babies, children and nonbeer drinkers. On the whole, it would be considerably higher when considering only adult beer drinkers. Bavaria brews (and consumes) the largest quantities and is considered the place in which the first German brewing occurred, when dutiful monks produced kegs of it during the Middle Ages in a monastery in Munich. Years later, Munich would also invent the *Brauhaus,* which was simply a restaurant operated by a brewery, so the inexpensive and thirst-causing food would encourage—you guessed it—more beer drinking.

Ask any American who has spent time visiting Germany about German beers, and he or she will likely comment on how fresh and good the beer tasted there and how different it seemed from American beers on draft. Why is that? It isn't because regular German beers are slightly higher in alcohol content, which they are (4.5 to 5 percent alcohol by volume instead of 4.4 percent for American and British beers). And it isn't because the draft beer in Germany is often dispensed in larger glasses. Or the colors of their beers are any different. It's because German beers are so wonderfully smooth and frothy—exactly what an ideal beer should be like.

Again you ask why? The answer is because German beer is fresh and pure. The manufacturing practice of pasteurization used to produce American beers entails heating the beer long enough to kill all the bacteria it contains. The pasteurized beer can be shipped all over the country and held in warehouses without spoiling. And occasional-drinking American consumers can keep a few cases of beer in their garages practically indefinitely, sipping only one or several bottles at a time. Pasteurization isn't so important in Germany, where even the smallest village can have its own brewery and where beer needn't be shipped far or warehoused for long times.

In Germany, there's a strict purity law that originated in the fifteenth century, when Bavarian dukes tried to regulate the prices of beer. The price-fixing law had a short section that also addressed what beer could be made of. No German beer could have any ingredient other than yeast, hops, barley malt and water. That was it, and that's still it. No chemicals, no sweeteners, no sugars that don't occur naturally, and no preservatives. That's not so with many American beers in which pasteurization and preservatives affect the beer's taste by lending it a slightly bitter or skunky flavor.

To allow German breweries to compete on an international basis, the purity law is relaxed for German export beer. That's why many German brands of beer sold in the United States taste differently from the "same" brands marketed within Germany. They *are* different.

There are two basic categories of German beer: bottom-brewed and top-brewed. Top-brewing is taking place when the yeast rises to the top during the brewing process. It's the earliest method of brewing and the trickiest because the beer could spoil quickly unless kept cold. Because of the cold temperatures required, beer brewing was once strictly a seasonal activity, with most beer produced during winter and spring, and stored in cool cellars, to be brought out later during those major beer-drinking hot summer months. That's how beer cellars came about—as places to store the beer. Beer cellars, in turn, were located next to the beer gardens, where the beer was served. After years and years of beer cellars and beer gardens situated alongside each other, the two terms became interchangeable.

Bottom-brewing came about when some sharp-eyed brewmaster noticed that when yeast settles to the bottom during the brewing process, the brew would keep indefinitely and wouldn't spoil. Later a brewing method was developed in Pilsen and Vienna in which the process started with the yeast on the bottom. Thus pilsner and lager (which hails from the German word *Lager,* meaning "to store") came into vogue and have been the leading German and European beers ever since.

Bottom-Brewed Beers

Helles Bier is a pale-colored lager with a thick, frothy head of foam. It's got a slightly sweet flavor that lends itself to American tastes. It's not as strong as many other German beers. A good lager beer should be stored between one and three months while it matures. This "lagering" is accomplished somewhere between 32 and 36 degrees Fahrenheit. Lagering helps produce the clear, clean-tasting and golden-colored brew so popular in Munich and the rest of the country.

Pilsner Bier, or "Pils" as the locals call it, is a stronger-tasting lager that results from considerable quantities of hops used in its brewing. Although it's the most popular beer in central and northern Germany, it's still available in the south, in special "Pilsbars" that resemble tiny neighborhood taverns or pubs. While in Germany, if you're in a hurry, avoid ordering a pilsner. That's because the traditional way of drawing it takes from five to eight minutes. The bartenders or maids inevitably draw it into thin-stemmed, wide-mouthed glasses in a manner that causes up to 85 or 90 percent of the beer to come out as foam. Then you wait for the foam to turn to beer before more is poured. More foam comes out, accompanied by more waiting. Many a visiting patron has thought he or she had been abandoned at the bar, while waiting to be served a pilsner.

Dunkles Bier is a dark lager with higher concentrations of malt and a relatively low alcohol content, between 3 and 4 percent. The burnt malt used in its brewing gives it a color resembling that of cola drinks. It's traditionally a Munich beer but can be found all over Germany, where it is affectionately known as *Munchner.*

Bock Bier is a strong beer, with an alcohol content of at least 6 and possibly 7 percent. The word *Bock* means "billy goat" in German. The breweries have taken the billy goat to heart, and most bock beers include a symbol of a goat or the astrological sign of Capricorn in their advertising. Bock beer explodes the belief that light-colored beers are not as strong as their darker cousins. Although bock beer is available year round, most is consumed during special celebrations such as Octoberfest.

Doppelbock is one of the strongest German beers available, with an alcohol minimum content of 7.5 percent, and usually more. One version is *Eisbock,* a beer whose alcohol content is about 13 percent alcohol, achieved during brewing by freezing the water in the beer so that the remaining liquids can be drawn off—liquids much higher in alcohol content than would otherwise naturally occur during the fermentation process.

Light beers, the newer German diet beers, have essentially been copied from American diet beer success stories. Most are versions of *Helles Biers,* with alcohol percentages of about 3.5 and up to 40 percent fewer calories.

Top-Brewed Beers

Alt is a rather weak beer, with an alcoholic content of between 3.5 and 4 percent. Its taste is on the bitter side due to high quantities of hops used in the brewing process. It's also flatter or less carbonated than *helles* and other lagers, a taste which has over the years attracted its northern German devotees. Its color is reddish. Again, this beer is not widely popular throughout Bavaria but is heartily consumed by small numbers of Munich and other southern beer drinkers.

Kolsch is a top-brewed beer that has a little more carbonation than *Alt* and a little more alcoholic content, about 4.6 percent. It's a pale brew, with a milder taste than the previously mentioned beer. It's name is a derivation of *Cologne,* the city with which it has been associated for years.

Weizen is wheat beer. Also called *Weiss* (white) *Bier,* it is a special highly carbonated brew favored on steamy summer days and nights, when a drier beverage is preferred, and is sometimes served with a slice of lemon or mixed with half lemon-lime soda. Another popular ale drink is *Weisse mit Schuss,* which is white beer with a shot of raspberry syrup. The alcohol content of *Weizen* is often higher than 6 percent and has traditionally hit unsuspecting visitors whose defenses against alcohol have already been weakened by summer heat and humidity. Its color is a light amber.

Wine

While beer may be the favorite German drink, German wines are among the world's finest. Germany distinguishes between three major types of wine: white wine made from white grapes, red wine pressed from red grapes, and rose wine made from red wine grapes that are pressed only to a light color.

Wine is fairly inexpensive in Germany, with locally bottled table wine costing less than orange or grape juice. By far, most wine produced and consumed in Germany is white, with the fruity Rieslings and Sylvaners leading the way.

White Wines

- *Rhine wines,* which are a deep golden color, are quite aromatic, and have a fruity and slight sweet taste.

- *Moselle wines,* which are light golden in color, are not as aromatic, and are slightly dry in taste.

- *Sekt* is a sparkling German wine prepared by keeping carbon dioxide in the bottle long enough to cause a second fermentation. *Sekt* is often the choice for parties and holiday celebrations.

- *Eis wines* are made from grapes whose water content has suffered a single freezing or frost on the vine. These wines are, essentially, prepared only with nature's cooperation and are rather scarce and expensive. They have an exceptionally clean, cool taste, and are sparkling clear.

Other Wines

Beyond white wines there are some reds and some pale and mildly sweet rose varieties, but the overall quality of German red wines is not as high as that of the white wines. Some fruit wines, including the ever popular apple wines that often come from the region around Frankfurt, are also produced.

Wine-Producing Areas

Excellent vines are cultivated on the sun-drenched slopes of river valleys and along the shores of small lakes. Although the Rhineland, Hesse, Palatinate and Baden regions are noted for their high-quality wine grapes and wines—mostly due to their association with the rich wine-grape–producing Rhine River and its tributaries—small stretches of land on which vineyards flourish can be found along most of the central and southwestern German riverbanks and in pockets of terrain elsewhere. Again, grape-growing river valleys of importance include the Rhine, Mosel, Saar, Ruwer, Main, Neckar, and the Upper Rhine. The Lake Constance region to the far south also produces extremely flavorful wine grapes.

Wine Grades

As with German beer brewing, German wine making is strictly regulated. In 1971 a new wine standard came out in Germany, which has since thoroughly confused all but the staunchest and most meticulous student of German wines. But simply and for our purpose, German wines are divided into grades of varying quality which must conform to specific measurable standards.

Table wines, for instance, can only be produced from officially approved vines that come from approved vineyards and must contain a minimum alcohol content of 8.5 percent. Yet another characteristic by which German wines are judged is the percentage of naturally produced sugar in proportion to the wine's total volume. The addition of some sugar to table wines is allowed.

Quality wines—those above the quality of table wines—also come from approved vineyard vines. Their alcoholic content is a little higher than that of table wines, at least 9 percent. Their flavor must conform to the specialty wine of the area from which they hail, and each bottle of wine carries an official examination number attesting that it has passed strict tests. Quality wines may also have extra sugar added.

Specially graded quality wines are the best available. These wines need, nor are they allowed to have, no additional sugar. In addition to the sugar content, wine graders pay attention to the time of the vintage, the method of harvesting and the ripeness of the grapes.

Specially graded quality wines include:

- *Kabinett,* or high-quality wines from grapes harvested during October, which is later than when most other wine grapes are harvested in Europe. The lengthy slow-ripening grapes help give these wines unique full-bodied flavors.

- *Spatlese,* or full-bodied wines, are wines from grapes harvested after the regular picking periods, after grapes destined for Kabinetts have been gathered. Spatlese wines have a higher sugar content than do Kabinett wines.

- *Auslese* wines come from the tedious process of selecting only fully ripe grapes from whatever grapes are harvested toward the very end of the season.

- *Beernauslese,* or dessert wines, are wines pressed from a particular combination of hand-sorted ripe and overripe berries.

- *Trockenbeernauslese,* or sweet, rather heavy and smooth dessert wines, are only the finest quality. They use tiny, shriveled grapes that have dried on the vine until they resemble raisins.

Other Beverages

Rum is an import that comes all the way from Central America to be used in hot toddies or grogs and other mixed drinks. It's traditionally used in areas along the Danish border.

Schnapps, in their various forms, are still the most popular alcoholic spirits in Germany. They're to Germany what whiskey is to Ireland and vodka is to Poland and Russia. *Kirsch* cherry brandy is often served, as are raspberry liqueurs and a host of clear fruit spirits, including pear, plum or prune, raspberry and even strawberry.

Mineral-water sales in Germany are on the rise too, as are sales of soft drinks.

Cherry Compote

Kirschkompott

When cherries aren't in season you can substitute 1 quart frozen, pitted sour cherries for fresh cherries. Adjust the sugar amount to suit your taste. Some people prefer a tart compote; if so, add sugar a teaspoon at a time. *Makes 10 to 12 servings.*

1 1/2 qts. fresh sour cherries, pits
    and stems removed
2 qts. water

1 cup sugar
1 (3-inch) cinnamon stick
5 whole cloves

In a large saucepan, combine cherries, water, sugar, cinnamon and cloves; bring to a boil over medium heat. Reduce heat to medium-low; cook, uncovered, 25 to 30 minutes. Serve hot or chilled. Spoon cherries into a medium glass so cherries fill one-fourth to one-third of the glass. Pour compote juice over cherries. Serve with a spoon in the glass.

Hot Cider

Heisser Apfelwein

What could taste better on a chilly October evening after a hay ride? Your main problem might be hiding the cider long enough for it to start turning hard—without someone drinking it before it does. *Makes 6 to 8 servings.*

1 1/2 qts. slightly hard cider or
    apple wine
6 (3-inch) cinnamon sticks

6 whole cloves
1/4 lemon, thinly sliced
Sugar

In a medium saucepan, combine cider or apple wine, cinnamon sticks, cloves and lemon. Bring to a boil over medium heat. Season with sugar to taste. Reduce heat to medium-low; simmer, uncovered, 15 minutes. Carefully strain cider into cups or glasses while steaming hot. Serve immediately.

Variation
Substitute apple juice for cider.

Eggnog

Hoppel-Poppel

Eggnog can be made in various alcohol concentrations by decreasing (or increasing) the amount of rum or brandy. When adding the tiny pinch of salt, just 6 or 7 grains will do if you're counting. *Makes 4 to 6 servings.*

1 qt. plus 1 cup milk	*1 cup rum or brandy*
4 egg yolks	*Pinch of salt*
1/2 cup sugar	*2 pinches of ground cinnamon or*
About 1 1/4 teaspoons vanilla extract	*nutmeg*

Heat milk in a medium saucepan over medium-low heat; do not boil. In a large bowl, beat egg yolks and sugar until combined and foamy. Add vanilla and hot milk, pouring in a little milk at a time while beating constantly. Stir rum into milk mixture. Add salt. Top with ground cinnamon or nutmeg. Serve hot.

Variation
For a sweeter drink, increase amount of sugar.

Hot Toddy

Grog

The longer cinnamon sticks remain in a drink, the more of their sweet, pungent flavor they'll impart. *Makes 4 servings.*

4 cups water	*Juice of 1 lemon*
1/2 cup sugar	*4 (3-inch) cinnamon sticks*
2 cups rum	

Bring water to a boil in a medium saucepan. Dissolve sugar in boiling water. Stir rum and lemon juice into hot water mixture; carefully pour drink into heatproof glasses or mugs containing 1 cinnamon stick each. Serve hot.

Variation
Substitute 1/3 cup maple syrup for sugar.

May Wine

............⊠............ ⊠............

Maibowle

This drink is traditionally dedicated to springtime. In herb gardens throughout cities and countrysides, *Waldmeister,* or sweet woodruff, is grown for this recipe and others, shaded by a tree or corner of a shed or barn. *Makes 8 to 10 servings.*

*2 (750-ml.) bottles Moselle or other
   dry white wine
2 tablespoons sugar
1/2 cup bottled spring water
2 oranges, halved lengthwise, then
   sliced*

*1 bunch day-old fresh sweet woodruff
   sprigs, or 1/2 cup dried woodruff
Ice cubes (optional)
8 to 10 fresh strawberries, halved*

Pour wine into a medium bowl. Dissolve sugar in spring water; stir into wine. Add all but 8 to 10 orange half-slices.

If fresh woodruff is used, tie sprigs together and immerse them so stems are sticking up from wine. Cover and refrigerate 30 minutes; remove woodruff. If dried woodruff is used, tie woodruff into a cheesecloth bag. Immerse woodruff bag in wine; cover and marinate at room temperature 30 minutes, then refrigerate 30 minutes. Remove dried woodruff.

Evenly arrange ice cubes, if using, strawberries and remaining orange slices in punch glasses. Ladle in wine mixture.

Cold Duck Punch Bowl

............⊠............ ⊠............

Kalte Entebowle

Serve this refreshing punch bowl at parties, receptions, reunions, picnics and holiday celebrations. *Makes 12 to 15 servings.*

*2 (750-ml.) bottles Moselle or other
   white wine, well chilled
1 bottle dry Sekt (sparkling wine),
   well chilled*

*Juice of 1 lemon, chilled
Peel of 1 lemon, carefully cut in a
   continuous spiral, chilled*

Chill a punch bowl. Combine wine, Sekt, lemon juice and peel in chilled punch bowl. Set punch bowl on a bed of cracked ice.

Turks' Blood

Turkisches Blut

The dramatic (some would say, romantic) name for this incredibly simple drink hails from a few centuries ago, and from some hard feelings between the Germans and . . . guess who? *Makes 12 to 15 servings.*

1 (750-ml.) bottle Burgundy wine, chilled

2 (750-ml.) bottles Sekt (sparkling wine), chilled

A few orange slices (optional)

Pour Burgundy into chilled punch bowl. Add Sekt. Serve garnished with orange slices, if desired.

Raspberry Buttermilk

Himbeer Buttermilch

It's hard to tell if this is a drink or a dessert. Perhaps it's a dessert you can pour into a glass. *Makes 4 to 6 servings.*

1 qt. fresh red or black raspberries

About 1/4 cup honey or maple syrup

1 qt. buttermilk

Pinch of nutmeg

Wash raspberries under cold running water. Using a blender or food processor fitted with the metal blade, process berries until pureed. Add honey or maple syrup. Process again. Pour buttermilk into raspberry mixture, a little at a time, processing in short bursts until blended. Add nutmeg. Cover and refrigerate 30 minutes to 1 hour. Serve chilled.

Fruit Punch

Fruchtpunch

Be careful or someone will steal the peaches and sherry right out of the refrigerator. It's been known to happen! *Makes 12 to 15 servings.*

4 ripe peaches, peeled and sliced
1/3 cup powdered sugar
2/3 cup dry sherry

3 (750-ml.) bottles dry white wine, chilled

Place peaches in a medium bowl. Evenly sprinkle with powdered sugar. Drizzle sherry over peaches. Cover and refrigerate 4 hours to overnight, turning peaches occasionally.

Transfer peaches to a punch bowl. Before serving, add wine. Gently stir to combine. Serve chilled in glasses, with several peach slices per serving, if desired.

Egg Beer

Eierbier

A bartender once told a veteran beer drinker that a person shouldn't drink on an empty stomach. The patron thought for a moment before declaring that he'd do both things at once, then. He'd have his egg and drink his beer at the same time, too. Here's how he did it:

2 qts. beer
Peel of 1/2 lemon, cut in 4 or 5 pieces
3/4 cup sugar

12 egg yolks
1 qt. milk

Place beer, lemon peel and sugar in a large saucepan; cook over medium-high heat until almost boiling. Reduce heat to low.

Place egg yolks in a medium bowl; beat until frothy. Slowly add milk to egg yolks, beating constantly until well blended. Add 1 cup beer mixture to blended eggs; beat until combined. Carefully remove lemon peel. Pour egg mixture into beer. Continue beating beer mixture over very low heat until smooth and foamy; do not let mixture get too hot, or egg yolk will curdle. Serve warm, in glasses or mugs. *Makes 4 to 6 servings.*

Metric Conversion Charts

Comparison to Metric Measure

When You Know	Symbol	Multiply By	To Find	Symbol
teaspoons	tsp	5.0	milliliters	ml
tablespoons	tbsp	15.0	milliliters	ml
fluid ounces	fl. oz.	30.0	milliliters	ml
cups	c	0.24	liters	l
pints	pt.	0.47	liters	l
quarts	qt.	0.95	liters	l
ounces	oz.	28.0	grams	g
pounds	lb.	0.45	kilograms	kg
Fahrenheit	F	5/9 (after subtracting 32)	Celsius	C

Fahenheit to Celsius

F	C
200–205	95
220–225	105
245–250	120
275	135
300–305	150
325–330	165
345–350	175
370—375	190
400–405	205
425–430	220
445–450	230
470–475	245
500	260

Liquid Measure to Liters

1/4 cup	=	0.06 liters
1/2 cup	=	0.12 liters
3/4 cup	=	0.18 liters
1 cup	=	0.24 liters
1-1/4 cups	=	0.30 liters
1-1/2 cups	=	0.36 liters
2 cups	=	0.48 liters
2-1/2 cups	=	0.60 liters
3 cups	=	0.72 liters
3-1/2 cups	=	0.84 liters
4 cups	=	0.96 liters
4-1/2 cups	=	1.08 liters
5 cups	=	1.20 liters
5-1/2 cups	=	1.32 liters

Liquid Measure to Milliliters

1/4 teaspoon	=	1.25 milliliters
1/2 teaspoon	=	2.50 milliliters
3/4 teaspoon	=	3.75 milliliters
1 teaspoon	=	5.00 milliliters
1-1/4 teaspoons	=	6.25 milliliters
1-1/2 teaspoons	=	7.50 milliliters
1-3/4 teaspoons	=	8.75 milliliters
2 teaspoons	=	10.0 milliliters
1 tablespoon	=	15.0 milliliters
2 tablespoons	=	30.0 milliliters

Index

Index / 311

German Recipe Index

About the Author

Marianna Olszewska Heberle grew up in
eastern Europe near the Russian border,
where she was influenced by the cooking
and cultures of Poland, Germany, Russia,
Hungary, and Czechoslovakia. Now living
in Erie, Pennsylvania, with her husband and
three daughters, she specializes in ethnic
cooking, particularly the foods of Germany
and Poland. In addition to cooking for a
large extended family, she is a private cook
and also caters special dinners and parties.
She enjoys sharing her expertise with others at community events and seminars.
Heberle is also the author of HPBooks'
Polish Cooking.